The Lives and Times of Bonnie and Clyde

E. R. Milner

Southern Illinois University Press
Carbondale and Edwardsville

Copyright © 1996 by E. R. Milner
Printed in the United States of America
Paperback edition 2003
06 05 04 03   4 3 2 1

Library of Congress Cataloging-in-Publication Data

Milner, E. R.
    The lives and times of Bonnie and Clyde / E. R. Milner.
        p. cm.
    Includes bibliographical references and index.
    1. Parker, Bonnie, 1910–34. 2. Barrow, Clyde, 1909–34.
3. Criminals—United States—Biography. I. Title.
HV6245.M54 1996
364.1'552'092273—dc20
[B]
ISBN 0-8093-1977-2 (cloth : alk.paper)   95-4305
ISBN 0-8093-2552-7 (pbk. : alk.paper)

Contents

Plates   vii

Acknowledgments   ix

Prologue   1

1   Bonnie and Clyde   5
2   A Legacy of Violence   8
3   Bonnie and Clyde Are the Barrow Gang   16
4   They Call Them Cold-Blooded Killers   33
5   Hang It on Bonnie and Clyde   46
6   They Say They Are Heartless and Mean   57
7   From Heartbreak Some People Have Suffered   75
8   From Weariness Some People Have Died   88
9   The Road Gets Dimmer and Dimmer   100
10   Sometimes You Can Hardly See   114
11   They Wouldn't Give Up 'Til They Died   122
12   Death Came Out to Meet Them   134

Epilogue   157

Notes   167
Index   175

Plates

Bonnie Parker   67

Clyde Barrow   68

Raymond Hamilton   69

Reenactment of the Lon Davis murder   70

Ambush site   71

The "death car"   72

Bonnie and Clyde   73

Crowds waiting to view Bonnie   74

Bonnie in her casket   117

Pallbearers removing Bonnie   118

Bonnie's headstone   119

Dual headstone of Clyde and his brother Buck   119

The McKamy-Campbell hearse and driver   120

Ambush site marker   121

Acknowledgments

I wish to express my gratitude to:

Dr. Delores Akin of Forth Worth, Texas, a supportive colleague, who introduced me to Mrs. Eva Campbell, owner of the McKamy-Campbell Funeral home that conducted services for both Bonnie Parker and Raymond Hamilton.

Julian Bach of New York City, an agent of great loyalty and keen wit, who offered many suggestions that improved the manuscript tremendously.

Carol M. Besler of Dubuque, Iowa, an outstanding copyeditor, whose expertise prevented many blunders.

Mrs. Eva Campbell of Cedar Hill, Texas, cited above, who granted me an interview about the Parker and Hamilton services.

Dr. Allen B. Campbell, Jr., of Cedar Hill, Texas, retired physician, who encouraged his mother to be interviewed, and who freely shared related photographs never before published.

Sophia (Stone) Cook of Ruston, Louisiana, who along with H. Dillard Darby was kidnapped by Bonnie and Clyde, and who took time to talk with me while carefully watching dinner on her stove.

Corbin Crews of Grapevine, Texas, who drove the ambulance on Easter Sunday, 1934, to Dove Lane and raced to get the two Texas Highway Patrolmen to a physician before they died of their wounds, and who talked with me though his health was declining.

Ralph Fults of Dallas, Texas, who was one of the first members of the Barrow gang and the last survivor; his interview brought an entirely different insight into the material already gathered.

Leonard Herring of Denton, Texas, who introduced me to his father, a personal friend of John Bucher (Clyde Barrow's first murder victim), whose interview and memories of Bucher opened new vistas; Leonard also hoped that the volume would never be published.

Ralph Irvine of Palestine, Texas, who shared information that proved conclusively that Bonnie and Clyde did not rob the Palestine Ice Company, when officers maintained their guilt.

Mrs. Charles Kilgo of Dallas, Texas, who shared her singular personal memories of Clyde Barrow when he was a young man without a record.

Drs. Carroll Y. Rich and J. Don Vann of the University of North Texas, who encouraged me tremendously from the beginning; Dr. Rich also freely shared his research and writings to add to my probe.

James Simmons and Teresa White of Southern Illinois University Press, who shepherded this work through the maze from raw manuscript to published work.

Librarians and volunteers at the following institutions, who helped me in my search:

Alma (Arkansas) Public Library
Atoka County (Oklahoma) Genealogical Society
Dallas (Texas) Public Library
Denton (Texas) Public Library
Ellis County (Texas) Public Library
Fayetteville (Arkansas) Public Library

Fort Worth (Texas) Public Library
Grapevine (Texas) Public Library
Hillsboro (Texas) Public Library Archives
Iowa State Department of History and Archives
Kansas City (Kansas) Public Library
Lincoln Parish (Louisiana) Public Library
McKinney (Texas) Memorial Public Library
Miami (Oklahoma) Public Library
Moffett Library, Midwestern University
Northwestern Louisiana State University Library and Archives
Palestine (Texas) Public Library
Sherman (Texas) Public Library
Tarrant County Junior College Libraries
Temple (Texas) Public Library
Texas State Library
Texas Woman's University Library
Tyler (Texas) Public Library
University of North Texas Library
Waco-McLennan County (Texas) Public Library
Willis (Texas) Public Library

And Dr. Sue Milner, wife, supporter, and first editor, who has graced my life for almost four decades.

Prologue

Clyde Barrow and Bonnie Parker burst upon the American Southwest in the Great Depression year of 1932. At the time of Clyde's first involvement in a murder, people paid little attention to the event. He was just another violent hoodlum in a nation with a growing list of brutal criminals, which included Al Capone, John Dillinger, Pretty Boy Floyd, and the Barker gang. Not until Bonnie and Clyde joined forces did the public became intrigued. The phrase "Bonnie and Clyde" took on an electrifying and exotic meaning that has abated little in the past sixty years.

Several books and dozens of articles have been published and five motion pictures have been produced about the youthful slayers. Some volumes are devoted entirely to Bonnie and Clyde; others briefly present the couple as minor figures in larger stories about other gangsters. Articles cover the entire spectrum of imagination from a history of Bonnie and Clyde's last stolen car to their victims' personal accounts of their own kidnapping and survival. Some of these writings are major contributions to the field. For example, no work on Bonnie and Clyde can be considered complete without including the research of Dr. Carroll Rich, retired professor of English at the University of North Texas. He grew up near the site where Bonnie and Clyde were slain and personally interviewed many of the eyewitnesses to major events in the outlaw couple's final days. His articles about this particular time as well as the unusual history of the car in which they died (known as the "death car") are indispensable.

The films range from a 1937 production loosely based on the

lives of the couple to a 1967 release, *Bonnie and Clyde,* that enjoyed worldwide success. None of the books, articles, or movies totally agree, and many are grossly inconsistent with historical facts, as verifiable in primary sources. The only extensive data available (which may be considered primary sources) about the early lives of Bonnie and Clyde are from a book and an article. The book, called *The Fugitives,* was written by Bonnie's mother and Clyde's sister, in collaboration with Jan Fortune, and was published soon after the two desperadoes died in 1934. It provides the most complete details about the killers' childhoods. However, the work is severely flawed: although the authors understandably offer explanations for their relatives' criminal acts, many of the dates and events are woefully inaccurate. A cursory examination of contemporary newspapers would have prevented a majority of the errors. The second primary source is "Riding with Bonnie and Clyde," a November 1968 *Playboy* article written by W. D. Jones. Jones knew Clyde as a child and later became a member of his gang. Jones brings a unique perspective of Clyde first as a youngster and later as a man sought by every law enforcement agency, including the Federal Bureau of Investigation. Jones's memories of how Clyde's unpredictable behavior made even fellow criminals anxious proved especially enlightening; he pointed out that Clyde might be smiling and relaxed one moment, but enraged and capable of killing anyone the next. Thus, Jones supports Clyde's sister when she states that the young criminal possessed a volcanic temper inherited from both his parents, a frustration that grew from his family's devastating and grinding poverty, a passion for fashionable and expensive clothing, and an insatiable lust for fast, sleek automobiles. All of these factors combined to create a charming, albeit criminal, personality that terrorized one entire region of America for more than two years.

Perhaps the main reason for the fascination of Bonnie and Clyde by their contemporaries was their romantic involvement. At heart, Americans, then and now, are so dreamy that lovers, even criminal lovers, evoke a tender response. Still another reason for the fascination was that Bonnie and Clyde encouraged and received a tremendous amount of publicity from reporters. Newspapers and especially the new medium, radio, charted and trumpeted their progress from state to state.

With Bonnie constantly at his side, Clyde drove his stolen cars at high speeds with skill and audacity and seemed able to escape every trap laid by police. Solid ranks of officers could not restrain the ghostlike couple who came and went at will, even frequently visiting their families in Dallas. Evidence indicates Bonnie and Clyde were aided by insufficient and inefficient lawmen who were intimidated by news reports, and who often, therefore, cautiously conducted their pursuits at a respectful distance. Though Clyde was a criminal by choice and swiftly and skillfully killed when angry or cornered, he never slew his victims in cold-blood. Almost a dozen hostage victims, many of them peace officers, were released unharmed. Compared with a 1990s juvenile gang-members' random drive-by shooting, Bonnie and Clyde's escapades were relatively moderate. Surely, the events relating to the deaths of Bonnie and Clyde added a permanent aura to their memories. The fact that they died side by side and virtually in one another's arms further contributed to the romantic charisma.

Finally, every life must be considered against the background of his or her time. Bonnie and Clyde were on the run from police during the worst economic times in the history of the nation. The New York Stock Exchange had crashed in October 1929, and economic chaos quickly followed. The banking system of the nation soon collapsed as nearly 10,000 banks went out of business between 1930 and 1933, swallowing nearly $3 billion in depositors' money, which simply vanished. Securities investors joined bank depositors in watching with disbelief as their life savings also disappeared.

The country's money supply declined by 33 percent, a significant amount, which led to great loss of purchasing power. Manufacturing firms reduced prices to the bone, cut back on production, and slashed their work forces. Unemployment in major cities like New York, Chicago, and Toledo ranged from 50 to 80 percent. Gaunt and dazed men roamed the city streets seeking jobs to be greeted by endless displays of No Help Wanted signs. Ultimately, these desperate souls, blaming themselves instead of the system that had failed them, gave up their quests and dropped out of the work force. Some committed suicide; others deserted their families in shame.

People who heretofore had considered their families to be part of the middle class found themselves signing up for relief programs (welfare), which soon collapsed. When cities proved unable to continue any meaningful help, desperate citizens turned to their states.

Here public officials pointed to declining tax revenues and offered little help. Breadlines and soup kitchens became jammed with starving people in almost every American city. Churches and charities attempted to cope with the flood of hungry people but were overwhelmed by the widespread sufferers. Total malnutrition resulted in many cases and citizens were admitted to hospitals in the final phase of starvation.

American rural areas were in just as desperate shape. Farmers had been in a severe recession for almost a decade when the Great Depression began in 1929. As farm income fell by nearly 65 percent from 1929 to 1932, hardship became desperation. Foreclosures forced more than 33 percent of farmers off their lands. Exacerbating the farm problem, a catastrophic drought struck the Great Plains region in 1930 and lasted for almost ten years.

By the time Bonnie and Clyde became well known, many Americans felt the capitalistic system had been abused by big business and government officials until it had failed the people. Now here were the charismatic Bonnie and Clyde who were striking back at what many viewed as a corrupted system. For Americans in the south, with a populist strain still quite strong in their bones and their psyches, Bonnie and Clyde became heroes, a modern day Robin Hood and Maid Marian; they terrified the bankers and businessmen who were perceived by more than a few as the people's tormentors.

The outlaws' mobility put everyone in the nation at risk. For two years, various law enforcement agencies attempted, without success, to capture or kill Bonnie and Clyde. Other gang members, even relatives, were caught or slain, but the two principals remained free. Finally Bonnie and Clyde smuggled weapons into the Texas prison system and led an attack that freed several dangerous criminals, including one of their most violent gang members, Raymond Hamilton. Texas, through its prison director, Lee Simmons, set into motion a plan to remove this couple. Simmons selected a former Texas Ranger captain, Frank Hamer, to track the outlaw gang; his advice to the lawman was to shoot Bonnie and Clyde on sight. For assistance, Hamer picked a Texas highway patrolman and four local lawmen for his posse and drove off after them. Within three months Bonnie and Clyde fell before the lawmen's guns.

1

Bonnie and Clyde

Shortly before 9:00 o'clock on the morning of 23 May 1934, a tan 1934 Ford sedan, stolen in Topeka, Kansas, a few days before, sped along the Sailes Road about eight miles south of Gibsland in northwest Louisiana. The occupants, Bonnie and Clyde, were high upon the list of most wanted criminals in America. In other circumstances the couple would be considered attractive. Bonnie was small, less than five feet tall and weighed about ninety pounds. Ringlets of strawberry blond hair surrounded the fragile features of her face; a spray of freckles crossed her nose and deep dimples adorned her cheeks. Conscious of her clothes, she usually donned a stylish red dress, shoes, bag, and hat. Most people considered Clyde a handsome young man with his impish, quick smile, and thick brown hair parted on the left side. His brown eyes had a slight squint, as if he had strained to see great distances far longer than his twenty-five years. A thin, small man, he weighed about one hundred and twenty-five pounds and stood only a few inches taller than Bonnie. Clyde usually wore a business suit, often with a vest, and a white shirt and tie. Frequently, he wore a light gray wide-band hat that was fashionable in the 1930s. But his well-dressed appearance and his smiling face concealed a slumbering volcanic temper waiting to explode.[1]

Bonnie and Clyde knew a posse was on their trail. They didn't know, however, that the six officers themselves had driven along this Louisiana road just seven hours before. The lawmen had carefully turned off the dirt lane and hidden their cars behind dense shrubbery on the east side of the road. The humid night was like black ink as the officers stumbled through the brush. The leader arranged the men in their ambush positions facing the road. As they lay down in the foliage, briars and stickers clutched at the fabric of their business suits. Huge mosquitoes and other flying insects gouged at the men's faces, and the officers responded with slaps and soft curses. The posse leader, Frank Hamer, chain-smoked as he walked along the line checking on his squad. A large man, he stood well over six feet and weighed more than two hundred pounds. Though his face was full and round, the skin was creased with wrinkles like shallow desert erosions, and contrasted with his hard but sad gray eyes. The hardness came from a lifetime of confronting criminals. He had killed several male outlaws in the line of duty, but he had never had to kill a woman. Accordingly, his eyes were touched with sadness when he considered that in the next few hours he would have to kill Bonnie Parker as well as Clyde Barrow.

These six officers represented the leading edge of an immense force of lawmen who pursued Bonnie and Clyde with orders to shoot on sight. Though the young outlaws had never been formally arraigned in a court of law for their crimes, a trial of sorts had been held in the newspapers and in the hearts and minds of most citizens of the Southwest. Even after excluding the unsolved crimes, unfairly assigned to the bandits, the evidence proved overwhelming and had been presented by legions of victims. Essentially, a regional jury of public opinion had found the pair guilty and assigned these half-dozen lawmen the task of carrying out the sentences of death.

Ironically, the condemned pair accepted the decision and recognized that their deaths were inevitable. They simply hoped to delay execution of the sentence for as long as possible and remain free on a sort of apocryphal appeal. The outlaws knew, however, that the end drew near. Bonnie passed the time on the road by composing primitive poetry. Her latest effort, "It's Death for Bonnie and Clyde," included the passage, "The road gets dimmer and dimmer. Sometimes you can hardly see." During their last family meeting, Bonnie implored her mother, "When they kill us, don't let them take me to an undertaking parlor, will you? Bring me home."[2]

The ambush site was on top of a knoll with a view that stretched for one-half mile to the north and one mile to the south. Located between Gibsland and Sailes, it was a rendezvous point for the Barrow gang. One month earlier a gang member's father had guaranteed the posse leader that he would betray Bonnie and Clyde in exchange for a pardon for his son. Receiving the father's message that the outlaws would be on the Sailes Road Wednesday morning, the posse hurried to the site.

In both Louisiana and Texas, other people, who within hours would be drawn into the vortex of violence, prepared for the day. In the southern part of the parish, William Lyons, an African American truck driver, started his vehicle. A logger, Lyons planned to pick up a load of pulp logs from woodcutters near Sailes and haul them to the mill. His trip would take him past the site where the officers waited. Several miles to the northeast in Arcadia, Louisiana, Dr. J. L. Wade slept fitfully after calling on several patients before going to bed after midnight. Dr. Wade also served as the parish coroner.[3]

Inactive members of the outlaw gang waited in various Texas jails. Raymond Hamilton, an original gang member, lay on a cell cot in the Denton County Jail; he had been captured after robbing a bank at West, Texas. Razor thin, sharp featured, with thinning blond hair and flinty brown eyes, Hamilton was arrogant, nervous, volatile, and impulsive. Forty miles away, W. D. Jones snoozed in the Dallas County Jail. A short, chubby, frightened, young man with thick, straight hair and deep brown eyes that constantly displayed trepidation, Jones had been in jail since his arrest near Houston the previous year. He claimed Bonnie and Clyde had forced him to join the gang and kept him chained. Jones eagerly told authorities everything he could recall about the young couple.[4]

Across town in west Dallas, Bonnie Parker's mother and Clyde Barrow's parents, their hair gray and faces creased with worry lines, rose from uneasy sleep. Before retiring the night before, Mrs. Barrow had prayed that God would allow her to see Clyde one more time before authorities caught up with him.[5]

2
A Legacy of Violence

Several factors had joined to form the heritage of Bonnie and Clyde and delivered them to this point. At the time of their births, most Texans' roots remained steadfastly planted in a diminishing frontier. Only a few years before, the state flaunted a macho-type individual. A singular and personal code of vigilantism dictated dependence upon no outside help for settlement of disputes. Every frontiersman wore a six-shooter strapped to his side and gunfights easily erupted from slight or imagined offenses. The usual violent atmosphere was fueled by a sturdy strain of racial hatred that resulted in frequent lynchings of Blacks and shooting and pistol-whipping of Mexicans, Indians, and Orientals. The rural background added to the intrinsic harsh nature of many Texans: some radical groups of the early ranchers used trackers and murderers to trail, capture, and execute cattle rustlers. And expanding exploitation of agrarians by landlords through the crop-lien system and farm tenancy further exacerbated the violent nature present in many Texas farmers. Against this turbulent and ferocious background, Bonnie's and Clyde's parents married and raised their families.

Clyde's father, Henry, had known nothing but wrenching poverty most of his life. A short, chubby, quiet man, he worked relentlessly on a few acres of leased land just outside Teleco, in Ellis County, Texas; he had never traveled far from home and his tenant farm was less than twenty-five miles from Palmer, the place of his birth. Like many Texas farmers, he had never attended school and could neither read nor write.

Cumie, his wife, a native of Nacogdoches, Texas, looked older than her years, with graying hair and a sun-lined face; she occasionally read the family Bible but had little time for other relaxation. While Henry labored in the cotton fields with mules, hoe, and cotton sack, she kept house, bore annual children, and frequently joined him and their offspring in helping with the crops. Perhaps because of the strain of survival, the couple was lax about discipline. Later Nell Barrow could remember none of the children ever being punished and speculated that perhaps the lack of correction led to her brothers' lives of crime.[1]

By 1909 the Barrows had four children and expected another. On 24 March, as Henry drudgingly plowed the black, crusty land near the crude and unpainted shack, one of the raggedly dressed children came running from the house with the message that Cumie was in labor and needed the midwife. Later that day Cumie delivered a son and named him Clyde Chestnut. Ironically, when the midwife notified a local physician, Dr. Jonas Palmer, of the birth, he recorded it incorrectly as "baby girl Barrow" in the *Vital Statistics* volume of the Ellis County Courthouse at Waxahachie.[2]

Three additional children followed Clyde's birth and the family's financial difficulties worsened as the price of cotton bounced up and down erratically. During some years, the Barrows found it impossible to provide for their children and sent them to live with relatives in east Texas. At one kinsman's home, Clyde developed two interests that remained with him to the end of his life: a passion for music and an obsession with guns. Even as Clyde drove along the lane in Louisiana, the backseat of his stolen tan Ford contained a saxophone and reams of sheet music as well as an arsenal of firearms—symbols of the celebration of life juxtaposed with the firearms as constant harbingers of death. Clyde loved and named his guns and regarded them as tokens of his power.[3]

Deciding they could stay on the tenant farm no longer, the Barrows loaded their household goods onto their ramshackled truck in 1921 and left the land for good. Since they migrated to Dallas with no prospect for jobs and with very little money, the family was forced to live under the Oak Cliff viaduct for several days until Henry found a job and rented a house. All the children attended Cedar Valley School, but Clyde frequently played hookey. At the age of sixteen, he dropped out of school to work at the Proctor and Gamble plant. One of his co-workers invited the youngster home for dinner and introduced him to his sister. The two young people began dating, always in the company of several of her middle-class friends who accepted Clyde as an equal. The following year, during the young woman's senior year at Forest Avenue High School, Clyde seriously considered marriage and gave her several gifts, including rings, a watch, and luggage. As was the custom among poor-class men, Clyde had the girl's initials, E. B. W., along with a dagger through a heart, tattooed on his left arm. The girl, however, had never considered Clyde anything except a friend, and the young couple drifted apart. She returned all the gifts except a watch, which Clyde refused to accept. In what can only be tremendous irony, the watch was stolen from her Dallas home by a burglar in 1975.[4]

Clyde's older brother, Marvin Ivan (nicknamed Buck), was a slow, plodding man with a gangly, saber-thin body; his emaciated face held clear, hard eyes that radiated coldness. Complex and significant differences separated the brothers. While Clyde was excitable and explosive, Buck was passionless and apathetic; though Clyde never drank whiskey, Buck was virtually an alcoholic; although Clyde dressed in the latest men's fashion, Buck preferred khaki or denim overalls; when Clyde constantly planned for the future, Buck drifted aimlessly; whereas Clyde became a leader, Buck remained a follower.

In 1926 Buck asked Clyde to help steal a small flock of turkeys in east Texas and transport them to Dallas to sell for Christmas money. Dallas officers, seeing the backseat filled with live fowl, forced the Barrow car over to the curb and arrested both men. Buck claimed full responsibility, swore that Clyde was unaware the birds were stolen, and went to jail for several days.[5]

Because Clyde looked so small and innocent, the lawmen believed the story and freed the youngster. Within a few weeks, Clyde made a trip to Wichita Falls, Texas, and met a girl named Grace; he brought her back to Dallas, told several people that he and the girl were married, and lived with her for several months before she returned home. After Grace left, Clyde's sister Nell begged Clyde to return to their parents' home. Since the Barrow family lived in the most dreadful depths of poverty, he refused and began rooming with a man of his same age, Frank Clause. Though the men became close friends, the contrast between the two was striking: while Clyde smiled much of the time, Frank always appeared sullen; his tight, thin lips and cruel, frosty, marble-gray eyes in a pale, hawkish face seemed never to have known a smile. An ambiance of intense hatred surrounded the young man like a vapor.[6]

Within a short time, Clyde quit his job at Proctor and Gamble and joined Buck, Clause, and Sidney Moore in burglarizing businesses in Dallas, Lufkin, and Hillsboro, Texas. Clyde's criminal career had progressed in brief and rapid steps from a reasonably conscientious worker to a turkey rustler, then burglar, then automobile thief. Although Clyde was introduced to crime by Buck and was later absorbed into the gang, he quickly evolved as the leader of the lawless group.

Shortly before noon on 29 November 1929, three of the outlaws left Dallas in a stolen, black Buick sedan and drove northwest. Clyde slouched under the steering wheel with a pistol lying beside him; occasionally, he nodded to his brother Buck sitting with him in the seat to guide the car while he rolled a Bull Durham cigarette. Buck frequently reached under the front seat, pulled out a quart fruit jar, and gulped a swallow of moonshine whiskey while he pointedly ignored Clyde's look of disgust. Sidney Moore rode in the backseat; a small, slight man with gray eyes and sandy hair, he drank from his own Mason jar while he solemnly examined the lonesome countryside. The cold and blustery late autumn weather and the clouded gray sky depressed the young man. Like Buck, Moore was awed by Clyde's drive and intelligence. A long-time friend of the Barrows, he also grew up in the singular squalor of west Dallas and was just as committed to a life of crime as were the Barrow brothers.

Their destination, Henrietta, the largest town in Clay County, sat about twenty miles south of the Red River, which divided Texas and Oklahoma. Authorities later told reporters that the gang needed a new car, since their auto, stolen earlier in Dallas, unquestionably was on every police officer's list. Clyde cruised through Henrietta for several minutes. Finally he pulled to the curb behind a black Model A Ford sedan. The three men craned their necks and carefully scanned the street in all directions. Clyde slowly nodded to Buck, who jumped out and dashed to the deserted car. Quietly raising the hood, Buck clipped the wires together to start the Ford and then got into the right front seat. The other two vaulted from their car, ran to the new auto, and climbed inside. Clyde drove around town for nearly an hour before stopping at the curb of an apparently vacant house in an exclusive neighborhood. He again nodded to Buck, who walked to the front door and knocked loudly.

When no one answered the door, Clyde turned into the driveway and pulled around to the back. Buck inspected the immediate area before following the car to the rear of the deserted house. They quickly forced open the back door and separated to ransack the house. Buck hurried into the living room, Clyde ran into the bedroom wing, and Moore looked in the kitchen. In the dresser of the master bedroom, Clyde found a case of jewelry articles that obviously were of very good quality. When the three men met in the front hall, Clyde's prizes were the only significant find. They returned to the car, hurriedly drove away and stopped in a city park. Pulling the jewelry from his pockets, Clyde divided it equally.[7]

By early evening the three were driving southeast toward Dallas. As the lights of Henrietta faded in the rear window, the three outlaws discussed their immediate problems: a shortage of cash and an uncertainty of when they could sell the jewelry they had stolen in Henrietta, or even how much they could expect to get for it. Somewhere along the darkening road to Dallas, Clyde decided they must create another opportunity. It was well past midnight when the car neared Denton, located forty miles northwest of Dallas. Disdainful of small-town policemen, Clyde decided to burglarize a business to find cash. Denton's police force was small but efficient, and two members patrolled in a squad car at night. Officers Clint Starr and T. E. Jones had reported for duty at midnight. They cruised the courthouse square and the first ring of streets before driving to the two local colleges for a slow inspection.[8]

Police concluded that shortly after 1:00 A.M., the Barrow gang drove along Denton's streets in search of a firm to burgle. After cruising a few blocks, Clyde coasted to a crawl near the Motor Mark Garage on Oak Street; he pulled around to the rear and turned off the lights and ignition. Buck and Moore hurried to the garage's rear door and attacked it with a wrecking bar. Clyde walked to the edge of the building, watched for a brief time, and returned to the back door. Within seconds the door gave way and swung open with a slight squeak. Leading the others inside, Clyde struck a match and cupped his hand as a makeshift lantern. Buck saw the small safe sitting against the back wall near the door, pulled a candle stub from his pocket, and lit the wick from Clyde's match; he knelt down before the safe and stood the candle nearby. At 1:50 P.M., as the bandits labored over the safe, Officers Starr and Jones stopped for coffee at the police station, located behind the city hall, before resuming their rounds.[9]

Moore rummaged in the tool bag and handed Buck a hammer and chisel as Clyde walked to the front of the building and looked out the window. Buck placed the chisel against the combination dial and brought the hammer down causing a loud clang to echo through the empty garage; he waited for a few seconds. Clyde surveyed the darkened street from the front window, turned, and nodded. Buck continued to hit the chisel until the dial fell to the floor. Moore stepped forward and pried the door with the pinch bar. When the safe refused to open, Clyde shrugged: "Well, just load the damn thing in the car." The men lifted the safe, wiggled through the back door, and staggered to the car. Moore jerked open the left door and backed into the car while he held his side of the safe. Clyde and Buck pushed the box through the door and allowed it to fall on the left side of the rear seat. Clyde climbed into the driver's seat as Buck ran around to the right front. The large clock on the Denton County National Bank building struck 2:00 A.M., as Clyde turned the car west on Oak Street.[10]

Leaving headquarters, the patrol car moved toward one of the main thoroughfares, Oak Street. The officers noticed the suspicious car speed up as it passed the cruising police vehicle. Skeptical of a car on the streets at that time of night, Officer Jones blew his whistle and signaled Clyde to pull over to the curb. Clyde ignored the policeman's order and raced along the deserted street; he warily watched the car's headlights in his rear-view mirror and frantically searched for a way to elude the policemen.[11]

Spotting Piner Street, a short connecting lane that ran south off Oak, Clyde turned the corner too sharply, struck the curb with the left front wheel, and broke the axle. He jumped from the disabled car, ran south down Piner, and disappeared into the night. Jones skidded the patrol car to a halt behind the wreck and Starr sprang out with his pistol drawn. Buck and Sidney Moore scrambled from the wreckage and ran down Piner. Leveling his pistol, Starr yelled, "This is the police. Stop or I'll shoot." When both men continued to run, the officer opened fire, and Buck fell to the pavement screaming with pain from a wound in his knee; Moore stopped and raised his hands. Still running, Clyde recognized Buck's cries and feared he had been killed. Jones and Starr temporarily bound Buck's wound, transported the suspects to the red stone jail located a few blocks away, and began their processing. While Starr searched Moore and Buck for hidden weapons, Jones telephoned the doctor.[12] The policemen then marched the two outlaws down the hall to a holding cell, and returned to the office to fill out their arrest reports. Sitting dejectedly on his cot, Moore thrust his hands into his pockets and felt the hard, sharp edges of the jewelry stolen in Henrietta. He jerked the gems out. Buck lay on his bunk, groaning in pain, and failed to notice. Moore looked at the cell door, then crouched beside his friend. "Buck, what are we going to do with the jewelry? They'll know we stole it." Buck stopped moaning and said, "You've got to throw everything out the windows." Reaching inside his own pockets, he withdrew a number of diamond rings and handed them to Moore.[13]

Officer Starr stepped out the front door of the police station to wait for the physician. A silvery, flashing movement caught his eye as he glanced at the window of the cell containing his two captives. Just then, more jewelry sailed out and landed near his feet. Gathering up the ornaments, Starr walked back into the station to show his partner the strange, shiny missiles.[14]

Dr. W. C. Kimbrough arrived shortly thereafter and worked on Buck's knee. Finishing about dawn, he walked out of the station and met County Attorney Earl Street.

"Well, how about my suspect, Doc? When can I have him?"

Dr. Kimbrough set down his black bag and stretched. "Well, since no bones were broken and no arteries damaged, I'd say he could face the Grand Jury and trial within a few days."[15]

Meanwhile Clyde hitchhiked back to Dallas where police arrested him the next day at his parents' home on charges of automobile theft. Nell states that on 3 December 1929, Lt. Douglas Walsh of the Dallas Police Department Fingerprinting and Photographic section, processed the young man. The picture indicated a small, good-looking boy who appeared much younger than his twenty years. His brown hair was clipped short and his dark eyes showed traces of sadness and fear. Clyde was soon tried for car theft; he was convicted and given a suspended sentence.[16]

During this same time, the grand jury had convened in Denton.

Newspapers reported that on Wednesday, 5 December 1929, Earl Street presented the cases of Sidney Moore and Marvin Ivan "Buck" Barrow. The arresting officers' depositions convinced the panel that the cases warranted trial. The following day the grand jury delivered fifteen felony bills, including those of Buck Barrow and Sidney Moore, to District Judge Ben Boyd. The court clerk set their trial to begin on Tuesday, 17 December 1929. Buck hobbled into the courtroom aided by crutches. When Judge Boyd asked for their pleas, Barrow and Moore stood with their attorneys and pleaded not guilty. The case moved along quickly as Denton police officers Starr and Jones testified about the capture and the safe found in the wrecked auto. Starr related how the two men had thrown jewelry from their cell window, and County Attorney Street introduced evidence from Henrietta connecting the defendants with the theft of the car and the burglary of the house. Neither Barrow nor Moore testified.

Shortly after noon, both the defense and the prosecution rested their cases, and the jury withdrew to consider the evidence. Within minutes the group filed back into the jury box and announced the verdict: both Barrow and Moore were guilty of theft of over fifty dollars and burglary of a habitation. Judge Boyd deferred sentencing for a week, and the bailiff led both felons from the courtroom. On 23 December 1929, Judge W. C. Boyd, sitting in for his ill brother, sentenced both men to four years for each count with the terms to be served concurrently. The two men returned to the county jail and remained there until they were moved to Huntsville State prison on 14 January 1930.[17]

Meanwhile, in Dallas, Clyde visited an injured girlfriend who had fallen on icy steps and had broken her arm. Her neighbor, Bonnie Parker, had moved in for a few days to help with the housework. On the night of 5 January 1930, Clyde called on the woman. Having an insatiable appetite for chocolate, he joined Bonnie in the kitchen to brew a pot of hot cocoa. Clyde fell in love with Bonnie almost instantly and never romantically considered another woman again.[18]

3
Bonnie and Clyde Are the Barrow Gang

Bonnie Parker was born in the small Runnels County town of Rowena, Texas, on 1 October 1910. Buster, her brother, was two years older, and her sister, Billie, three years younger. Her father, Charles, worked as a brick mason and her mother, Emma, was a housewife. The family lived quietly, attended First Baptist Church, and seldom went out except to participate in church activities.[1]

In 1915 Bonnie's father died suddenly, and Mrs. Parker faced the prospect of raising three children alone. Mr. and Mrs. Edward Krouse, Bonnie's maternal grandparents, who lived in a suburb of Dallas called Cement City, encouraged the family to come live with them. Since job prospects were much better in Dallas than in Rowena, the widow accepted the offer. In school Bonnie became a good student and frequently won prizes for writing essays, reciting poetry, and spelling. She had no formal dates until she was fifteen years of age. Within a short time, however, she began seeing a school mate, Roy Thornton. He was a thin, small boy with an elongated head that was topped with dark, curly hair; his appearance was accented by large, protruding ears and a long, narrow nose. The following year Bonnie and Roy, both sixteen, were married. Thornton soon discovered that Bonnie could not bear to be away from her mother. Though the couple lived only two blocks from the Parker home on Olive Street, Bonnie insisted that Thornton check on her mother every day. After several weeks of having her son-in-law visit her at all hours, Mrs. Parker suggested that the couple move into her home, and Bonnie readily agreed.[2]

Perhaps because of Bonnie's obsession with her mother, Thornton temporarily left her early in August 1927. After waiting at home for several weeks, Bonnie got a job as a waitress at Marco's Cafe on Main Street in downtown Dallas, near the county courthouse. Within a few months, Ted Hinton, a subsequent member of the ambush posse, met Bonnie while eating his noon meals at the cafe. He considered her pretty and an enthusiastic worker. Bonnie told Hinton that she wanted to be an entertainer or poet.[3]

Bonnie's husband continued to drift in and out of her life. Near the end of January 1928, she decided that if he ever returned, she would send him away for good. When Thornton reappeared in January 1929, Bonnie ordered him to leave. As a youngster, Thornton had served a term in the Oklahoma Reform School at El Reno. After leaving Bonnie, he had joined an outlaw gang. In early 1929, he was arrested by police during a robbery in Red Oak, Texas. Following a brief trial, a Dallas County jury sentenced him to the Texas prison system for five years.[4]

Mrs. Parker appealed to Bonnie, "Honey, why don't you divorce that man?" Bonnie shook her head. "I didn't divorce him before he went to jail. I feel like it would be wrong to file while he's in prison."

In November 1929 Marco's Cafe closed. The New York Stock Exchange had crashed in October, and the economy had begun to shrink. Bonnie diligently looked for another job but could find none. Because she had not found employment, Bonnie readily agreed to stay with the neighbor who had fallen and broken her arm; here she met Clyde. Mrs. Parker visited the girl's home in mid-January 1930 and met Clyde, who was spending a great deal more time with Bonnie. Even at this first meeting, she sensed the attraction between the couple, noticing an urgency in Bonnie's voice when she introduced him and the way the couple looked at one another and touched.

Within a few days, the neighbor recovered, and Bonnie returned home. On Wednesday night, 12 February 1930, Clyde came to visit Bonnie at her home. He hesitantly told her, "I'm going to leave Dallas in the morning."

Bonnie gasped. "Honey, you can't leave just when we are getting to know each other. Please stay in town a little longer."

"You don't understand, Sugar," he said. "The laws are bound and determined to pin something on me."

He got up to leave. Bonnie rushed over and kissed him. "Please stay with me a little longer." The couple sat talking so long that Mrs. Parker came into the living room.

"Listen, Clyde," she said. "It's so late now that you might as well spend the night. You can sleep on the couch."[5]

Meanwhile, Dallas authorities had issued an all-points bulletin for Clyde. Police were helped by informants to trace him to the Parker residence, where they arrested Clyde on suspicion of several burglaries, including the Motor Mark Garage in Denton.   Disturbed that the police had come to her house, Mrs. Parker asked Bonnie not to see Clyde again. Bonnie vehemently shook her head. "It ain't his fault, Mama. The laws are out to get him. You'll see that Clyde will clear up the charges and never do anything wrong again."

In her letters to Clyde, Bonnie said, "When you get out I want you to go to work, and for God's sake, don't ever get into any more trouble." Another message read, "Honey, if you get out OK, please don't ever do anything to get locked up again."

When Clyde responded that the Dallas police were hounding him, Bonnie replied, "You could go somewhere else and get a job and work. I want you to be a man, Honey, and not a thug."[6]

The evidence against Clyde in the Denton garage burglary proved inconclusive, and Waco and McClennan County authorities asked that he be transferred there for a hearing. On 2 March 1930 the Waco police moved Clyde from Denton. Learning of the move, Bonnie went immediately to her mother. "Mama, loan me the bus fare to Waco." Horrified, Mrs. Parker answered, "Bonnie you can't go off to Waco just because Clyde is there. In the first place you might not be safe. In the second, it would not be proper."

"Now, Mama, don't forget that Cousin Mary moved to Waco here a while back. I could stay with her."

"What about Mary's husband?"

Bonnie shook her head. "He's a musician and travels all the time. You know she asked me to stay with her some."

Mrs. Parker sighed. "Honey, Clyde might not even be convicted. He got off in Denton."

Bonnie pressed her lips and shook her head. "No, Mama, this is different. You know they are out to get him."

Emma Parker cocked her head. "I just don't have the money right now, Honey."

Bonnie persisted. "Well, just say it's okay for me to go. I'll ride down with Clyde's mother. She needs somebody to go with her anyhow. And staying with Mary, I won't need any money."

After several arguments, Mrs. Parker relented. Bonnie rode to Waco with Clyde's mother on 3 March 1930 and moved in with her cousin. That night she wrote Clyde a letter in which she promised to get a job in town to be near him until he was transferred to the state prison in Huntsville. Bonnie closed the note by declaring her love and promising to do anything she could to help him; she soon learned that he expected her to break him out of jail.[7]

On Saturday, 8 March 1930, officers placed William Turner and three other prisoners, all first offenders, in the block with Clyde. Turner, a stiff, lanky man with blank eyes, began his criminal career in 1926, when he was convicted of burglary. Paroled the following year, he was immediately convicted of auto theft by another jury. Officers returned him to Waco in November 1927 for another trial for receiving and concealing stolen property. After going back to prison, Turner escaped and remained free until arrested in Houston. After again being imprisoned, he received a second parole and soon returned to Waco to commit a new series of robberies of private businesses as well as of the United States Post Office at Mount Calm, Texas. Evidence indicated Lee Black and Pat Beweley joined in the crimes. Facing a lengthy federal prison sentence, Turner offered to testify against Black and Beweley in return for a reduced term.[8]

Bonnie continued to visit Clyde in the cell block as often as the jailers would permit. When she came on Saturday, 8 March, Clyde put his hand through the bars and patted Bonnie's cheek. "How're you doing, Sugar?"

She placed her small hand on his. "Oh, I'm alright. I just can't stand to see you cooped up like this."

Turner walked over to stand beside Clyde. He peered along the corridor, then in a low voice, said, "Maybe you won't have to much longer."

Glancing at Clyde, Bonnie saw no change in his mien; she looked back at Turner. "What are you talking about?"

Turner leaned closer to the bars. "I'm talking about a way to get us out of here. It's possible, but it all depends on you."

Frowning, Bonnie said loudly, "Me? Why on me?"

Clyde put his finger to his lips as a signal to be quiet. "Just listen to him, Sugar."

She looked from Clyde to Turner and asked, "Well?"

Turner's eyes narrowed. "My folks live at 625 Turner Avenue over in east Waco. They're going to be gone until late tonight. You can slip in there about dark, get my gun, and bring it back to us." Bonnie looked at Clyde; she saw him watching for a reaction. "Is this what you want, Clyde?"

He shrugged. "It's a way to get me out of here, Honey." "Maybe it's a way to get you killed, too," she said softly. Clyde shook his head. "Naw, with a pistol we can walk out of here slick as a button." Bonnie took a deep breath and exhaled in resignation. "Okay," she said, "tell me what to do." Turner again glanced along the corridor to ensure no officer was listening. "The front door will be locked." He grinned, "You know, there's crooks everywhere these days."

Bonnie stared at him coldly.

"Anyhow," Turner continued, "the key is over the front doorsill on the lefthand side." From his pocket, he removed a pencil stub and a ragged sheet of paper. "I can make you a layout of the house." He quickly drew the floor plan of the Turner house. In one bedroom, he drew an *X* and held the paper through the cell facing Bonnie. "You'll find a closet here," he said. "Under a whole bunch of junk there's a gun." Bonnie looked at the drawing for several seconds. Sagging against the cell door, she took the drawing, folded it, and put it into her purse. "Why is it that I have to get it. Why don't your folks bring it in here?"

Turner spread his hands. "Because they're working late. They don't get home till nearly ten o'clock."

Clyde patted her hand. "I told Bill we could count on you, Sugar. Get the gun and bring it back tonight. You just never know when a chance to bust out might come up."

Bonnie nodded, kissed Clyde, and walked down the corridor; she hurried to the car where Mary waited, reading a newspaper. Jumping inside, Bonnie said, "We need to go over to Turner Avenue in east Waco to pick up something for the boys." Her cousin folded the newspaper, nodded, and started the car. The sun was sinking in the west when the two girls pulled up in front of the Turner home. The small frame dwelling sat quiet and without lights in the early evening of 8 March. They walked casually up the sidewalk, located the key over the doorsill, and stepped inside. Once inside, Mary turned to Bonnie and asked, "What are we going to get."

Bonnie looked at her evenly and murmured, "A gun."

"A gun?" asked the other girl in a loud voice. "What on earth for?"

"Shhh," cautioned Bonnie. "Pull down the shades and I'll turn on the light."

Mary lowered the paper blinds and turned back to Bonnie. "I want to know why you're looking for a gun."

"For Clyde, of course."

Mary began to tremble. "Good gracious, Bonnie. What if somebody came home and caught us here?"

Bonnie looked at the sketch of the house and walked toward the indicated bedroom. As she stepped out of the living room, she said, "They won't." Mary followed her into the bedroom as Bonnie pulled down the shades and flicked on the light. Bonnie turned to her cousin. "Listen, Mary. I'm going to find that gun if it's the last thing I ever do. If you help me we can get out of here quicker." She opened the closet door and rummaged among the items stacked on the floor.

Mary stood in the middle of the bedroom wringing her hands as Bonnie came out of the closet and glanced around the room.

"Well, I can't find the darn thing."

"Okay," said Mary, "let's get out of here."

Bonnie ignored Mary's statement and started into another room, "Don't just stand there, Mary. Help me look for it."

The girls went from room to room until they finally located the pistol and bullets in a window seat. Bonnie dashed for the front door with Mary close behind. They stopped briefly and looked back at the strewn house. Bonnie shook her head. "I hate to leave the house torn up like a wild sow's bed, but we have to get out of here."

They ran out the front door, locked it, and placed the key above the sill. Driving back toward the jail, Mary felt her hands shaking as she held the steering wheel. "My Lord, Bonnie," she said. "I feel like everybody is looking at us."

"That's just your imagination. Nobody's paying any attention to us."

Mary glanced at Bonnie. "Thank goodness it's getting dark. How can you be so calm?"

"I'm thinking. The hardest part is still ahead. How am I going to get this gun into Clyde?"

"Oh, my Lord," groaned Mary.

After they had driven for several blocks, Bonnie snapped her fingers. "Pull over to the curb. I think I've got a way figured out." When the car had stopped, Bonnie held out her hand. "Let me have your belt."

Mary shook her head, but handed over the article. Bonnie put the belt around her waist and buckled it tightly; she lowered the pistol down the inside of her dress between the outer garment and her slip. Patting her bosom, she turned to Mary. "Do you think the jailer will be able to see anything?"

Mary struck a match and held it up for light. "Good gosh, Bonnie. Of course he can."

Bonnie turned back to the front. "Well, I'll just have to take a chance. I'll put my sweater on and keep my arms folded across my chest." She slipped her arms into the sleeves as the car arrived at the jail; she climbed out and crossed the street while buttoning the front of her sweater. Bonnie entered the jail and asked permission to see Clyde again. When the jailer consented to a short visit, she delivered the gun, hurried back downstairs, and they drove away. Neither Bonnie nor Mary could sleep and spent the night pacing the floor.[9]

They had burglarized a private home and had smuggled a deadly weapon into a county jail to aid in an escape. Evidently these were the first felonious actions of Bonnie's young life, and the implications probably troubled her. Up to this point, Bonnie Parker still had two choices: she could either live as a law-abiding citizen without Clyde Barrow or she could continue to support him in a troubled life that almost certainly would lead to more serious criminal acts; Bonnie chose to go with Clyde.

Police told *Waco Tribune-Herald* reporters that the following day another prisoner had been placed in the cell block. This expedited the escape plan. Emery Abernathy towered over Turner and Clyde and appeared dark and brooding with black eyes, a knife-blade nose, and a pulsing vein in his forehead like a small blue snake. He bragged to his new cell mates of his lucrative crimes and various capers. Though he was already serving a six-year term in the state penitentiary, officers moved him to Waco to face trial on new charges. A fellow prisoner, Monroe Routen, had written to District Attorney Dick Holt implicating Abernathy in another burglary. In interviews with authorities, both Abernathy and Routen confessed to the crime as well as to the robbery of the First State Bank of Reisel in 1925. On Sunday, 9 March 1930, law enforcement officials brought Abernathy back to the McClennan County Jail on a bench warrant to stand trial for the Reisel bank robbery. The following morning Federal Judge C. A. Boynton sentenced Clyde's other cell mate, William Turner, to three years in Leavenworth Federal Prison for his part in the Mount Calm Post Office robbery. Later that same day, Turner appeared in District Court before Judge R. I. Munroe, who sentenced him to twenty-five four-year terms for the burglaries. The sentences were to run concurrently. That evening Clyde, Abernathy, and Turner held a whispered conference. Clyde said, "Now's the time to make our getaway. There ain't no telling when we will be moved."

Turner nodded. "Besides that," he said, "there's a good chance that the pistol could be found in a routine shakedown."

Abernathy narrowed his eyes. "Okay. Start thinking about a plan to bust out." They soon devised a scheme to bring the night jailer to their area and get the door open.

The second floor block contained several cells, but the jailers allowed inmates to circulate throughout the cell block prior to being locked into individual cells at bedtime. At about 7:00 P.M. Turner asked for milk to settle his upset stomach. Following McClennan County Jail procedures, night jailer I. P. Stanford left his weapon in the downstairs office, opened the door, and placed the milk just inside the cell. Standing near the bars, Turner reached over to get the milk and suddenly rushed to the cell door and jammed his head and shoulders through the still-open door.

Abernathy ran to the door, brandishing the pistol, and growled, "Hold up your hands, Screw."

Stanford considered calling out to the city jail turnkey, Huse Jones, who was seated in the hall on the first floor. But Abernathy placed the end of the gun barrel to his head and said, "I'll kill you if you make a sound."

Recognizing the deep desperation in Abernathy's face, Stanford raised his hands and kept quiet. Clyde, Turner, and Abernathy ran out of the cell and pushed the jailer inside. The three other prisoners in the block, men accused of nonviolent crimes (petty theft, counterfeiting, and embezzlement), rushed to Stanford's side and said, "We are going to stay with you." All three later testified that they noticed the pistol for the first time that morning and denied any knowledge of how it got into the cell.

As the escapees carefully slipped down the stairs, Turnkey Jones sat at his desk on the first floor reading the daily newspaper. The jail keys, unseen by the crooks, lay on the desk top. A trustee sat nearby reading a magazine. The jailer heard a strange noise and looked up from his evening paper. Abernathy stood on the landing pointing the gun and glaring.

"Stick 'em up," he ordered.

Intending to stall until his friends came to help, the jailer slowly raked the keys off the desk into his lap as he lowered the newspaper. Abernathy kept the gun pointed at Jones as Clyde ran to the jailer's right side and Turner to his left. Each grabbed an arm and twisted it until Jones told them the keys were under his feet. Rushing to the front door, Clyde unlocked it, removed the heavy oak cross-bar, and ran outside. Abernathy and Turner quickly followed.

As the desperadoes passed through the front door, Jones jerked open a desk drawer, pulled out a pistol, and hurried after them. Reaching the front door, he heard a shot and dodged back inside. Looking around the edge of the jamb, he saw the men running into an alley alongside the jail. Jones aimed one shot, ran to the alley, and fired three more times at the retreating shadows; all the bullets missed.

Chief Jailer Glenn Wright had been asleep upstairs in his living quarters that adjoined the jail; he awoke when Jones fired at the bandits and came to help. Leaving Jones to pursue the bandits, Wright and the trustee went upstairs to find Stanford locked in the cell.

Meanwhile, the criminals continued up the alley and soon outran the jailer. Giving up the chase, Jones returned to the jail, where Wright ordered him to spread the alarm by telephoning surrounding towns. Wright himself placed long distance calls to Dallas, Fort Worth, Austin, and Houston.

Earlier in the evening, Mrs. J. M. Byrd had arrived at her home at 724 North Fifth, a few blocks from the county jail, and had parked her green Ford coupe in front. Spotting the car as they ran along the street, Clyde and Turner jumped inside the auto as Abernathy raised the hood and crossed the wiring to start the car. When the motor coughed into life, he climbed into the auto and they sped off into the night. Before leaving Waco, they stole another car, drove west through Goldthwaite, and then turned north. They stole several additional cars along the route: one in Wichita Falls, Texas; another in Joplin, Missouri; and a third in St. Louis, Missouri. The fugitives continued northeast through Illinois, robbing and burglarizing businesses along the route. As they entered Nokomis, Illinois, Clyde felt he was far enough from Waco to notify Bonnie and stopped at a Western Union office to send her a telegram.[10]

Coming home to Dallas to await a message from Clyde, Bonnie upset Mrs. Parker with her severe personality change; she constantly walked the floor, grabbed newspapers as soon as the delivery boy passed, and occasionally went downtown to get the early editions. Later Mrs. Parker recognized that Bonnie's role in the Waco jail escape probably seemed daring and romantic to the girl, and she saw clearly that the girl loved Clyde desperately and would do anything to please him; Mrs. Parker also understood that the jail break probably made a singular impression on the girl, since Bonnie was an overly dramatic person and enjoyed being the center of attention.[11] Within a short time the telegram arrived advising Bonnie that Clyde had escaped unharmed. He sent his love, promised to write, and requested that she notify his mother that he was okay.[12]

Meanwhile, the fugitives crossed Illinois, robbed several businesses in Indiana, and on 18 March 1930, reached Middleton, Ohio. Newspapers later reported that along the route, Clyde stole automobile license plates and changed them frequently to confuse pursuers, a practice that he would use extensively later. The three Texans in the stolen Missouri car bearing bogus Indiana license plates slowly cruised through the Ohio town searching for stores to burgle. Shortly after midnight, they broke into three gasoline stations but found nothing more than small change; they had more success at the Baltimore and Ohio Railroad Ticket Office, where they took nearly sixty dollars. At the train office, however, the bandits left their car nearby, and a suspicious Middleton citizen noted the license number. Leaving the railroad building, the men broke into a ladies' ready-to-wear store; they found no cash but took several silk articles for their girlfriends. Before dawn the robbers raced out of Middleton, drove west until they found an all-night diner, and stopped for breakfast.

Upon opening their firms the next morning in downtown Middleton, businessmen found their stores burglarized. When police arrived to investigate the series of crimes, an alert citizen recalled the suspicious car, produced the license number, and officers began the search.

The three Texans, having finished their morning meal, casually prepared to continue their escape. Apparently the road appeared different in the morning light than it had in darkness, because Clyde drove east toward Middleton instead of west. About 8:00 A.M. two patrol car officers noticed the men driving through the west edge of the city; the lawmen began pursuing the bandits and tried to force them to halt by firing their pistols into the air. Deciding to split up and possibly divide the pursuers, Clyde slowed the auto to allow Turner and Abernathy's escape. The officers, unable to keep up with Clyde, concentrated on the two suspects escaping on foot. Within a short time, the pair was trapped by officers, and they surrendered without resistance. Unaware that Turner and Abernathy had been captured, Clyde continued to cruise the area searching for them. Two Middleton officers spotted Clyde about 10:00 A.M. and blocked his escape. He drove his car up onto a curb, veered between two houses, smashed through two citizens' backyards, and stalled on the bank of the old Miami and Erie Canal. Clyde jumped from the car and ran; he paused occasionally to fire at the policemen with the pistol that Bonnie had smuggled into the jail cell. As the officers closed in, Clyde threw the revolver into the canal.

Meanwhile, Abernathy and Turner openly answered all the questions posed by detectives about their crimes; they craftily told officers that Clyde was just a hitchhiker they had picked up on the road. When the other officers brought Clyde into the police station, he supported the story by claiming to be Robert Thomas of Indianapolis, Indiana. The detectives, already in contact with Waco authorities, continued to question Clyde. After extensive grilling, he admitted to being the third Waco escapee.

On Wednesday, 19 March 1930, McClennan County Sheriff Leslie Stegall and Assistant District Attorney Jimmy Stanford boarded the 3:30 P.M. Missouri-Kansas-Texas train bound for Ohio. The Texas authorities arrived at Middleton about 12:30 A.M. Friday, 21 March and picked up their prisoners; they started back at once and reached Waco late the following day. The handcuffed prisoners were walked from the train depot to the jail, just a short distance away, and were placed in a secure section on the north side of the third floor.

Stanford told reporters that the bandits' car had contained food, stolen license plates from various states, and burglar's tools. Three days after returning from Ohio, Clyde's problems increased as he found himself accused of a murder that had taken place in Houston, Texas, almost a year earlier.[13]

On the evening of 2 July 1929, Howard Gouge, aged twenty, and Lillian Bissett, aged eighteen, both of Houston, had driven to Morgan Point, a resort area twenty miles east of town. After parking their car, the couple removed a cushion from the auto and sat down in a secluded beach area. About 10:00 P.M., someone fired a shot from near the auto and struck Gouge. When the couple jumped up another bullet grazed the girl's neck. Neither Gouge nor Bissett saw the attackers. No attempt was made to rob the couple, and the car was not damaged. Wounded less severely than Gouge, the girl hurriedly drove them to the nearest hospital; her friend died a short time later. Bissett required hospitalization for several days; just before being released, she issued a statement to the press outlining all the information she recalled about the incident. The Houston police arrested several suspects but released them later for lack of evidence. Howard Gouge's father offered a reward of $3,000 for apprehension of the killer or killers.

Shortly after Clyde's jailbreak from Waco, Houston authorities learned that another suspect in the Gouge case, who had been sought since the murder, was being held by federal officers in Shreveport, Louisiana. On 22 March 1930 Assistant District Attorney Frank Williford traveled to Shreveport; he soon returned with a signed statement from the secret witness that implicated both Frank Clause and Clyde Barrow. Clause was then being held in the Dallas, Texas, jail on a burglary charge. Clyde, interviewed by Harris County officers on 24 March, later told reporters that he had visited Houston only two times in his life and left before dark both times. He charged that the Harris County officials were looking for someone to blame for the murder and had picked him after the Waco jailbreak. Clyde's claims proved correct. Authorities later discredited the depositions of the alleged witness and dropped the investigation of Frank Clause and Clyde.[14]

Clyde Barrow's mother, Cumie, and Bonnie Parker arrived at the Waco jail on 27 March 1930 to visit before the state transferred him to Huntsville. Hoping to receive better treatment as a younger prisoner, Clyde misrepresented his age to authorities by saying he was only eighteen, when in fact he was twenty-one. Mrs. Barrow supported his lie. She told newsmen that her son had reached his eighteenth birthday the previous Monday. She also blamed all of her son's troubles on the bad characters he had befriended.[15]

On 21 April the state of Texas transferred Clyde to Huntsville and assigned him the number 63527. Completing the questionnaire required of each arriving prisoner, Clyde declared his middle name was Champion instead of Chestnut and entered Bonnie's name in the space allotted for his wife. The second lie made it possible for Clyde to get letters from her. He continued to claim that he was only eighteen years of age and listed his birthday as 24 March 1912. Clyde indicated that he neither smoked, drank liquor, nor gambled. Examining the young bandit, officials noted that he was 5 feet 7 inches, weighed 127 pounds, and had brown eyes and dark hair. Distinguishing marks included three tattoos; one on his outer left forearm with the letters E. B. W., another revealing the letters U. S. N. on his inner right forearm, and the third a design of a girl's head on the outer part of his right arm. Within a few hours, authorities assigned Clyde to the Eastham Prison Farm in the southern tip of Houston County, forty miles north of Huntsville, where he began serving his fourteen-year term.[16]

Bonnie was heartbroken. Devastated by the thought of being separated from Clyde for fourteen years, she cried almost constantly and spent hours each night writing him long letters. Within a short time, however, her anguish disappeared; she returned to work as a waitress and dated other men. The long, heartrending letters to Clyde grew shorter and less frequent, and in a few months she stopped writing altogether.

Unaccountably, during the winter of 1930, Bonnie resumed her correspondence with Clyde. He responded with a letter on 11 December expressing his joy and surprise at hearing from her after such a long period of silence. Clyde asked Bonnie to keep faith in him because his mother had pleaded with District Judge R. I. Munroe in Waco to reduce his sentence from fourteen years to two. Apparently Munroe had promised Mrs. Barrow that he would do all he could to help her.

Ten days later Clyde further encouraged Bonnie by relating that his mother had virtually accomplished the reduction of his term to two years and reminded Bonnie that he had already served eight months. Despite the renewed correspondence, Bonnie continued to see another young man. Several weeks later Clyde became depressed when he witnessed the murder of a boy by an older convict who wanted the youngster to become his lover.[17]

Meanwhile, Buck moved to clear his record; he had escaped from Eastham Prison Farm earlier by simply walking away from a work gang. After his getaway Buck met and married a girl named Blanche Caldwell. When he told his new wife that he was an escaped convict, she joined his mother in begging him to return and complete his sentence. Two days after Christmas in 1931, the family delivered Buck to Huntsville, and he surrendered himself to authorities.[18]

In the meantime, Clyde started to grow more anxious. He became increasingly despondent for several reasons: the state's delay in reducing his fourteen-year sentence, his tenuous relationship with Bonnie, and his inability to keep up with his workload in the fields of the prison farm. Unaware that his mother's efforts neared conclusion, Clyde conspired to get off the farm and into the regular prison by persuading a fellow convict to chop off two of Clyde's toes with an ax. As expected, officials moved him to the Huntsville Prison Hospital for treatment. With Judge Munroe's recommendation and the mother's pleadings, Governor Ross Sterling agreed to the parole. The speed of the official action surprised Clyde; he still walked with the aid of crutches when word arrived on 8 February 1932 that he would be released.[19]

When Clyde returned to Dallas, his family noticed an extraordinary and disturbing change. He demanded, for example, that relatives spend their meager savings, during the depths of the Great Depression, on silk shirts and other fancy clothing. Dressed in his new clothes, Clyde hobbled over to the Parker home, where he found Bonnie seated in the family living room with the young man she had been dating while he was in the penitentiary. When Bonnie saw Clyde standing at the door, she acted as if he had never been away. This reunion bitterly frustrated Mrs. Parker.

During February 1932 Clyde visited Bonnie regularly. Toward the end of the month, his sister Nell obtained a job for him with a construction firm in Wooster, Massachusetts. Both the Parker and Barrow families felt happy about Clyde's new employment. That he planned to work and be separated from his old criminal cronies elated Bonnie. Clyde traveled to New England and worked for the construction firm for a short time. Within a few days, however, Cowan's friend wrote her expressing concern that Clyde didn't seem too interested in the work. Two weeks after beginning the job, Clyde quit and arrived back in Dallas on 17 March 1932. He went directly to his parents' home, where he found Nell furiously pacing.

"What do you mean, quitting that job in Massachusetts? I bent over backwards to get it for you," she demanded.

Clyde scratched his chin. "I know it, Sis, and I'm sorry. But I was so homesick I could die."

"That's no excuse, Clyde Barrow."

Barrow backed away from his sister as she advanced. "I know it's not, but it's the way I felt." He looked carefully at Nell to see if his words were having any effect on her rage, then continued. "There were times I wanted to die when I was at Eastham because I missed home so bad. And there I was again about a million miles from the family."

Nell stood erect with eyes flashing and arms folded. "You didn't seem too concerned about the family when you first got out of the Pen and wanted that silk shirt and fancy gloves."

Clyde bowed his head and didn't answer.

Nell stomped her foot. "You don't know how hard it is to find a job nowadays. There's a depression on, in case you haven't heard."

Clyde looked at his feet. "I know it's tough times," he said softly. "But I'll find something around here." He looked out the window, and his eyes stared into the distance; his voice hardened as he continued, "Nothing means a damn to me but all of you. If I have to be away from you all, I might as well be dead." He stood dejectedly with his hands thrust deeply into his pants pockets and his head tilted to the left in a manner that Nell knew so well. Almost in a whisper, he said, "Sometimes I think everybody would be better off if that con in the joint had chopped off my head instead of my toes."

The thought of harm coming to Clyde melted Nell's heart. She went to him and put her arms around his neck as she had done when he was a small boy. "It's okay, Honey. I know how you felt. We missed you too." She stepped back and held his shoulders with both hands as she looked into his eyes. "I'll tell you this, Clyde Barrow, you better not get involved again with that bunch you were running with before you went to the Pen. You really will end up dead."

Clyde held up his hands with the palms toward his older sister. "You don't have to worry about that, Sis. I've learned my lesson."[20]

Three days after Clyde returned to Dallas, Bonnie greeted her mother at the front door of her home with a surprise. "Mama, I've got a job in Houston demonstrating cosmetics. I have to go down there tomorrow."

Mrs. Parker leaned against the door. "Bonnie, you don't know anything about selling face powder."

"I can learn. But I have to live in Houston."

"Oh, Honey, I can't stand to see you move off."

"I can't find a job around here, Mama. You know I've tried hard enough."

Emma Parker finally agreed that the scarcity of jobs made it necessary for Bonnie to move to Houston. Mrs. Parker didn't know that Clyde was in Dallas and forming an outlaw gang with two young criminals, a Dallas bootlegger and automobile thief, Raymond Hamilton, and a McKinney burglar, Ralph Fults.[21]

On 22 March 1932 Bonnie, Clyde, Raymond, and Ralph Fults attempted a robbery in Kaufman, a small town a few miles east of Dallas. At about 1:00 A.M. the three men broke into a hardware store near the courthouse square to steal guns. Bonnie served as a lookout. A night watchman spotted them and set off the alarm.

They ran to the car, raced out of Kaufman, and turned down an unpaved country lane. Spring rains had turned the road into a quagmire, and the car got stuck. With the police close behind, the four bandits tried to escape through adjoining fields. Finding a group of mules, they jumped onto the animals' backs and attempted to ride away, but the animals refused to move. Meanwhile, the authorities found the getaway car and tracked the gangsters to the field. Crouching in a ditch as officers fired over their heads, Clyde warned Bonnie, "This looks like where we get ours, Honey." They crawled along the muddy gully for several yards. When officers spotted them, Clyde confidently said, "You stay here. I'll get another car and come back to get you." He escaped by running between two officers who had stopped firing to reload their guns. Though Hamilton also escaped by the ditch, lawmen captured Fults. Bonnie remained hidden in the culvert all that day and night, but Clyde never returned. Later, Raymond also escaped.[22]

The next morning Bonnie walked to the nearest highway and began hitchhiking. The driver of the first car that offered her a ride was a posse member; he drove her to Kaufman for questioning. Placed in adjoining cells, Fults told Bonnie to admit nothing and offered to confess in order to protect her. She agreed and asked the jailer for permission to call her mother in Dallas.

Two days after Bonnie ostensibly left for Houston and a new job, Emma Parker received the call from the Kaufman jail. When Mrs. Parker arrived to arrange for Bonnie's release, the jailer's wife, a Mrs. Adams, took her aside. "Don't go borrow money for bail. Wait until the grand jury convenes in a few weeks. If you want my opinion, the lack of evidence indicates she probably will get no-billed. This means that no formal charges will be filed and she will be released. Besides, several days in jail might bring Bonnie to her senses." Emma Parker accepted the friendly advice.[23]

While Bonnie waited for the grand jury to meet, she became temporarily disenchanted with Clyde. She wrote a poem called "Suicide Sal" about a girl named Sally, whose lover, Jack, used her and then allowed her to take the blame for his crimes. Obviously viewing herself as Sal, Bonnie waited in jail while Clyde and Raymond were free to follow their lives of crime. Ralph Fults bravely assumed full responsibility for the attempted burglary of the hardware store and received a term in state prison.[24]

Meanwhile, Clyde and Raymond joined with Frank Clause, recently released from state prison, in committing several crimes. During April 1932 they sketched out a scheme for the robbery of the Bucher store in Hillsboro, Texas, an event that would have a profound effect on their lives.

4

They Call Them Cold-Blooded Killers

For several years John and Martha Bucher had owned and operated a small service station and gift shop at the intersection of Highways 77 and 81 on the outskirts of Hillsboro, the largest town of Hill County, Texas. The couple lived above the store. Later Mrs. Bucher and her employees told the *Hillsboro Mirror* details of the crime that took her husband's life.

During the afternoon of 30 April, John Bucher inventoried stock at the rear of the store while two of his employees, Bedell Jordan and Marvin Kitchens, worked near the front. Shortly after five o'clock, Clyde, Raymond, and Clause drove up to the entrance in a dark 1932 Ford sedan and stepped inside. Jordan greeted the men and asked, "Can I help you?"

Raymond grinned. "I want to look at some watches." The clerk led them to a display counter and placed several watches on the top of the case. Raymond carefully looked at the items; he compared the faces and bands and handed them back.

"These ain't good enough for me," he said, "I want the best."

Jordan called Bucher from the back and told him what the customer wanted. Leading the three men to the rear of the shop where the safe was located, Bucher said, "Our best watches are in here."

Raymond looked at the diamonds and watches in the safe; he glanced back at Barrow and Clause and rolled his eyes. The men continued to look at the jewelry for several minutes then left without making a purchase.[1]

Subsequent court testimony revealed that late that night the

Bucher store stood quiet and dark as the black Ford sedan again came to the store entrance. Clyde sat in the driver's seat with Frank Clause beside him and Raymond in the back. Nervously, Hamilton jumped out and hurried to the front of the store; he banged loudly on the door while Clyde slowly walked to join him.

The knocking soon awakened the Buchers. Getting out of bed, Bucher said, "Who can that be at this time of the night?" His wife turned over. "Why don't you ignore them and maybe they'll go away."

"Naw, Mother. Somebody might need help." He walked to the front window. Looking below, he saw two men, standing in the shadows and another waiting near the car. "What do you want? I don't like to be called after 10:30 at night."

"It ain't much later than that," said one of the men.

Mrs. Bucher looked at the clock. It indicated a few minutes after midnight.

At the window Bucher thought he recognized the men. "Don't you live over at West?"

"No, sir. I'm sorry it's so late but we've been to a dance and the strings broke on the fellow's guitar."

"Well, I'll be down in a minute." Bucher slipped a pistol into his robe pocket and went downstairs; he opened the front door and flicked on the light switch. He found Raymond Hamilton offering a ten dollar bill while picking up a set of guitar strings from a display on the counter. Clyde Barrow stepped inside and stood in the shadows as Bucher locked the door. Having no reason to feel concerned, since the customers were well-dressed, clean-cut, and had money to pay for their purchase, Bucher relaxed; "I can't make change for a ten," he said, "don't you have anything smaller?"

Raymond shook his head. "No, sir. I sure don't." Bucher sighed. "Well, I'll have to get my wife to come downstairs and open the safe. My eyes are so bad I can't work the combination."

Raymond and Clyde nervously glanced at each other as Bucher called to his wife; they didn't want another witness, but there was no backing out now. As Mrs. Bucher came down the staircase, the handle on the front door rattled. Bucher looked at the door. "We'll be through here in a minute," he said.

Raymond yelled, "It's alright." He fondled the pistol he carried in his pocket while anxiously waiting for the woman to work the dial;

after what seemed a long time, he watched her turn the handle and swing the door open. Pulling the gun from his pocket, Raymond pointed it at Bucher; his hand shook and he licked his lips as the merchant reached into the safe and brought out the cash box. He opened his mouth to order Bucher to hand over the money, but his fingers twitched on the trigger and the gun fired. Striking the safe door, the bullet ricocheted off and slammed into Bucher's heart. The old man fell to the floor in front of the safe, dead. Mrs. Bucher screamed and collapsed as Clyde glared at Raymond.

"What the hell did you do that for?" asked Clyde.

"It was an accident, honest," whined Raymond.

"Well, never mind that now, get busy."[2]

The two men pushed the sobbing woman out of the way and plundered the safe of jewelry and money; they dashed out of the door and jumped into the car where the third man waited.

"What happened?" asked Clause.

Clyde slammed the car into gear and sped away. "Never mind," he snapped.

Raymond cringed in the corner of the backseat and wept. "I swear it was an accident," he whimpered.

Martha Bucher crawled to her husband and checked for signs of life. Finding him dead, she ran to the phone and called the Hill County sheriff's office. The officers came within minutes and recorded all the details. Sheriff John Freeland telephoned all adjoining counties descriptions of the killers. A few days later, Mrs. Bucher picked the pictures of Clyde and Raymond from a group of police photographs.

Sitting hunched behind the steering wheel of the stolen Ford sedan as it sped off into the night toward Dallas, Clyde realized he had reached a significant point in his life. He could surrender to police, but his involvement in a homicide, even as an accomplice to an accidental killing while just out of prison, meant facing almost certain conviction and execution. The only alternative was to elude the police for as long as possible. Clyde made the choice to run for freedom. He never deceived himself about the ultimate outcome, however, and later told his sister Nell, "I'm just going on 'til they get me. Then I'm out like Lottie's eye."[3]

After all their previous crimes, Clyde and Raymond had acted cocky and confident. Murder, however, was different. Clyde hurried to his parents' home to hide. Nell visited the home on 1 May 1932, the day following the Hillsboro killing, to see if Clyde had contacted their parents.

"Clyde is hiding out behind the house in a ditch," said Mrs. Barrow.

Nell went out to confront him. "Did you have anything to do with that Hillsboro killing?"

Clyde looked scared. "No. Sis, I swear."

"Don't lie to me, Clyde Barrow. That killing sounds just like some fool stunt you and Raymond would pull."

"Well, I was in on it in a way."

"What does that mean?" she asked.

"I was just the driver. Me and Frank and Raymond went to the store to check it out. But Mrs. Bucher recognized me because I ran with her son when they lived in Dallas."

"Are you sure?"

"You bet. We all agreed that since she knew me, I would stay in the car as the driver and keep the motor running. But while the boys were inside, guns began to pop and somebody screamed. I just goosed that foot feed and took off."

"How did the other boys get away?"

Clyde shook his head. "I don't know and I don't care."

Nell walked back to the house and told her mother. The entire family chose to disregard the reports in the newspapers that the Buchers were pioneer merchants in Hillsboro and had lived there since 1902. They had never lived in Dallas.[4]

Five days after the Bucher killing, Clyde emerged from hiding to join Frank Clause in a robbery scheme. Early on the afternoon of 5 May, they drove to Lufkin in far east Texas and stopped at a Magnolia service station. After asking the attendant to fill the gas tank, both men walked into the station office, carefully concealing themselves from passersby and waited. The attendant entered the office and found the two men with guns pointed at him.

Clause ordered the man to open the cash register, hand over the money, and get into the back of the car. Clause sat down beside the victim while Clyde slipped behind the steering wheel and drove four blocks west to a Gulf gasoline station. Clause remained in the back seat with his pistol hidden under his coat. Clyde flashed the pistol at the Gulf station manager and ordered him to empty the cash drawer. Hiding his gun inside his coat, Clyde walked the second victim to the car and forced him into the back seat. The outlaws jumped into the front and drove west out of town. A short time later they released the two station operators, unharmed, on Highway 69 near Central.[5]

Clyde continued to commit crimes with Clause and Hamilton, yet he never traveled too far from Dallas and returned frequently. He hid in an abandoned farmhouse near Grand Prairie, a small town just west of Dallas, and marked time until the Kaufman grand jury decided Bonnie's fate.

On 17 June 1932 the grand jury heard Bonnie's case. At the request of panel members, she testified in her own behalf. Just as Mrs. Adams had predicted, the jury issued a no-bill in Bonnie's case because of lack of evidence, and the judge ordered her released. When Bonnie returned to the Parker home in Dallas, her mother noticed a significant change in the girl's conduct; she acted quieter and more mature than she had before she entered jail.

Emma Parker looked lovingly at her daughter and sighed. "Bonnie, if Clyde's going to keep on the way he's going, you're going to have to stay away from him."

Bonnie shook her head. "You don't have to worry. I'm never going to have anything to do with him anymore."

Later that month, Emma Parker came home from work to learn that Bonnie had left for Wichita Falls, about two hundred miles northwest of Dallas. Ostensibly, Bonnie went to apply for a job as a waitress in a new cafe that was rumored to be opening soon. Though extremely uneasy and suspicious, Emma Parker relaxed somewhat when, several days later, she received a postcard mailed from Wichita Falls. In the message Bonnie explained that she had gotten the job; she described the rooms she had rented and outlined her working hours and conditions. Emma Parker hoped that Bonnie would keep her pledge never to see Clyde again.

The entire letter was a lie. Bonnie, Clyde, and Raymond had rented a two-bedroom house in Wichita Falls. They lived together throughout the month of July while the men committed various crimes in the north Texas area. The outlaws got up early on 1 August 1932 and drove to Dallas. Arriving shortly before 3:00 P.M., they picked up a fellow gangster named Everett Milligan and left Bonnie at her mother's house. When he drove away, Clyde called out to Bonnie to listen to the radio and learn if the holdup he planned was successful.[6]

The *Dallas Morning News*, quoting the Dallas Police, reported that the men then hurried to the Oak Cliff section of Dallas; they cruised up and down various streets searching for a likely automobile to steal. In the one hundred block of North Winnetka, they spotted a light- colored sedan parked at the curb. Raymond jumped out and ran to the parked vehicle. He started the auto in a short time and signaled his two friends. The two cars moved off in tandem toward north Dallas. They crossed the Oak Cliff viaduct and turned north on Industrial. Both drivers carefully observed the traffic rules. Driving past the northern city limits, the autos moved east for two blocks then turned south on Alamo Street, where Clyde pulled his car onto the shoulder; he and Mulligan jumped out and climbed into the light-colored sedan. Clyde's watch indicated 4:00 P.M. as Mulligan slid behind the wheel of the stolen car and drove to the parking lot of the Neuhoff Brothers Packing Company. The outlaws knew that the firm always paid their employees in cash on the first of each month. Pulling their pistols, Clyde and Hamilton entered the front door of the main office. Elsie Wullschleger sat at a front desk counting money for the payroll. The two men violently slammed the front door and wildly waved their guns about.

Raymond looked at Joe and Henry Neuhoff, the firm's owners, who sat at their desks in the rear. He loudly demanded, "Where's the money?" Clyde noticed Wullschleger at her desk counting the payroll and waved Raymond into her office.

The Neuhoffs looked up as Raymond yelled. Leveling his pistol at the two men, Clyde stepped toward the rear of the offices so he could cover all three victims while Raymond scooped up the cash. When Raymond finished and dashed into the hall, Clyde followed him to the front and yanked out the telephone line from the wall connections. Glaring, he yelled, "Where's the other telephone?" Joe Neuhoff pointed to a second desk at the rear of the room, and Clyde ripped out that cord as well. Both bandits ran out and jumped into the sedan. Milligan drove away quickly and stopped near their original car. The three men hurriedly changed cars and raced down Alamo Street with Clyde at the wheel. They sped west to Industrial Boulevard and dashed past a police car that contained Captain A. F. Deere and Sergeant Roy Richburg.

Deere and Richburg had checked out a squad car from the police motor pool and left the downtown station just off Commerce a few minutes before 4:00 P.M. They planned to go into the country north of Dallas for pistol target practice. The officers arrived at a short country road that linked Alamo and Industrial just as the bandit car raced past them at a high rate of speed. Quickly turning their car around, the two policemen followed the fleeing gangsters onto Industrial Boulevard with the siren at full volume. They continued the chase for several miles until Clyde's impetuous driving at seventy miles per hour left the squad car far behind.

Meanwhile, back at the crime scene, Henry Neuhoff ran two blocks to a sheet metal shop to telephone authorities. The Dallas Police dispatcher broadcast an all-points bulletin, which Deere and Richburg received as they returned from the pursuit. Captain Deere radioed the dispatcher that they had unsuccessfully chased the suspects' auto. The officers relayed a description of the getaway car as they raced to the packing plant; they discovered the abandoned light-colored automobile as they neared the crime scene. While interviewing the Neuhoff brothers, the officers determined that the car was used by the outlaws in their escape from the robbery. The dispatcher alerted officers in nearby cities but the daylight bandits escaped without a trace.[7]

After picking up Bonnie at her home, Clyde, Raymond, and Everett Mulligan hid out at the abandoned farmhouse near Grand Prairie for several days. The following Friday, 5 August 1932, Clyde returned Bonnie to Emma Parker's home for a few days. Subsequent Police investigation revealed that Raymond and Mulligan drove to Corsicana, about eighty miles southeast of Dallas, and stole another car. They returned via Lancaster, then headed toward Dallas. North of Lancaster, two Dallas County Sheriff's Department detectives on patrol recognized Raymond. He saw the lawmen at the same time and sped away. The officers turned their patrol car around and pursued the outlaw's stolen auto but failed to catch it.[8]

After eluding the detectives, Raymond became nervous and wrecked the stolen car shortly after entering the Dallas city limits; he quickly took another. In the second car, Raymond and Mulligan continued through south Dallas to the Parker home and picked up Clyde. With Clyde driving, the three headed north toward Oklahoma. Convinced that police had issued a report on the car he was driving, Clyde stopped in north Texas where Raymond stole a third car. Ultimately, the gangsters took and abandoned at least three other automobiles before they left Texas.[9]

Crossing the Red River into Oklahoma, the gangsters cruised along country roads in the southeastern area of the state while they looked for businesses to burgle. As usual, Clyde drove. Slouching beside him in the front, Hamilton drank moonshine whiskey from a Mason jar; he occasionally passed it to Mulligan in the backseat. As the car neared a crowded open-air dance floor just outside Stringtown, Hamilton bolted upright in his seat and asked Clyde to stop long enough for them to dance.

Clyde studied the dance floor and tried to persuade Raymond that it was dangerous. Raymond countered with the argument that they would not have to stay for a long time. To stop Hamilton's whining, Clyde reluctantly turned the car into the parking area near the hall. They went inside and danced several tunes with local girls. At about 11:00 P.M. Clyde and Hamilton went outside to the car while Milligan talked with an Oklahoma man. Hamilton swigged whiskey from the fruit jar and offered it to Clyde, asking his friend to relax. Clyde pushed the jar away, for he rarely drank. As the major driver, he was interminably concerned about maintaining a clear head in case a fast getaway became necessary.[10]

Prohibition still existed at that time and most Oklahoma officers enforced the national drinking laws with great enthusiasm. When Sheriff C. G. Maxwell and Deputy E. C. Moore saw Hamilton drinking from the Mason jar, the universal container of illegal whiskey, they walked toward the bandits. Without drawing his gun, Maxwell called out, "Here you can't do that. Consider yourselves under arrest. Now get out of the car."

Both outlaws grabbed their pistols and opened fire. Moore crashed to the ground with a mortal injury to his forehead, and Maxwell collapsed with severe wounds in the chest, side, arm, and leg. Clyde quickly started the motor and jammed the car into reverse. Though severely wounded, Sheriff Maxwell pulled his gun from the holster, partially raised himself upon his wounded arm, and fired all his bullets at the fleeing car.

On the dance floor, Milligan was dancing with a Stringtown girl when the shooting began; he immediately suspected that his friends were involved and tried to merge into the anxious dance crowd. He asked the new Oklahoma friend for a ride into town. The man agreed, and they left the hall as the crowd milled about in disbelief. Meanwhile, the fugitives' car, damaged by a shot from Sheriff Maxwell's gun, began to wobble. Clyde lost control and ran the car into a ditch. A passing motorist, Cleve Brady, who lived near Stringtown, stopped to offer aid. Clyde jerked out his gun and told Brady to sit down in the car and relax and he wouldn't get hurt; he asked Raymond to get in the backseat. They raced off toward the northeast until the car stalled near Stringtown. Leaving Brady with his disabled auto, the outlaws spotted a small farmhouse. Clyde ran to the front door and knocked loudly. He creased his forehead in anguish and greeted the owner, John Redden, "I just wrecked my car and need to get a friend to a doctor."

Redden's son, Lonnie, came to the door. "I'll take them, Daddy." Once out of sight of the house, Clyde took over the car at gunpoint and put Redden in the back so Raymond could guard him. Continuing to drive very fast, the fugitives arrived at Clayton, Oklahoma; there they stole another automobile belonging to Frank Smith, who was visiting from Seminole. Clyde left Redden standing beside his car and sped off into the night.

Meanwhile, Milligan arrived in Stringtown and hurried to the ticket window of the bus station and asked, "When's the next bus for Texas?"

The clerk glanced at the customer. "Whereabouts in Texas?"

Milligan shook his head. "Anywhere in Texas. Just so it's out of here."

The clerk consulted a list. "A bus is leaving for McKinney in a few minutes."

Milligan reached for his wallet. "I want a ticket."

Back at the dance, an ambulance rushed Sheriff Maxwell to a hospital in McAlister, and police officers and local citizens drove about searching for the slayers. The McAlister Police Department notified Governor William Murray of the tragedy and gathered a pack of bloodhounds in case the men had fled on foot. The governor ordered all members of the Oklahoma Bureau of Investigation to go immediately to the crime scene and assist local lawmen. Within hours of the shooting, state investigators as well as sheriffs and deputies from Antlers, Colgate, and McAlister arrived and joined in the investigation and manhunt. Physicians at the McAlister hospital hurried Maxwell into surgery. After an extensive operation, they told reporters that the sheriff might recover.

Authorities at Stringtown systematically questioned every witness and learned that another man had arrived with the killers but apparently had not left in the getaway car. A bystander told Special Officer L. C. Harris that he remembered seeing the stranger talk with a local resident and gave the officer the man's name. Harris quickly obtained the man's address and drove to his home; he learned about the ride to the bus depot and rushed to question the ticket clerk. The clerk remembered the excited passenger who had bought a ticket for McKinney, Texas, and told Harris the bus had departed only a short time before. Harris notified the McKinney police and contacted Atoka County Attorney J. B. Maxey. The two Oklahoma lawmen jumped into a squad car and sped toward McKinney. Aided with the description provided by Special Officer Harris, two Texas policemen waited near the driveway of the McKinney bus terminal when the bus from Oklahoma arrived. Milligan was halted by the officers when he departed the bus; he offered no resistance but refused to talk. When J. B. Maxey and L. C. Harris arrived from Atoka, he ignored their questions as well. Waiving extradition, Milligan and the two officials returned to Oklahoma and arrived at Atoka on Saturday morning, 6 August 1932.[11]

While Oklahoma officials were capturing Milligan, Clyde and Raymond raced to Texas. Using back roads, they continued southwest until reaching Grandview, about thirty miles south of Fort Worth; they abandoned the Smith car, stole another, and drove to Dallas.[12]

At about 8:00 P.M. on Saturday, 6 August, Bonnie sat with her mother on the porch of the Parker home; she planned to return to Wichita Falls on the Sunday morning bus. Driving up to the front walk, Hamilton signaled Bonnie, who ran out to talk with him. Raymond told her that Clyde was waiting for them at the Grand Prairie hideout.

Bonnie looked at her mother sitting in the rocking chair on the front porch and said she wanted to tell her mother goodbye. She ran back to the porch and said that she had a ride to Wichita Falls and would not have to take the bus. She returned the bus fare that her mother had loaned her, kissed her goodbye, ran to the car, and rode off.[13]

On Sunday morning, 7 August, Constable H. A. Hunt of Grandview, Texas, received a call about an abandoned automobile. Checking the list of cars reported stolen within the last week, he realized it was Frank Smith's vehicle and telephoned Fort Worth police. The authorities rushed a fingerprint team to check the stolen auto and discovered several prints that matched file copies of those belonging to Clyde Barrow and Raymond Hamilton.[14]

That same evening two Dallas detectives arrived at McAlister to question Milligan. Realizing his precarious position, the prisoner finally revealed to them the trail that led from Corsicana, Texas, to Atoka, Oklahoma. The Dallas officers asked Milligan, "Aren't you afraid your friends will come back and put you on the spot since you named names and implicated them in several crimes?"

Milligan shook his head and replied, "Naw. I'm not afraid. In the first place, you'll have me cooped up for quiet a while. Besides, you'll catch the boys soon, but you ain't going to take them alive. They told me that."[15]

Clyde seemed more determined not to be captured than Raymond; following the Bucher killing, he understood clearly that he had little chance of getting off with a long prison term. But unquestionably, after the shootings at Stringtown, there was no chance of his ever turning back.

Bonnie, Clyde, and Raymond decided that they needed a hideout in an area where they weren't so well known. Emma Parker's sister, Nettie Stamps, lived on a farm outside Carlsbad, New Mexico. The fugitives thought no officer would look for them on a farm, so they went west, hiding out until the search parties calmed down. The outlaws drove through Carlsbad on Saturday, 15 August 1932. Joe Johns, a deputy sheriff, was on city patrol and saw the coupe with Texas license plates pass through town. Out-of-state license plates were less common in America during the Great Depression, and the lawman checked the number when he returned to the sheriff's office. As he had suspected, the car had been reported stolen in Texas several days before. Johns kept the number in his pocket in case the automobile returned to Carlsbad.

The three gangsters spent Saturday night at the Stamps farm.

Early the next morning, Raymond drove into Carlsbad to buy a block of ice for making ice cream. Johns, once again on patrol, spotted the car and followed it to the Stamps home.

Arriving back at the farm, Raymond carefully locked the car because all the weapons were hidden behind the seat and in the trunk; he went inside the farmhouse to join the others. Mrs. Stamps, unaware of the impending trouble, strolled to the garden to gather vegetables for lunch.

Just before noon Johns arrived at the farm and knocked on the door. Bonnie answered the knock and saw a pleasant, middle-aged man dressed in western clothing. A holstered pistol hung by his side. The man's face was weathered the color of rustic oak, but his eyes were sparkling and clear. Inside, Clyde and Raymond took Stamps's hunting shotgun and dashed to the back door.

When Bonnie opened the front door, Johns tipped his hat and flashed his badge. "Morning, Miss. I'd like to talk to the owner of the car with Texas plates that's parked in your yard." Bonnie smiled. "Why sure, Officer. It belongs to a friend of mine who is visiting. He's dressing and will be out in a few minutes."

"Thank you," said Johns as he touched the brim of his hat; he stepped off the porch and walked toward the suspicious car.

Bonnie closed the door and ran to the back where Clyde and Raymond waited. "It's the law, and he's headed for the car."

Clyde nodded grimly. "Stay here 'til I call you." He and Raymond eased out the back door and closed it carefully.

Mrs. Stamps watched in surprise as Clyde, carrying the family shotgun, ran from the back door. Raymond followed closely behind. Johns looked in the car window and tried to open one of the doors; he was so intent with the search that he failed to notice the two men coming from the house. Pointing the gun directly at the officer's stomach, Clyde said, "Alright, Mister, drop that pistol, or I'll drill you."

The deputy dropped his weapon. When Clyde moved to retrieve the pistol, his finger slipped and the shotgun fired. The shot went wild. Clyde turned toward the house, "Honey, get a move on." He ordered Raymond to get the officer's gun. Raymond scooped up the pistol as Clyde rushed to the car and unlocked the door. Bonnie came running from the house. Clyde signaled Johns toward their car. "Now that you've stuck your nose in our business, Hotshot, you can just come along with us." Clyde got behind the steering wheel with Johns sitting in the middle. Raymond sat on the right with Bonnie in his lap. They drove away rapidly and turned east. Mrs. Stamps hurried to notify authorities, who quickly placed long distance calls in several directions. Officers all over New Mexico and Texas searched for Johns for the next several hours. The body of a murdered hitchhiker found in west Texas temporarily led police to believe the fugitives had killed Johns and dumped the body. By Monday night the deputy's office openly predicted that Johns was dead. But at 8:00 P.M. he called from San Antonio to say that the outlaws had released him, unharmed, after a wild ride of several hundred miles. Johns told reporters that the harrowing ride, which included detours onto obscure side roads to avoid roadblocks, often at speeds of seventy miles per hour, exhausted him but seemed to greatly excite his three captors.[16]

5

Hang It on Bonnie and Clyde

The desperadoes continued through San Antonio and turned south-east on Highway 87. Spending Monday night in a tourist court, they went on to Victoria, where Raymond stole a new Ford sedan. Early Tuesday they turned north toward Houston. Clyde decided their escape would be more certain if they had another car. Raymond stole a Ford coupe from a parking area on Highway 59, and they headed north. Bonnie and Clyde led in the coupe and Raymond followed in the sedan. Since the owner of the sedan reported the theft to police almost immediately, the police saw a pattern in the escape route. It ran in a direct line from San Antonio to Victoria toward Wharton and probably Houston. Authorities set up roadblocks and searched for the fugitives along the apparent route. About two miles southwest of Wharton, the Colorado River swept into a horseshoe bend where a long two-lane bridge crossed over. The officers planned an ambush at this point, with half of the posse hidden at the southwestern end of the bridge and the rest at the northeastern edge; they hoped the outlaws would drive onto the bridge and into their trap. The lawmen concluded that capture would be relatively simple once the gangsters were trapped between crossfire on the elongated bridge. They confidently settled down to wait. The message from Victoria about the stolen sedan led authorities to expect all three bandits would be riding in only one car. When the small Ford coupe came into view, posse members were surprised and hesitated to act. Clyde, however, continued at the same fast speed, spun the steering wheel, skidded the car around in a complete turn, wounded one officer with his pistol, and raced back toward Victoria. Meeting Raymond in the sedan, Clyde signaled him to turn as well. The officers ran up the highway, momentarily stopping to fire a fusillade of bullets at the sedan as Hamilton turned around. Racing to their concealed squad cars, the lawmen tried to catch the fleeing autos. A short distance away, Bonnie and Clyde abandoned the coupe, damaged by lawmen's gunfire, and joined Raymond in the sedan as he pulled up beside them. Clyde jumped into the driver's seat, raced southwest on country roads, and vanished. Posse members took the wounded lawman to the Wharton hospital. After the escape, Bonnie, Clyde, and Raymond dropped from the newspaper headlines for a time. They continued to rob various businesses in Texas, but they neither killed nor kidnapped any of their victims.[1]

During the first week in September 1932, Hamilton decided to visit his father, who had moved to Michigan to find work. Since Bonnie and Clyde couldn't bear to be away from their families except for brief periods, Raymond asked another west Dallas criminal, Gene O'Dare, to go with him. O'Dare was three years older than Hamilton and although he had recently married a woman named Mary, he readily agreed to make the trip. Hamilton bought Pullman tickets, and they traveled to Bay City, Michigan, located on Saginaw Bay of Lake Huron.

Within a month, Clyde left Bonnie at a Denton County hideout, picked up two accomplices, Frank Hardy and Hollis Hale, and drove to Sherman, Texas. There, during a robbery attempt, Clyde killed a grocer named Howard Hall.[2]

A burly man who enjoyed life immensely, Hall's benevolent attitude reminded young people of their grandfathers. Hall was a native of McKinney, Texas, and had lived in Sherman for thirty-five years; for more than a decade he had owned and operated a grocery store on East Brockett Street. In 1929 Hall sold his business and accepted a position as meat market manager for the Little Food Store at the corner of Vaden Street and Wells Avenue in suburban Sherman.

Business at the store on 11 October 1932 was sporadic. At about 6:20 P.M., A. B. Little, the market owner, removed part of the daily receipts from the cash register and carried them to his home nearby. Hall and Homer Glaze, a young sales clerk, prepared to close the market for the day. Glaze swept out the front of the store. Hall scrubbed the chopping block in the meat market section. While they worked, a black Buick sedan bearing Kansas license plates drove east along Wells in front of the store, traveled one block further east to Hazelwood, turned south, and pulled up to the curb. Clyde sat behind the steering wheel with Hollis Hale beside him and Frank Hardy in the back; he planned to pick up Bonnie after the robbery of the market. Shortly before 6:30 P.M., Clyde got out of the car and walked north on Hazelwood. He turned west on Wells Avenue to Vaden Street and briefly paused in front of the Little Food Store to survey the store layout. A long narrow building with the slender end facing Vaden Street, it had two entrances, one in the narrow end opening onto Vaden and the other facing Wells Avenue about halfway along the building.

Clyde entered the Vaden Street door and glanced at the store's interior. A long counter ran along the north side of the market from the front to the meat section in the rear. A short glass display case sat perpendicular to the long counter. An opening between the long counter and the display case allowed employees to move in and out of the section behind the display areas. The cash register sat on the end of the long counter near the opening. Glaze had finished sweeping and began checking the day's bills near the cash register. Hall continued to clean the meat area. Neither Glaze nor Hall gave careful attention to Clyde as he picked up a loaf of bread and walked to the rear of the store. Glaze sensed Clyde's hesitancy but later said he attributed it to confusion experienced by customers in a strange store.

When Clyde placed the bread on the counter top, Glaze turned to him and smiled. "Will you be needing anything else?"

Clyde looked around the store. "Maybe half a dozen eggs and some lunch meat."

Hall looked at Clyde for the first time and asked, "How much lunch meat do you need?"

The man shrugged and answered, "Oh, I guess about ten cents worth will be enough." Handing Glaze a dollar bill, Clyde continued, "That's all I want."

The clerk stepped to the cash register, added up the bread, eggs, and meat and rang up the total; he counted out the change and turned back to face Clyde, who now stood with a large shiny .45 caliber pistol pointed directly at him. Speaking so softly that Glaze barely heard, Clyde said, "This is a stick-up. Move away from the cash box."

Stepping back from the cash register, Glaze made room for Clyde, who moved behind the counter and scooped out about sixty dollars from the cash drawer. Hall finished his cleaning and looked up; he noticed the young man with the pistol. Coming around the display case, Hall said, "You can't do that."

Clyde, expecting no trouble from the older man, was enraged and waved the gun about menacingly. "Alright, smart alecs, get out from behind the counter." With the two clerks walking in front, Clyde moved toward the Wells Avenue exit.

Outside, Mrs. L. C. Butler, coming to the market to pick up a few items before closing time, drove up near the Wells Street entrance and parked her car. As Mrs. Butler got out of her car she noticed the clerks being forced forward by a gunman. Running to the southeast corner of the building, she nervously watched.

Apparently Clyde was still upset over Hall's resistance. When they reached the front door, he swung his fist and struck the older man. The blow was so hard that Hall's glasses flew out the door and landed on the sidewalk. The man staggered but didn't fall. Clyde drew back his arm to hit him again, and Hall grabbed at the outlaw's arm to halt the punch; Clyde's temper boiled, and he opened fire. Both Glaze and Mrs. Butler reeled in shock as Clyde fired three shots into Hall's chest; he fell through the door and onto the sidewalk near his glasses. On Wells Avenue near Hazelwood, two boys playing on the sidewalk heard the shooting and looked at one another.

Clyde stepped through the doorway and fired another bullet into Hall's prone body. Mrs. Butler gasped and bit her knuckle to keep from screaming. The outlaw turned to Glaze. The young clerk ignored him and ran to help his fallen friend. Barrow pointed the gun at Glaze and pulled the trigger, but the gun refused to fire; Clyde then ran east on Wells Avenue past Mrs. Butler, continued on to Hazelwood Street, past the wide-eyed boys, turned right, and hurried to the parked Buick. Frank Hardy stood by the back door trying to see what had caused the gunshots. As Clyde neared the auto, he shouted, "Everybody, get in the car." Sitting under the steering wheel with the motor idling, Hollis Hale slid over to the right side. Clyde drove away at a fast speed and turned east as the two boys ran to tell police what they had seen.

Back at the market, Glaze called police and an ambulance, which a nearby funeral home dispatched at once. The attendants placed Hall on a stretcher and carried him to the St. Vincent's Sanitarium located directly across the street from Little's market. The police raced to the scene and questioned Homer Glaze, Mrs. Butler, and the two boys. Sheriff Frank Reese arrived shortly and joined in the investigation; he asked Glaze to describe the gunman. Glaze thought for a moment and said, "He was small, about 5 feet 6 inches tall, weighed about 130 pounds, was clean shaven and light complexioned, wearing a gray felt hat, tan lumber jacket, and dark trousers, and looked to me to be between twenty and twenty-five years old."

Across the street from where police talked with witnesses, Howard Hall remained conscious for some time. However, despite physicians' best efforts to save him, the man died at about 7:30 P.M. Sherman Police Chief Gradie Thompson instructed an aide to call other police departments in the immediate area and to ask the Dallas radio stations to broadcast a description over the air. Then the chief, Patrolman B. V. Atnip, and Deputy Sheriff O. J. Nearberry drove their patrol car to Bonham, Texas, located twenty-two miles away; they hurried to the entrances of two bridges that crossed the Red River at Telephone and Ravina. Bridge toll collectors assured the officers that no persons fitting the descriptions of the suspects had passed by them. The lawmen drove along the river bank searching for clues; finding nothing, they finally abandoned the probe about 11:00 P.M.[3]

Meanwhile, the gangsters drove east from Sherman on Highway 82 toward Bells, Texas, in eastern Grayson County. About three miles out of Sherman, Clyde noticed the car drifting to one side as if tire pressure was down. Pulling over onto the shoulder of the road, he jumped out and discovered that one of the tires was extremely low. He flagged a passing motorist and asked to borrow a tire pump. The motorist offered the use of his patching kit, but Clyde declined. Hardy pumped up the low tire as Clyde watched. Handing the pump back to the owner, Clyde jumped into the driver's seat and sped off toward the east. They continued onward through Bells and at about 7:00 P.M. passed a night watchman who noticed them because the car was going so fast. East of Bells, Clyde turned south along country lanes and doubled back toward Denton. Just before midnight, he stopped to pick up Bonnie, changed the license plates on the Buick, and continued westward before turning north into Oklahoma. The car crossed the Red River about daybreak on Wednesday, 12 October.

After committing robberies in Oklahoma, Hollis and Hale returned to Texas while Bonnie and Clyde drove north to Kansas. They planned to reunite in Missouri.[4]

On Wednesday, Grayson County Sheriff Reese, District Attorney Joe P. Cox, and A. B. Little, the market owner, posted a $200 reward for information leading to the capture of the gunman. Later that day the sheriff received a group of police photographs from Dallas County Deputy Dennis Seals, which included lineup pictures of suspects fitting the description broadcast on Tuesday. Reese immediately carried the photos to Little's market for Homer Glaze to view. The clerk made a positive identification. Reese later showed the photographs to the motorist who had loaned the tire pump. Both Glaze and the motorist selected pictures of Clyde Barrow.[5]

Bonnie and Clyde continued to commit robberies in Kansas during October. The day before Halloween in 1932, they were driving along a rural lane when Bonnie said, "I'm so blue, Honey. I'd really like to see my Mama."

Clyde did not speak but simply turned the car and headed south toward Texas. While Bonnie slept, he continued to drive throughout the night and by morning had reached the outskirts of Dallas. They drove past the Barrow home and threw out a bottle containing a note advising the family where they would meet them that evening. Nell visited the outlaws at the rendezvous. Always suspicious, Nell asked, "Were you involved in the Hall murder at Sherman?" Clyde said, "The laws are just trying to hang something else on us. We've been in Kansas for the past three weeks."

Mrs. Parker was unable to get off work early, and Bonnie became upset during the afternoon because she could not see her mother until late in the evening. By dusk, she could wait no longer. Clyde refused to allow her to go alone and shortly after sundown, they drove to the Parker home near Lamar Street, one of the busiest thoroughfares in the city. Clyde circled the block several times while Bonnie dashed inside to share a few minutes with her family. On Halloween night Bonnie and Clyde left Dallas and drove to Carthage, Missouri, where they were reunited with Hollis Hale and Frank Hardy.

Renting tourist cabins, which they used as a base of operations, the three men committed various robberies and thefts throughout November. Near the end of the month, Clyde decided to rob the Oronogo, Missouri, bank. Though he did not allow Bonnie to participate in actual robberies, Clyde permitted her to go to the bank to look over the floor plan and report back on the positions of guards and other strategic information. On 30 November 1932 the men drove into town and stopped in front of the bank. Hale remained in the front seat to act as sentry and to drive in case of trouble. When Clyde and Hardy walked inside and pulled out their guns, the guards apparently expected a robbery and opened fire. Since the gangsters were completely out of money, Clyde fired back at the guards as Hardy dived into the teller's cage and scooped up all the money he could find. Clyde ran outside to the driver's seat and jumped inside as Hardy followed closely behind. The guards cautiously followed and fired at the back of the fleeing auto. Hardy counted the money as they escaped and said, "Well, there ain't much here. It only amounts to eighty dollars."

Clyde looked in the rear view mirror. "Go ahead," he said, "and cut it three ways."

When they arrived at the cabin, both Hardy and Hale insisted on returning to Oronogo to buy more ammunition. They hitchhiked into town, stole a car, and Clyde never saw them again. Reading the newspaper the following day, he discovered that the total cash stolen amounted to $115. Since the rent on the cabins was due and food was needed, Clyde selected another bank in a nearby town. Posting Bonnie as a guard with orders to sound the horn in the event of trouble, Clyde went inside and found one gray-haired man sitting in the corner studying ledger sheets.

Clyde brandished his gun. "This is a stick-up. Give me all your money." The man looked at him sadly. "Son, this bank failed several weeks ago. There's no money here." After being cheated by his fellow criminals and attempting to rob a bankrupt bank, Clyde decided the time had come for the couple to return to Texas.[6]

Meanwhile, Raymond Hamilton and Gene O'Dare traveled across Michigan. After visiting his father, Raymond suggested they find some girls; he met a striking young lady who worked as a waitress in a restaurant. Hoping to impress the girl, Raymond told her of his adventures in Texas and flashed a roll of money that he claimed to have netted from robberies.

Unknown to Hamilton, the girl's steady boyfriend was a Bay City policeman; he suggested she and another girl arrange a double date to go skating with the Texans while police planned an arrest.

When the officers approached the two men as they were skating, O'Dare reached into his pocket as if to draw a gun, and one of the policemen knocked him down. Even though Hamilton was armed with a loaded revolver, he made no attempt to resist arrest. When the officers questioned him, Hamilton gave his correct name, told them he was wanted in Dallas, said he was glad they had arrested him, and waived extradition.

Early Monday morning, 9 December 1932, Sheriff W. S. Day of Midland County, Michigan, sent a telegram to the Dallas sheriff. Thinking the two arrested men were probably Clyde Barrow and Raymond Hamilton, the Texas officers prepared photographs, finger-prints, and records for identification and rushed the packets to Love Field near Dallas for air shipment to the Michigan lawmen.[7]

On Wednesday, 11 December, Dallas County Deputy sheriffs Denver Seale and Ed Caster and Hill County Deputy Sheriffs P. F. Wilkerson and Kelly Rush left by automobile enroute to Michigan; they arrived in Bay City on Saturday, 14 December. After one day spent resting and processing the extradition papers, the Texas law-men started the return trip on Monday and arrived back in Dallas on Wednesday, 18 December. During the trip Raymond rode between two officers in the front, and O'Dare sat in the middle of the back seat; neither prisoner created a problem during the three-day journey. Upon arriving in Dallas, Wilkerson and Rush immediately departed for Hillsboro. They planned to return to Dallas within two days with Mrs. John Bucher so that she might view Hamilton to determine if he was one of the men who robbed and killed her husband on 30 April 1932.[8]

Meanwhile, Bonnie and Clyde also traveled to Dallas for a Christmas reunion with their families. During the visit the couple added another member, W. D. Jones, to their small gang. Just sixteen years of age, Jones had known Clyde for more than ten years. The Barrows had migrated to Dallas about the same time the Jones family arrived in town from Henderson County. Both groups had camped out under the Oak Cliff viaduct because they had no money for rent. Later, when Henry Barrow found a job and rented a house in west Dallas, the Jones family rented a house on the same street. After the experiences with Hale and Hardy, Bonnie and Clyde felt they needed someone who could be trusted to stand guard while they slept. Jones was not only a family friend, he also had a criminal record. On

Christmas Eve of 1932, Bonnie, Clyde, and W. D. Jones drove south out of Dallas along Highway 77, through Waco, the scene of the daring jail break, and continued south.

Arriving in Temple, Texas, late on 24 December, they rented a tourist cabin for the night; Bonnie and Clyde slept on the double bed while Jones bedded down on a quilt pallet on the floor. After breakfast Clyde ordered Jones to change two tires on their car and later gave him a .41 caliber pistol.[9]

Since Clyde believed in keeping open every avenue of escape, he frequently took extra cars to be used in case of trouble. On Christmas day of 1932, he decided to steal an auto, which set in motion a chain of events that led to the murder of a man named Doyle Johnson.

Doyle and Tillie Johnson had every reason to be very happy on the twenty-fifth of December 1932. They had celebrated their fifth wedding anniversary on 28 October, and they had an infant daughter. Johnson had a good job with the Strassberg Market and liked his work. The couple enjoyed living in Temple, which had been Johnson's home since 1918. At about 2:25 P.M. Johnson was napping in his home at 606 South 13th Street when a black Ford coupe stopped in front. As usual Clyde was driving, with Bonnie sitting in the middle and Jones next to the right door. Looking up and down the street, Clyde told Jones, "Jump out and check to see if the keys are in the ignition of that Model A Ford roadster parked at the curb."

Jones bounded out, ran to the automobile, peered inside, and signaled Clyde that he had found the keys. Bonnie and Clyde continued to sit in their Ford with the motor idling. Accustomed to the professional approach of Raymond Hamilton's thievery, they expected no trouble. Jones, however, with less expertise and experience, couldn't get the roadster motor started.

Henry Krauser, Johnson's father-in-law, heard a noise and looked out the front window. Spotting Jones in the auto, he ran from the house in an attempt to stop the thief. Krauser's son, Clarence, also ran out to assist his father in chasing the outlaws away from the car. Soon Mrs. Johnson joined the others on the sidewalk and also began yelling.

Clyde jumped from his car and ran to Jones, who was struggling with the ignition; he yelled, "What the hell are you doing? Get out of the damn car and help me push it 'til it starts." When they got the vehicle into the street, Clyde climbed into the driver's seat, and Jones jumped in beside him. Henry Krauser continued to yell at the thieves from the sidewalk while Clarence ran alongside screaming. Jones jumped onto the running board, waved his pistol about, and shouted, "Shut your damn mouths or I'll drill you."

Henry Krauser retreated toward the Johnson house while Clarence stepped behind a tree near the sidewalk. Running inside, Mrs. Johnson awakened Doyle to warn him of the theft of his new car. Johnson jumped up and ran from the house, rubbing his sleep-filled eyes just as Clyde got the motor started; he ran up to the auto on the driver's side, leaped onto the running board, grabbed Clyde's arm to prevent him from driving away, and yelled over his shoulder, "Clarence, go call the police."[10]

Bonnie sat in the black Ford coupe and watched the unfolding scene of three people standing on the Johnson front lawn screaming for help, Jones standing ashen-faced in fright on the right running board of the roadster, and Clyde and Doyle Johnson engaged in a wrestling match for control of the steering wheel; she became progressively more alarmed and called out to Clyde, "Why don't you just forget the car and let's get out of here." Bonnie had no qualms about leaving Jones and told relatives later that she knew he would be charged only with attempted auto theft if captured. With the entire neighborhood alerted, however, Bonnie feared the police might appear any moment; she slid behind the steering wheel, drove the car near the other automobile and yelled to Clyde, "Honey, just knock him down and forget about the car."[11]

Holding the revolver in his left hand, Clyde jammed it against Johnson's body. As they struggled, Johnson pushed the gun away from his body and pointed it toward the front of the car. Clyde pulled the trigger and the bullet passed through the front fender, ricocheted off the brake, and fell to the street where police later found it.

Jones, reacting to the explosion of Clyde's gun firing, also pulled the trigger of the .41 caliber pistol. The bullet struck Johnson on the right side of the neck about center, moved slightly downward, striking and severing the spinal column, and halted on the left side of the neck just under the skin. As Johnson fell to the pavement, Clyde drove the car away. From her position Bonnie saw the car escaping, and unnoticed by witnesses who crowded around Johnson's crumpled body, eased her auto away and followed the speeding roadster. She caught up with Clyde and Jones at the intersection of P and 17th streets; the two men jumped out of the stolen car as she pulled along-side. Clyde and Jones climbed into the Ford coupe, and Bonnie sped away to the south. A Temple resident, driving her car near the scene, saw the men abandon the auto and called police.[12] As he sped out of town, Clyde screamed at Jones, "You idiot. A killing wasn't called for. What the hell were you thinking about?"[13] Four men had now fallen before Clyde's guns.

6
They Say They Are Heartless and Mean

Except for Raymond Hamilton, who had been transferred to Hillsboro, Texas, to stand trial for his part in the Bucher murder, many of Clyde's criminal friends continued to be active as the year drew to a close. Four days after the murder of Doyle Johnson, Odell Chambless and Les Stewart strolled into the Home Bank of Grapevine, Texas, and brandished pistols; they forced tellers and customers onto the floor and escaped with almost $3,000. Grapevine, located about twenty miles northwest of Dallas in northeast Tarrant County, was a remote area, and officers quickly set up roadblocks. Chambless eluded the police barricades by kidnapping two Grapevine farmers, W. A. Schumaker and Jesse Trigg, and forcing them to drive to Dallas. Forcing the farmers to pose as possemen, the three passed the roadblocks. Enroute to Dallas, Chambless told his victims that he had a pocketful of bullets and planned to use them to prevent being captured. Just before reaching Dallas city limits, Chambless forced Trigg and Schumaker out on Highway 114 and continued on to Dallas alone. Officers found Schumakers's abandoned auto on the city's outskirts later that night.[1]

Stewart's attempt to escape was less successful. Police caught him within hours of the robbery and took him to Dallas for questioning. At first the outlaw refused to talk with officers. Later, however, he admitted being involved in a Cedar Hill bank robbery with Raymond Hamilton; he confessed that he and Chambless committed the Grapevine crime and suggested that Chambless might be interested in making a deal with the authorities. In return for amnesty,

Stewart volunteered to contact Bonnie and Clyde or members of Raymond's family who allowed their homes to be used as hideouts. Stewart even offered to help trap Bonnie and Clyde. Stewart's proposals intrigued the interrogation team because they supported information gathered by neighboring county officials. Tarrant County deputies Dusty Rhodes and Walter Evans, both of whom worked for the district attorney's office in Fort Worth, advised Dallas officers they had learned that Lillie McBride might be able to furnish further information about the Cedar Hill Bank robbery. Dallas officers were interested because McBride was Raymond Hamilton's sister.

Chambless, however, left Dallas before lawmen had a chance to act on their information. After abandoning the farmer's car, he went to Lillie McBride's home at 507 County Avenue where she invited him in, hid him for several hours, and went downtown to purchase new clothing for him. As Chambless changed the muddy pants, boots, and lumber jacket that he had worn during the bank robbery, she borrowed a car to aid him in escaping.[2]

On the morning of Friday, 6 January 1933, Bonnie, Clyde, and W. D. Jones, returned to Dallas for what would be a disastrous visit. They first went to the Parker home near Lamar Street. Clyde, and Jones circled the block while Bonnie dashed inside to visit her mother. Mrs. Parker, concerned about police stakeouts or an accidental spotting, warned Bonnie, "Baby, Lamar Street is one of the busiest streets in town. The law is along here all the time. And every one of 'em has memorized Clyde's picture. You've got to leave here right now."

Bonnie sat down on a couch and sighed. "We're going to leave in a minute. I just want to see you for a while. Clyde's got to make contact with some of Raymond's family." After visiting for a few minutes, Bonnie watched at the door until Clyde circled the block; she dashed out the door and jumped in beside him. The bandits drove to the McBride house on County Avenue and gave Lillie a radio containing a hidden saw blade; they promised to return later that night. While Bonnie, Clyde, and W. D. hurried to their hideout, the secluded and abandoned farmhouse near Grand Prairie, McBride borrowed a car and drove to Hillsboro, Texas, to leave the radio with Raymond at the Hill County Jail.[3]

Dallas and Tarrant County officers, unaware that Chambless had escaped from the city, planned a trap for him at the McBride home.

Shortly after nightfall on the evening of Friday, 6 January 1933, five lawmen arrived at the home. J. A. Van Noy, a Texas Ranger stationed at Belton, represented the state of Texas; he was a tall, thin man with hawklike eyes that moved constantly. Deputies Dusty Rhodes and Walter Evans, who came from the Tarrant County Sheriff's Department, like Van Noy, were six feet tall. Deputies Fred T. Bradberry and Lon Davis, agents for the Dallas County Sheriff's Department, were also men of tremendous size. Bradberry knocked on the door and was greeted by Maggie Farrie, another sister of Raymond Hamilton. Flashing his identification card and badge, Bradberry said, "We would like to speak to Mrs. Lillie McBride."

"She's not home right now," said Mrs. Farrie, "but I expect her soon."

Bradberry looked at the woman carefully. "May we wait inside until she gets back?"

Mrs. Farrie stood back from the door. "Well, I guess it'll be alright. Come in."

The five men hid their police cars in the neighborhood and entered the house to begin their vigil. Bradberry and Rhodes sat on a divan while Van Noy waited in a chair facing the front door. Farrie, who was babysitting her own six-year-old daughter and McBride's infant son, remained in another chair in front of the radio near the front door. Evans and Davis moved to the back part of the house to cover the rear door.

Shortly before midnight, Clyde drove his Ford coupe by the McBride house several times to assure himself that the area was safe. Spotting the small car, Bradberry turned to Farrie and whispered, "Turn off all the lights in the house."

She switched off all the lights except one small red bulb in the living room. "I need to leave the little red light on because my daughter is afraid of the dark."

Bradberry shrugged. "Alright."

Van Noy went into an adjoining room and watched the street from a window. Seeing the car circle the block again, Bradberry turned to Mrs. Farrie. "You've got to turn that red light out." Farrie glared at Bradberry as she flipped the switch.

Clyde drove up to the front of the house and left the motor idling; he emerged from the car carrying a shotgun at his side. He carefully looked around and quickly walked toward the house. Ranger Van

Noy spotted Clyde when he neared the porch, and he slipped back into the living room. "Get ready for action, Boys. He's got a sawed-off." Bradberry stood up and turned to Farrie, "Open the door, Ma'am." Before she could move, however, Clyde saw Bradberry's massive hulk through the living room window. He jerked the shotgun up to his waist and fired one shot through the front glass at the deputy. Chaos erupted in the house. Both Farrie and her small daughter screamed as the three officers returned Clyde's fire.

In the car Jones grabbed a gun and fired in the direction of the shots from the window. Bonnie hit his gun hand. "Stop shooting, you dunce. You might hit Clyde." She slipped behind the steering wheel and quickly drove away to circle the block.

Warily stepping backward from the front porch, Clyde hurriedly pumped another shell into the shotgun chamber and looked for a target. At the rear of the house, Davis and Evans reacted to the shots by drawing their pistols, then dashing out the back door; they cut through the backyard and ran alongside the left wall of the house toward the street. Arriving at the front of the house ahead of Evans, Davis glimpsed Clyde's form retreating into the darkness; he stopped and called out, "Halt in the name of the law."

Clyde wheeled toward the voice and fired a blast at close range. Davis fell face down on the porch with a tremendous load of buckshot in his stomach and chest. Clyde rarely wounded his victims; he usually fired at close range and shot to kill. Evans dropped to the ground and fired several shots at the outlaw.[4]

Bonnie drove the car around the corner while searching for Clyde. Speeding down the street, she saw him running toward the car from between two houses; she halted the car and slid to the middle of the seat as he jumped in behind the steering wheel. Clyde sped past Westmoreland onto Industrial Boulevard and turned north.[5]

Back at McBride's house, officers tried to bring order to the chaotic residential street as neighbors piled out of their houses and ran to number 507. As Van Noy and Rhodes worked to hold back the crowd, Bradberry and Evans lifted Davis into a car and rushed him to Methodist Hospital. Doctors pronounced the deputy dead on arrival. The notches on Clyde's gun had reached a total of five.

While some officers spread the all-points bulletin, others ordered the curious neighbors to return to their homes and continued to wait for the McBride woman. McBride arrived about 3:00 A.M.. and admitted having traveled to Hillsboro to visit her brother. Telephoning the

Hill County Jail, a Dallas deputy learned that the woman had delivered a radio to Raymond Hamilton and had shortly departed. The officers arrested McBride, Farrie, and Lillian Hilburn, who also lived at the County Avenue address; they again called Hill County authorities to warn them that Hamilton previously had escaped from a jail in McKinney, Texas, by sawing his way through the bars with the noise covered from the music of a radio. Hill County Sheriff Freeland quietly slipped to Raymond's cell and found him with the radio volume turned high to obscure the sawing on the window bars. Freeland seized both radio and saw.[6]

Continuing their flight, Bonnie, Clyde, and Jones turned northeast after leaving Dallas and passed near Sherman about one o'clock in the morning. Throughout the remainder of the night, Clyde sat hunched over the wheel of the speeding car and stopped only for food or fuel. By dawn they had reached central Oklahoma, where they rented a tourist cabin and remained out of sight for almost two weeks.[7]

On the night of 31 January 1933, Clyde had a less violent meeting with a lawman. Driving through Springfield, Missouri, he was just above the speed limit. Unless he was fleeing from a crime scene or officers, Clyde usually obeyed all traffic rules. When escaping, however, he customarily drove at seventy miles per hour, a tremendous speed considering the roads and automobiles of the early 1930s. In Springfield, a motorcycle policeman, Thomas Persell, spotted the car traveling slightly over the limit and chased it; he pulled up beside Clyde's car while they were crossing a bridge. "Pull over to the side," he said.

Clyde disliked bridges because they limited his avenues of escape; he wanted to get off the overpass before stopping his car. He smiled at the officer as he said, "Just a minute, sir." Persell became angry when Clyde kept driving and yelled, "I said pull over."[8]

Clyde slowed down as he said, "I'll be across the bridge in just a minute, sir." Clyde turned up a dark side street and pulled over. He turned to Jones and whispered, "Let's take him, W. D."[9] Persell put his motorcycle on its stand and walked up to the car. "Where are you going in such a hurry?" he asked.

As Clyde pointed the sawed-off shotgun in Persell's face, Jones jumped out of the car and took the officer's pistol; he forced him into the backseat where he covered him with a blanket and propped his feet on the man's head. Clyde slowly and carefully drove away, leaving Persell's motorcycle parked at the curb for his companions to worry about. Thirty minutes later, a passerby found the vehicle and reported it to authorities. Springfield officers organized a manhunt in the general area for Persell.

Meanwhile, the bandits and their captive continued through southwestern Missouri. They traveled a twisting route that included stops at Buffalo, Golden City, Fairplay, and Carthage. During the night the car's generator quit working. When the car halted near Orogono the battery would not start the motor. Clyde turned to Jones and said, "Walk into town and steal a new battery."

As Jones reached for the door handle, he asked, "Why can't he go with me to carry the thing?"

Clyde nodded, "A damn good idea."

The men walked the few miles into Oronogo and found a car with a battery that appeared new; after taking it, they walked back to the stranded car, removed the old battery, and installed the new one. When Clyde started the car, he said, "Get in, kid," and waved Persell away. The officer, who by this time had guessed his captors' real identities, expected to be murdered. When Clyde drove away into the night, Persell wiped his forehead and said softly, "Much obliged."[10]

Buck Barrow was paroled from Huntsville State Prison on 22 March 1933. His family hoped that he would not return to his criminal ways. Heeding the pleas of Blanche, his wife, Buck had willingly surrendered to prison officials after an escape and had completed the sentence received in Denton; he had never really cared for guns and primarily had committed only petty thefts. Feeling responsible for Clyde becoming a major criminal, Buck was especially troubled when, during his sentence, his duties included sweeping the death chamber that contained the electric chair.

After his release Buck planned to take Blanche to visit her parents in Missouri. Since he had no transportation, Nell gave him the money to buy a used car. The family liked Blanche and hoped that Buck would settle on his father-in-law's Missouri farm and become a respectable citizen. Unfortunately, Buck had been out of prison less than a week when he said, "I want to visit Clyde."

Blanche pleaded with him, "Forget any visits and come with me to Missouri."

Nell cautioned, "Buck, you better listen to Blanche."

Reassuringly, Buck said, "I don't want to join the gang. I just want to see him on the way to Missouri." Using the west Dallas connection of Floyd Hamilton to contact Clyde, Buck set up a rendezvous. The arrangement terrified Blanche and she sobbed constantly in an attempt to change Buck's plans. They drove from his parents' home in Dallas on 2 April 1933 with Blanche weeping. Before leaving the city, Buck stopped at Nell's beauty salon and told her, "A man will call later and ask for me. Tell him that I've left town. That's the signal to Clyde that the meeting will be kept." When the mysterious man called later that day, Nell gave him the coded message.

The relatives met near Fort Smith, Arkansas, and drove to Joplin, Missouri; they rented a stone garage apartment in the Freeman Park Addition. Clyde, Bonnie, and Jones discussed their criminal acts, and Blanche responded with news of their families. Since Bonnie and Clyde enjoyed eating Texas dishes such as pinto beans, boiled cabbage, and cornbread, the women cooked several servings. Having been on the move extensively prior to the meeting, Bonnie, Clyde, and W. D. used the opportunity to rest and sleep. Blanche had been terribly apprehensive about the visit but soon began to enjoy the vacation; she had brought a small white dog and spent several hours each day romping with him.

Bonnie loved poetry and music; while a student at Cement City High School, she had sung at every opportunity. On the road, she read pulp fiction and wrote several poems that had a certain childlike intensity. While living at the Joplin apartment, she completed several new verses and copied some written earlier.[11]

Within a few days the Joplin police became suspicious of the group. Neighbors reported seeing different cars with various license plates as well as occasional glimpses of guns. Missouri State Highway Patrolmen George B. Kahler and W. E. Grammer arrived on 10 April to talk with witnesses; they agreed that the group deserved watching. Kahler checked out the registration of the Kansas plates. He also learned the suspects had registered with the power company under one name, with the gas company in another, and applied for a telephone hookup under still another. After reporting their decision to maintain surveillance to headquarters, the patrolmen began an around-the-clock stakeout of the garage apartment. During the evening of 12 April 1933 one of the suspects' cars left the garage apartment. That night, three men committed a robbery near Neosho. The robbers' descriptions matched those of the suspects. By late afternoon on 13 April, the state officers concluded that local officers should be included in the action and the suspects confronted.

Municipal and county officials agreed that the suspicions of the neighbors and state lawmen justified further investigation. Joplin Police assigned plainclothesmen Harry McGinnis and Tom De Graff to represent the city, while Newton County assigned Constable Wesley Harriman to join in the investigation. The officers drove their cars up to the entrance of the garage; Constable Harriman led the group from one car as Patrolman Kahler coasted his automobile into the driveway, blocking their escape.[12]

Buck and the two women were completely unprepared for action; he had removed his shoes and was asleep on the couch. Dressed in a negligee and carpet slippers, Bonnie mixed a recipe of cornbread and placed it in the oven. A pot of pinto beans boiled on the burner. Blanche spread the cards out for a new game of solitaire with the tiny white puppy asleep near her feet.

Suddenly, several different events occurred simultaneously. Looking out the window, Clyde spotted the approaching lawmen, snatched up his rifle, and said, "The law is outside. Everybody grab your guns and let them have it." Buck jumped from the couch, picked up a gun, and ran to a window.[13]

Constable Harriman, within a few feet of the apartment, called out, "I'm a peace officer. Open up."[14]

Upstairs Clyde and Jones broke the windows and opened fire; they struck Harriman with several rounds and he fell to the ground dead. Clyde and Jones ran downstairs to prepare for the escape while Bonnie threw items into suitcases. Curious, she looked out of a window and saw one officer duck back out of sight. Another sent a bullet through the windowpane just above her head and showered the top of her head with glass fragments. Buck ran to her side and forced her away from the window.

Blanche sat petrified for several seconds, unable to understand what was happening. Then, still clutching the deck of cards, she ran about the apartment screaming in a loud voice. The tiny dog, frightened by both the noise of the guns and Blanche's actions, chased after her barking as loudly as he could. Shortly, both woman and dog ran downstairs, through the gunfire, and into the street. With other officers putting down a cover fire, Detective McGinnis ran to Constable Harriman's motionless form on the ground. Downstairs

Clyde and Jones prepared for the gang to escape the ambush. They partially opened the garage door and fired at the lawmen with Browning automatic rifles stolen from National Guard armories. Between bursts Clyde yelled, "Bonnie, you and Buck come downstairs." They ran down the steps and jumped into the waiting car. Clyde crashed the car through the entrance, side-swiped the officers' car, and careened into the street. They spotted Blanche running parallel and pulled her into the car before racing out of town toward the southwest.[15]

The scene the gang left behind in Joplin was disastrous. Constable Wesley Harriman had died as he fell to the driveway. Detective Harry McGinnis's left arm had been shot away, and he died in the hospital that night. Officers Tom De Graff and George Kahler were badly wounded but survived. Despite their numerous wounds, the officers noted that the killers' escape car was a dark green 1932 Ford V-8 sedan and broadcast an all-points bulletin. Officers who searched the apartment found an interesting and assorted collection. A preliminary inventory produced a large number of firearms, stolen property, and evidence clearly implicating the Barrows. Weapons included a Browning automatic rifle, four regular rifles, a sawed-off shotgun, and a revolver.[16]

Officers discovered five diamonds that were part of a robbery committed the previous day at Neosho, Missouri. Blanche Barrow's purse was found and contained both her marriage license and the papers signed by Texas Governor Mirian Ferguson granting a full pardon to Buck on 20 March 1933, only three weeks before. In another room, officers found a motor vehicle certificate in the name of Carl Beatty. Further investigation revealed two rolls of exposed photographic film. Strangely, several posters of wanted criminals, including Bonnie and Clyde, were scattered about the apartment. After checking the posters, the Joplin Police Department notified the Dallas Sheriff's office. Dallas officers revealed that Clyde Barrow had used the alias Carl Beatty on several occasions in the past. This evidence plus the pardon indicated to both Joplin and Dallas law enforcement agencies that the escaped killers were unquestionably the Barrow gang.[17]

Moving quickly to capitalize on this new information, Sheriff Smoot Schmid called Deputy Bob Alcorn and instructed him to travel to Joplin, review the evidence, and look for a trail. Alcorn asked permission to take along Deputy Ted Hinton, who was also familiar with the Barrow case. The sheriff agreed and the two deputies left Dallas within an hour of the gun battle.[18]

Of all the evidence, the two rolls of photographic film proved the most interesting and helpful. With his knowledge of various west Dallas gangsters, Alcorn was able, indisputably and for the first time, to identify W. D. Jones. This young outlaw had been described by witnesses to the murder of Doyle Johnson in Temple, Texas, the killing of Deputy Malcolm Davis in west Dallas, the kidnapping of Motorcycle Officer Thomas Persell in Springfield, Missouri, and finally the bloody gun fight in Joplin, Missouri. Police in Texas had arrested Frank Hardy, who had the same general features of Jones, for the Doyle Johnson killing. Hinton's identification prompted officials to conclude that Jones, not Hardy, was present and involved in the Johnson slaying in Temple. The pictures also revealed to the public that these young killers showed little remorse for their crimes. Apparently the gang boastfully displayed officers' weapons they had stolen during kidnappings. One of the prints showed Bonnie with a cigar clenched between her teeth while she brandished two pistols. The photo was made as a joke. Bonnie chain-smoked Camel cigarettes but never cigars. The media, however, immediately labeled her a gun carrying, cigar-smoking gang thug.[19]

Meanwhile, the Barrow party raced toward Texas. After eluding roadblocks in Kansas, Oklahoma, and Texas, their dark green Ford stopped in Amarillo, in the Texas panhandle, only eight hours after the Joplin shooting. Clyde's practice of driving great distances in a very short time, sometimes as much as one thousand miles from a crime scene, helped the gang to escape; he led the group so far away that officers never sought them in their new resting spot. In Amarillo Clyde bought medicine for Jones, who had received a slight head wound in the gun battle.[20]

Later that day the city of Joplin, Jasper County, and Newton County each offered $200 for the arrest and conviction of the two Barrow brothers.[21] Clyde was now, directly or indirectly, responsible for the deaths of six men. Four of these had been law officers. Buck, who had claimed that he wanted simply to visit his brother Clyde, now found himself wanted by police throughout the southwest. Within two weeks both he and Blanche would be involved in additional gang activity, including a double kidnapping.

Bonnie Parker. Courtesy of Dr. Allen B. Campbell, Jr.

Clyde Barrow. Author's collection. Photograph by W. D. Jones.

Raymond Hamilton, on the left, shaking hands with his brother, Floyd (Dallas County Jail, 1934). From the collections of the Texas/Dallas History and Archives Division, Dallas Public Library.

Reenactment of the murder of Deputy Sheriff Lon Davis (the Lillie McBride home, Dallas, Texas). From the collections of the Texas/ Dallas History and Archives Division, Dallas Public Library.

Ambush site, looking north. Photograph by E. R. Milner.

The Warren Ford sedan after the ambush near Arcadia, Louisiana (known as the "death car"). Courtesy of Dr. Allen B. Campbell, Jr.

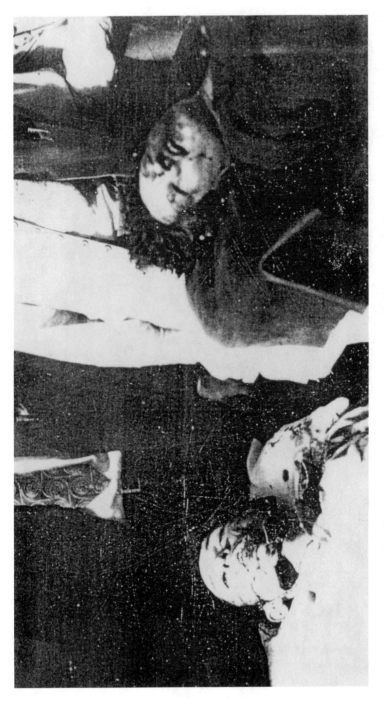

Bonnie and Clyde, two hours after the ambush, Conger's Furniture Store and Funeral Parlor, Arcadia, Louisiana. Courtesy of Dr. Allen B. Campbell, Jr.

Crowds line up to view the remains of Bonnie at the McKamy-Campbell Funeral Home, Dallas, Texas. Courtesy of Dr. Allen B. Campbell, Jr.

7

From Heartbreak Some People Have Suffered

The town of Ruston, arranged north and south of U.S. Highway 80, was replete with lovely old homes and friendly people. It was pleasantly warm on the morning of 27 April 1933 when the Barrow gang arrived. Clyde drove with Bonnie beside him in the front. Buck, Blanche, and Jones sat in the back. Since the Joplin shootings, the group had driven constantly for two weeks with no rest. Witnesses reported that they appeared extremely haggard.

Clyde drove through town memorizing the layout and fixing in his mind possible escape routes. Parking for more than an hour near the Ruston State Bank, he studied the flow of people into and out of the building as well as traffic in the area. Around noon Clyde turned to the group and said, "It's time we go to work." Needing a new car to use in the escape, he drove through the residential area of the town searching for one to steal.[1]

Shortly after noon H. Dillard Darby left the B. H. McClure Funeral Home, where he worked as a mortician. He drove to the L. K. Brooks Boarding House on North Trenton Street, where he, his wife, and several other boarders lived. Parking his new Chevrolet auto up beside the house, Darby went inside to lunch. As was common at this time in small southern towns, he left the automobile keys in the ignition switch. The virtual absence of crime allowed people to confidently leave their cars as well as their houses unlocked. Normally Mrs. Darby ate lunch with her husband; on this day, however, she was visiting her mother, Mrs. Kitty Taylor, in DeQuincy, approximately 150 miles away.[2]

One of Darby's fellow boarders, Sophia Stone, a home demonstration agent for Lincoln Parish, finished her lunch early and walked out to the Brooks' front porch. Enjoying the pleasantness of the spring day, she sat down in the porch swing. Darby joined her about 1:15 P.M.[3]

Within five minutes the Barrow gang drove along North Trenton looking for a suitable car to seize. Spotting Darby's new auto, Clyde turned to Jones: "When I slow down, you jump out and steal that Chevrolet." Clyde allowed the car to coast. Jones leaped out and ran to the Chevrolet. He saw the keys in the ignition and clambered inside. Quickly starting the car, Jones hurriedly backed up.[4]

Darby sat dumbfounded for several seconds; he then ran from the porch and tried to jump on the running board of his car. But before he could grab the door handle, Jones stomped the accelerator and the car shot away from the driveway. Running back to the Brooks' yard, Darby shouted, "Mr. Brooks, call the sheriff. Somebody just stole my car."

Stone called out, "I'll help you catch them."

Darby looked at his departing car and his temper boiled.

"Okay," he said, "let's get them." Darby and Stone ran to her car and sped off after the disappearing auto. Brooks called Lincoln Parish Sheriff A. J. Thigpen, who quickly notified authorities in surrounding communities and requested that roadblocks be set up.[5]

Jones raced along the Ruston-El Dorado highway until he noticed barricades some distance ahead; he turned west on the Hico road. Hurrying to catch up to Jones, Darby and Stone saw the Chevrolet turn left and quickly followed. After traveling along the Hico Road for several miles, however, they realized catching the stolen auto was impossible; they turned around and drove back toward Ruston. Reaching the El Dorado highway, Stone turned right. Within minutes they met a black Chevrolet coach parked on the shoulder of the road. Standing beside the car, a man waved vigorously to Darby and Stone. Darby thought he recognized the man and asked Stone to pull over. When she stopped the car, he jumped out, ran to the black Chevrolet, and discovered four strangers.

Clyde grabbed the front of Darby's shirt and demanded, "Why are you chasing that other car?"

Angry and indignant, Darby said, "If it's any of your business, I'm chasing my own car. It was stolen."

Clyde struck Darby on the back of the head and shoved him into the coach. He ordered Bonnie to get the woman. Bonnie ran to the other auto, jerked Stone out by pulling on her hair, forced her back to the Barrow car, and shoved her inside. As Stone fell into the gang's car, she noticed that the backseat held enough ammunition to fight a large battle. Neither Darby nor Stone made a sound when kidnapped. A farmer witnessed the crime from his cotton field nearby, and when the bandit car drove away with the captives, the farmer hurried to telephone authorities.[6]

When Sheriff Thigpen received the call from the boarding house, he first assumed the crime was the work of mischievous pranksters. Several youngsters in the preceding months had stolen autos for joy rides. After the farmer reported the kidnapping, however, Thigpen concluded that there was more to the theft of Darby's automobile than a group of youngsters; he quickly organized a widespread search for Darby and Stone.[7]

Meanwhile, Clyde turned off onto a gravel road that led to the town of Bernice. When out of sight of all other traffic, he turned to the captives in the back. "I guess you know we're going to have to kill you for messing up our plans."

Buck, who was seated next to Stone, said, "I say let's kill them right now." For the next several minutes, the bandits argued about whether or not to kill the kidnapped couple. As the car neared Bernice, Clyde decided to buy more gasoline. Before driving into the entrance, Clyde turned to the captives and frowned. "Unless you keep quiet I'll kill you and everybody working at the station." While paying for five gallons of gasoline, Clyde asked the attendant, "Have you seen a black-headed kid about sixteen come through here in a new black Chevrolet?"

The station worker shook his head. "Naw, it's been pretty slow all day. I ain't seen anybody like that."

Clyde drove to the exit and waited for the traffic to clear. Charles Goyne, mayor of Ruston, and W. D. Risinger, city marshal, passed by in a police car. Watching them drive out of sight, Clyde looked back at Darby and Stone: "I know that they're the Ruston law. I just as soon they would try to stop us so I could fill them full of lead." Barrow carefully watched the captives in the backseat for their reactions. He turned onto the highway, drove through the Dubach community, and continued on until he reached a point in northwest Louisiana that was unfamiliar to both Darby and Stone. Clyde constantly searched for W. D. Jones. Crossing the state line into Arkansas, he continued to travel the back roads. Several times during the trip Buck asked Clyde to stop the car and kill Stone and Darby. While driving through Arkansas, Stone noticed that though the gang talked less about killing her and Darby, she became extremely nervous and found herself talking incessantly. Seeing someone else frightened seemed to entertain the gang and they soon were talking normally with the young people. When the car arrived in El Dorado, Arkansas, Clyde stopped again for gas and oil. Both Barrow brothers got out and went behind the car where Darby and Stone could hear them talking in hushed tones. When they returned to the car, Clyde said, "We're not going to kill you after all. We're going to let you go pretty soon."

Bonnie asked, "How do you all make a living?"

Stone said, "I'm a home demonstration agent."

Concerned about the gang member's reaction, Darby hesitantly answered, "I'm an undertaker."

Laughing aloud, Bonnie said, "When the law catches us, you can fix us up. You probably recognize us after seeing our pictures everywhere." Hooking her arm through Clyde's she boasted, "If they ever take us alive, they'll put us in the electric chair. So what's the use?"[8]

Clyde continued through small towns such as Magnolia and Waldo and then turned toward Prescott. Five miles out of town, he stopped the car. "I figure it'll be at least two hours before you can get in touch with the law. Now hop out." He closed the door, started to drive away but then slammed on the brakes. Darby held his breath and Stone clutched her throat as Buck got out and came toward them. Instead of threatening them, however, he pulled out five dollars, handed it to Darby, and said, "Here's some money to help you get back home." The frightened couple watched the red taillights disappear into the night and began walking toward a spot where earlier they had seen a man changing a flat tire. The man agreed to take them to Waldo for five dollars. When they reached town, Darby tried to contact the city marshal. The officer was out of town, but the Waldo mayor drove the pair to Magnolia, where Darby called his brother-in-law, Nick Mialos. Within an hour, they were enroute to Ruston.[9]

Several days later authorities found Darby's undamaged car near McGee, Arkansas, with only the spare tire missing. On Friday, 28 April 1933, Sheriff Thigpen received a message from the marshal at Logansport, Louisiana. From the descriptions furnished by Darby and Stone, officers tentatively identified the outlaws as the Barrow gang. Later that day the victims positively identified the male kidnappers from wanted posters sent to Marshal Risinger. The next morning, Sheriff Thigpen received photographs from the police at Joplin, Missouri. Darby and Stone categorically identified Blanche Barrow and Bonnie Parker as the women in the group.[10]

On 3 May 1933 an interstate bus pulled into the Dallas terminal on Jackson Street. As several passengers got off and walked into the station, nobody noticed a lovely, slender, auburn-haired woman as she passed through the building and hailed a taxicab. Giving the driver the address of her husband's parents in west Dallas, Blanche Barrow settled back in the seat as the car drove away; she was troubled by the turn her life had recently taken. Blanche had never been in trouble before. Then, in the space of a few dreadful minutes at Joplin, Missouri, her life had drastically changed.

Arriving at the Barrow's service station-apartment, Blanche paid the driver and dashed inside; she brought the message that the outlaws wanted to see their relatives for a brief visit. She would guide the families to a prearranged site on a country lane near a bridge just outside Commerce, Texas, a small town about sixty miles northeast of Dallas. Since relatives had not seen the couple for several months, the plan caused great excitement.

Mrs. Barrow telephoned Bonnie's mother as well as Clyde's sister Nell. Suspecting the police had tapped the phone lines, she said, "I'm cooking pinto beans for supper. Why don't you come over?" This was a prearranged code that alerted family members to an impending rendezvous with their outlaw relatives. While the families gathered and planned the trip, Blanche went into the city to purchase some clothing. One new item, a pair of English-type riding breeches, would become well known within a few weeks when lawmen captured Blanche and a mortally wounded Buck in Iowa. A picture taken by a news photographer at the point of arrest showed her in boots and the riding breeches as she struggled to break free of the restraining officers in order to get to her dying husband.[11]

When the families arrived at the meeting place near Commerce, the joy of seeing their children was tempered by the dread of having to leave them in a very short time. Nell later told her mother, "I compare that meeting to visiting relatives in prison who are condemned to die." Everyone enjoyed moments of humor when Bonnie and

Clyde told stories of buying pinto beans and cornbread from a farm wife and about Blanche running down the street during the terrible gun battle at Joplin. Talking seriously, Bonnie and Clyde openly discussed the Malcolm Davis killing in Dallas, the Doyle Johnson murder in Temple, the Persell kidnapping in Missouri, the Johns kidnapping in New Mexico, and the Darby-Stone kidnappings in Louisiana; they denied several crimes that newspapers had attributed to them.

During most of the meeting, the families stayed in their cars to avoid being seen too clearly by people passing by. At one point Mrs. Parker and Bonnie left the parked cars to walk down the country lane for a private conversation. Emma Parker walked with her arm around Bonnie's shoulder. "Honey, I want you to think about leaving Clyde and giving up to the law. A prison sentence is a whole lot better to how he's going to end up. You know it's sudden and certain death."

Bonnie shook her head. "Clyde will never give up. He knows he'll be killed. We both know it. When he dies, Mama, I won't have a reason to go on living. So you see, I can't give up. We'll just go on."

The meeting broke up near dusk with the parents returning to Dallas and the bandits turning north toward Oklahoma. Buck and Blanche left the others for a brief period to spend a few days with her parents, the Caldwells, in Missouri. Buck had intended taking a job on their farm when he came home from prison. Now he and Blanche were inextricably intertwined in the gang.

As the families returned from their reunion early in May 1933, Sheriff Freeland, Deputy Bob Wilkinson, and Officer Fred Long transferred Raymond Hamilton to La Grange, Texas, where the outlaw went on trial in district court for a November 1932 bank robbery. He was found guilty and sentenced to a life term in prison. The officers returned to Hillsboro late Friday night, 13 May 1933, and since Hamilton earlier had used part of a bunk to aid his escape, they placed him in a cell by himself with only a floor mattress.[12]

Within two weeks of Hamilton's return from La Grange, one of the witnesses against Hamilton, Marvin Kitchen, was kidnapped in Hillsboro. While walking on Walton Street, Kitchen saw a man coming toward him from the west. The man passed Kitchen, then whirled, put a gun to his back, and said, "Take it easy; I don't want to hurt you." An auto hurriedly drove up and the gunman forced Kitchen inside. As the car pulled away from the curb, the man said, "You had better be more careful what you say and do." The kidnappers drove Kitchen to a point one and one-half miles west of Periola on the Bethel Road, where the outlaws put Kitchen out and bound his hands and feet with wire. As the abductors walked toward their car, Kitchen heard them talking of going for another victim. Two passersby, Knox Smith and R. Q. Dehart, discovered Kitchen about 2:30 A.M. and freed him. The kidnappers were never heard from again.[13]

After a mistrial, because the jury was unable to reach a verdict over the punishment, a new trial for the murder of John Bucher began in May. Otto Hanna, a garage owner in the small town of Malone, served as foreman. The jury heard the same testimony as before and at 9:30 A.M. on Friday, 2 June 1933, found Hamilton guilty of murder with malice and sentenced him to another life term.[14]

Within a week Judge Wray ordered a grand jury to begin investigation of the Kitchen kidnapping. Though no further evidence was found and neither of the kidnappers was ever located, people in Hillsboro speculated that Clyde and W. D. Jones had kidnapped Kitchen and had gone back for Bedell Jordan.[15]

Several days after the Hillsboro kidnapping, on 10 June 1933, Clyde, Bonnie, and W. D. Jones were speeding east on Texas Highway 203 between Quail and Wellington. They were enroute to a prearranged meeting with Buck and Blanche following the trip to Missouri to visit her parents. Six miles east of Wellington, a bridge over a ravine had been destroyed and the warning sign had been moved. Driving about seventy, Clyde crashed over the edge and into the ravine. The car rolled over two times and landed at the bottom of the deep ditch. Bonnie's door was ripped partially open and she was pinned under the car. Clyde had been thrown clear of the wreck and miraculously was unhurt; he pulled W. D. from the car and got the guns out. With the auto tilted at a precarious angle, gasoline began to run onto the ground and a spark caused the fuel to ignite. Bonnie, who had been dazed by the accident, began to regain consciousness and screamed for Clyde and W. D. to save her. They tried to lift the car but it was too heavy.[16]

Fortunately, Tom Pritchard, a local farmer had been sitting on his front porch talking with a neighbor named John Cartwright. Both men saw the car go over the embankment and rushed down the hill to help; they noticed the large number of weapons thrown clear, glanced guardedly at one another, and suspected that the three were outlaws. Jones threw sand on the fire as the other three men lifted the car off the badly burned Bonnie. Clyde carried her to the farmhouse where Mrs. Pritchard prepared a bed. Ordering the men into the other room, the farm wife treated the burns as best she could. Bonnie's face and arms were blistered but her right leg concerned Mrs. Pritchard most. Much of the skin from Bonnie's hip to her ankle had been terribly burned and in some places had exposed the bone. Using an accepted home remedy of the time, the woman bathed the wounds in bicarbonate of soda.[17]

While Clyde returned to the wreck to retrieve their guns, John Cartwright slipped away and ran to a neighbor's house to telephone Collinsworth County Sheriff George T. Corry. Returning to the Pritchard home, Clyde immediately demanded to know where their neighbor had gone.

Pritchard nervously looked at his wife. "I think he's gone to call a doctor," he said.

Mrs. Pritchard wiped her hands. "Mister, you sure should get this woman to a doctor. What we need is an ambulance."

Clyde shook his head. "No. We don't need any ambulance. Just do what you can for her."

The farm wife gathered up her medicine and bandages. "I'm sorry, but I've done all that I can."

W. D. walked in the front door. Clyde frowned at him. "Any sign of that neighbor?"

Jones shook his head. "Nope."

Clyde pulled a shotgun from a canvas bag. "I could kick your butt for letting that guy leave. Now keep an eye on these two."

W. D. pointed the shotgun at the Pritchards as Clyde squatted down near the bed where Bonnie lay. "Sugar, I don't know what to do about moving you."

Bonnie reached out her hand. "I can travel. It'll hurt for sure. But we can't stay here."

"Well, these people don't even have a car." He looked at W. D. "There ain't no telling where that neighbor got off to." W. D., visibly upset over Clyde's tongue-lashing, began to tremble and complain about a headache. His nerves seemed to become more frayed with each passing moment. Clyde glared at him for several seconds before going outside.

The pressure on Pritchard was also intense. He feared the imminent confrontation that would surely occur when the lawmen arrived.

Wanting his wife to escape danger, Pritchard leaned near to her ear and whispered, "Slip outside and hide."

When W. D. leaned against the wall to recover from his tremors, Mrs. Pritchard started out the back door. W. D. turned at the noise of the door and fired, hitting her in the hand. Pritchard grabbed cloths and tried to halt the bleeding.

He glared at W. D. "That's a fine way to show appreciation for us helping you."[18]

Bonnie, startled by the sound of the shotgun, jumped off the bed and tried to run. Clyde dashed in from the porch and yelled, "Somebody's coming. Get out here with me." Going back outside the two outlaws hid behind a hedge until Sheriff Corry and Wellington Town Marshal Tom Hardy stopped their car in the front yard; they watched the two officers go to the back of the house with drawn guns and start onto the porch. Stepping from behind the bushes, Clyde and W. D. seized the lawmen, took their weapons, and bound their wrists with their own handcuffs. Clyde went into the house and came out with Bonnie in his arms; he ordered Hardy to get in the backseat and hold Bonnie. After placing her in Hardy's lap, Clyde waved Corry into the front between W. D. and himself. He rapidly drove the car out of the Pritchard yard and headed east toward Wellington.

Following a three-hour drive in which Bonnie moaned in constant and excruciating pain, Clyde pulled up next to Buck's car just outside Erick, Oklahoma. W. D. jumped out and cut a length of rusty barbed wire from a nearby fence. Clyde ordered the officers to move to a nearby tree and bound their cuffs together with the fence wire. Blanche tried to comfort Bonnie while Buck walked to the tree and asked Clyde if he planned to kill the lawmen.

Clyde looked at the officers for their reactions. "Naw, they treated Bonnie pretty well. I guess we'll let 'em work their way loose." After carrying Bonnie to Buck's car, the gangsters drove away to the east. Corry and Hardy struggled to free their hands. After thirty minutes, they broke the rusty wire and hurried to notify local authorities that Clyde Barrow and Bonnie Parker were traveling east from Erick, Oklahoma. The alarm spread rapidly, but once again Clyde and his small band slipped through the net and drove to Fort Smith, Arkansas, where they rented a tourist cabin.[19]

Knowing Bonnie needed an immediate family member to help her, Clyde left Fort Smith at about noon on 11 June and drove to Dallas. Both Mrs. Barrow and Mrs. Parker insisted on returning with him at once. But apparently Clyde had decided that Bonnie's sister, Billie, was the choice. Unfortunately, she was attending a movie. Clyde paced the floor and wept in anguish until Billie returned. Quickly packing clothing, she and Clyde left about midnight.[20]

Dallas County Deputy Sheriff Ted Hinton, who was on night patrol, spotted the couple as they drove through Dallas. Briefly confused because he didn't recognize Billie, he hesitated before trying to intercept them. The brief hesitation was all that Clyde needed. While Hinton turned around, Clyde increased speed and disappeared into the night. Meeting no more lawmen, Clyde and Billie arrived at the Fort Smith tourist cabin at about dawn on 12 June 1933. Though Clyde had not slept for forty-eight hours, he appeared concerned only about Bonnie and didn't leave her bedside for several days. Three days passed before Bonnie emerged from her delirium and recognized Billie.[21]

Ten days after Clyde made the round trip to Dallas, Buck and W. D. Jones drove northwest along Highway 64 from Fort Smith determined to raise money to pay for Bonnie's medical care and to furnish the group operating funds.

Meanwhile, at about 2:00 A.M. on 22 June 1933, two unidentified bandits captured the Alma, Arkansas, town marshal, Henry D. Humphery, and forced him to go with them to the local bank and enter the building in front of them. After lashing the officer to a column, they placed the safe on a two-wheel mover, pushed it outside, and loaded it onto a waiting truck. Inside the safe waited more than $3,000. The outlaws ran to the truck and drove out of town north along U.S. Highway 71 toward Fayetteville, Arkansas. They halted on a country lane near their previously hidden car, blew the door off the safe, removed the cash, jumped into their auto, and drove away.[22]

Late the evening of 22 June, Buck and W. D. pulled into a secluded area near Fayetteville and spent the night in the car. The next day, they drove into town and looked over the R. L. Brown Grocery Market in the northern part of the city. The robbery worked as planned and the thieves sped away from Fayetteville along Highway 71 back toward Alma. Employees of the store contacted the police and relayed a description of the robbers, their car, and the license number. Fayetteville police broadcast an alarm and alerted officers in the nearby area.[23]

Fifty miles to the south, Marshal Humphery was monitoring the radio in Alma and recognized the descriptions of the grocery store robbers as the men who had humiliated him the previous day and vowed to avenge himself by capturing the robbers; he picked up a friend named A. M. Saylars, an employee of the Mississippi Valley Power Company and reserve officer, and hurried to Highway 71 to search for the outlaws. He and Saylars parked on the west side of the road facing south and watched the cars go by for some time until a passing friend, Webber Wilson, pulled up beside the patrol car. Wilson called out to Humphery, but the marshal signaled him to move on by and to get off the roadway. Humphery glanced at his rearview mirror and saw another car traveling at a high rate of speed bearing down on Wilson's car from behind.

Wilson slowly began to roll forward, apparently intending to park in front of the patrol car and question Humphery about his strange actions. But before he could get off the pavement, the oncoming auto struck the back of his car. Wilson, shaken by the crash, was unable to move for several seconds. Realizing what had happened, he became furious because his car had been wrecked. He jumped from his car, gathered up two large rocks that were lying beside the highway, walked toward the rear auto, and evidently intended to bash the two men inside, the car itself, or both. As he neared the car, however, Wilson saw that both men were aiming guns at him; he dropped his stones, yelled a warning to Humphery, and ran away. Humphery and Saylars got out of the patrol car and walked toward the auto. Nearing the bandit auto, he automatically scanned the license number and realized it was the same as that broadcast by the police in Fayetteville.

Humphery jerked out his gun and called to the men to raise their hands. Buck, holding a rifle, opened the door on the driver's side, while W. D., carrying a machine gun, pushed open the passenger's door. Both men leveled their guns while using their car doors as shields and began firing. Buck's fire went wide to one side, but Jones's shotgun pellets caught Humphery in the chest. The marshal was blown backward, landing near his car, and died almost instantly.

Finding himself standing alone against two of the most desperate men in the country, Saylars opened fire at the gangsters; he avoided being hit by dodging and jumping while he continued to shoot. Jones had a clear shot at Saylars once, but the shotgun was empty. When

Jones reached for another gun, Saylars tried to shoot him and found his gun empty as well. The officer dashed across the highway to a nearby barn and began reloading his revolver.[24]

Buck and W. D. used the opportunity to run to the marshal's auto, the only car that had not been damaged, and vaulted in with Jones behind the steering wheel. By the time they got the car motor started and turned around, Saylars had reloaded and resumed shooting at them. From a distance of about one hundred yards, the lawman's bullets caught the horn button and clipped one of Jones's fingers as he struggled to get the automobile onto the highway. A few miles north of Alma, the patrol car blew out a tire. W. D. pulled the car to the side of the road while Buck jumped out and flagged a passing motorist. When the driver stopped the auto, Buck waved his gun in the man's face and ordered him out. The motorist quickly climbed out and stood on the highway while the outlaws escaped in his car. They turned left off the main road and went west into the mountainous area in the southern part of Washington County. When they reached the foothills, the stolen car stalled. Seeing Mrs. Frank Rogers picnicking by a grove of trees near the base of the Boston Mountains, they stole her car at gunpoint, then wrecked the auto when Jones struck a tree.[25]

In the meantime Saylars had alerted townspeople of the marshal's slaying and had formed a posse. Learning from the hijacked motorist that the gangsters had driven into the mountains, the search party was confident they had the outlaws in a trap. The road Buck and Jones had taken into the Boston Mountains was a dead-end lane. Throughout the night of 23 June 1933, heavily armed members of the posse, guided by torches, searched the area.[26]

Buck and W. D. realized they had made a mistake by going into the mountains. Once out of sight of Mrs. Rogers, they abandoned her wrecked car, walked back down the hill to the highway, and hitched a ride with a farmer carrying a truckload of vegetables to Fort Smith. The three men drove through excited groups of people gathered along the highway, but no one questioned the farmer and his passengers because the officers expected the killers to be flushed from the mountains or at least to be headed in the other direction.

The two murderers rode all the way to Fort Smith with the unsuspecting farmer. When they arrived back at the tourist court, Clyde knew that the group must move to a new hiding place. He was also worried about officers capturing Bonnie's sister, Billie, as part of the gang and charging her with all their crimes. Since the gang had only one car, a Ford coupe with very worn tires, Clyde considered the logistics and then began the move. He told Billie to get into the front seat and set Bonnie in her lap; he then put Blanche into the trunk with all the goods she could squeeze in with her. Clyde instructed Buck and W. D. to stay at the court and finish gathering up all their remaining possessions; he promised to come back for them as soon as he found a safe hiding place for the women. Driving the small car into the nearby hills, Clyde had to stop three times when tires blew out. Each time he pulled off the road, took out the jack, hand pump, and patching kit and repaired the tubes. The women were terrified, since each car that passed was a potential source of danger. Clyde remained calm and worked rapidly and deliberately. Finally locating a solitary spot, he left the women, and despite his fatigue, drove back to the tourist court, picked up Buck and W. D., and motored to the new hideout.

During the second trip to the new hiding place, Clyde decided that Billie must get away. There were too many in the group and too much danger of her being dragged into a fatal situation. As he climbed from the car, Clyde called out to Billie to get her things together and told her that as soon as he could steal another car he planned to take her back to Dallas. Billie protested that she could continue to help Bonnie, but Clyde was adamant. Without eating or resting, Clyde ordered Jones into the coupe, and they drove toward Enid, Oklahoma. They cruised through the city in the late evening of 24 June 1933 and soon spotted a dark sedan. After stealing the auto and leaving the coupe in its place, they found a physician's bag in the backseat and realized that the car had belonged to a doctor. Within the next three weeks the bag would prove to be extremely beneficial. Clyde and W. D. returned to the hideout and rested for several hours.

Late on Sunday night, 26 June 1933, Clyde changed the license plates on the physician's auto and ordered everybody to prepare to break camp and move. They drove south and passed near Oklahoma City. Throughout the night Clyde continued to drive and just before dawn on 27 June, the group arrived at the Sherman, Texas, railroad depot. Clyde gave Billie money for train fare and left her at the station. Watching the car's lights disappear into the darkness, Billie feared she would never see Bonnie alive again.[27]

8

From Weariness Some People Have Died

The gang headed north back into Oklahoma and drove for several hours. Occasionally, Clyde left the main roads and sped along country lanes. Since he had little ammunition, he robbed the Oklahoma National Guard armory at Enid and continued on. Toward evening they located a deserted spot in a wooded area and pulled in. Shortly after midnight Clyde awakened the others and prepared to move again. Once more the direction was north. Leaving Oklahoma, they entered Sumner County, Kansas, and Clyde turned northwest to avoid Wichita with its large number of police officers.

Before sunset on 29 June 1933, the gang arrived at Great Bend, Kansas. Clyde located a tourist court on the edge of town and rented two connecting rooms. The funds needed to pay for room, board, and Bonnie's medical care for several days were substantial, so Clyde called Buck and W. D. to a conference. He told them they were going to need money but that he could not leave Bonnie and was going to depend on them. Buck and W. D. again agreed to do the robbing. Clyde, feeling they would be safe in Great Bend for some time, advised them to rob firms in northeast Kansas and Nebraska and avoid the southeast part of the state that was near Joplin.

The outlaws continued to write messages to their families, and Buck dropped the letters into mailboxes all over the Midwest as he and W. D. ranged widely to locate businesses to rob. Bonnie's mother also received messages from Dallas authorities warning that someone would find Bonnie on a deserted road with a bullet through her head. They pointed out that a man as hard, cruel, and heartless as Clyde

Barrow would never put up with a wounded girl who was a dead giveaway and a burden to him.

Bonnie, however, continued to rally physically and within two weeks had improved to the point that she was able to travel. Clyde drove southwest on 17 July. They camped in a farmer's woods in Edwards County, where Clyde changed Bonnie's bandages and threw the old dressings on their campfire. The landowner found the partially burned bandages the next day and called authorities. The Kansas State Police warned all lawmen to be on the lookout, but Clyde continued to move toward the southwest. Early on the morning of Tuesday, 18 July 1933, he drove the dark Ford sedan up to three separate service stations in Fort Dodge, Kansas, and systematically held up one after another. Witnesses at each station recalled the three male robbers and the two women, one with large bandages, that waited in the car. Beyond question, the Barrows were the robbers.[1]

The gang raced out of town, eluded roadblocks, and drove north with Clyde again occasionally leaving the main roads to travel the rural back lanes. He gradually steered the car toward the northeast and crossed the Missouri border late that same evening.

Around 10:00 P.M. the gang arrived at the Red Crown Tourist Camp and Service Station a few miles outside of Platt City. Delbert Crabtree was on duty at the court desk when a pretty, trim redhead entered the office. She asked for two rooms, paid the rent for one night in coins, and left. Crabtree customarily looked over the rest of the party when the registering person returned to his or her car. This night he glanced out the window, saw the bandaged girl sitting in the car along with the three men, watched them pull into the shed between the cabins, and go inside. Within a short time, Blanche returned to the station and bought five sandwiches and five bottles of beer.[2]

On Wednesday morning the woman returned to the private office to pay for another night and once again paid with small change. The men had not appeared since arriving, their auto was hidden in the car shed, and the cabin curtains were tightly drawn. All the secrecy proved to be too mysterious for Crabtree; he wondered if the secretive guests were doing something questionable and decided to tell his employer, H. D. Hauser, who telephoned Captain William Baxter of the Missouri Highway Patrol.

Learning of the bandaged woman, the officer correctly guessed that the seclusive renters were the Barrows and warned Hauser to do nothing. Baxter drove from his office in Kansas City to Platt City and contacted his friend Holt Coffey, the sheriff of Platt County. They agreed to join forces to capture the fugitives and called on several other law enforcement officers to join the posse. The Platt City Police Department sent two officers, Sergeant Thomas Witherspoon and Officer L. A. Ellis. The sheriff called upon Deputies George Borden, George Highfill, and Lincoln Baker as well as Constables Byron Fisher and Thomas Hullet. Sheriff Coffey's son, Clarence, came along to watch. The posse, ominously numbering thirteen, gathered to plan the assault.[3]

Inside the cabins Bonnie's burns needed fresh dressings, but Clyde had no more salve. Since the group had only the physician's auto stolen in Enid, Oklahoma, he hesitated to drive into town. After a short discussion, he walked to the highway and hitchhiked the six miles into Platt City. Stopping at the first pharmacy, Clyde bought ointment, gauze, and adhesive tape, then hitchhiked back to the tourist court. It was just past 8:00 P.M. when he arrived back at the cabin. Blanche went to the station for the usual five dinners and drinks, while Clyde bandaged the dressings on Bonnie's burns, and the group went to bed.[4]

The authorities began to draw their cordon tightly around the tourist court shortly before 10:00 P.M. as an armored car coasted up to block the garage containing the outlaws' only automobile. Inside the cabins the lights had been out for over an hour; in the left room, Bonnie, feeling better after the new dressings had been applied, had been asleep for some time. Clyde, still fully dressed, had fallen into a light sleep. W. D. slumbered on a pallet on the floor. In the next cabin Buck snored softly as Blanche lay awake.[5]

At approximately 10:00 P.M. Sheriff Coffey stepped up to the entrance of the first cabin and banged loudly on the door. Deputy George Borden switched on the spotlight and aimed it at the cabin door. The sheriff knocked again and called out, "This is the police. Open up."[6]

Blanche jumped out of bed and began flinging her belongings into a bag as she shouted, "You'll have to wait until I get dressed."

Clyde was awakened by Blanche's shouting. He leaped up and gathered up the weapons. W. D. bolted up on his pallet, wide-eyed. Clyde clamped his hand over Jones's mouth and whispered, "I'll carry Bonnie. You get behind the steering wheel."

Coffey rapped on the door again and yelled, "I need to talk to your menfolks."

Blanche screamed, "They're sleeping in the other room." The last exchange awakened Buck, who jumped up. Blanche grabbed him and covered his mouth.

Exiting from the cabin by the side door that opened to the garage, Clyde loaded Bonnie into the backseat. W. D. looked out the front and turned to Clyde. "They've got us blocked in by a armored car."

Clyde snatched up the automatic rifle taken from the Enid armory, aimed the weapon at the armored car, and opened fire. The heavy caliber bullets ripped through the light metal, penetrated the car, and wounded Deputy Highfill in the knees.

In the other cabin, meantime, Buck fiercely attacked the lawmen who were exposed by the spotlight reflecting off the cabins. The officers returned the fire with machine guns, and one volley crashed through the window near Buck and struck him twice in the head. The lawmen were also having trouble, since Clyde and W. D. continued to blast a devastating field of fire with the Browning rifles. One of the shots ripped into Sheriff Coffey's neck and knocked him to the ground. His son, Clarence, ran to aid his father and caught another round in his arm.[7]

Inside the armored car, Highfill was in deep trouble; he suffered terrible pain in his wounded knees and bullets from the Brownings continued to penetrate the vehicle. The deputy decided to back up slightly to escape the intense fire coming from the cabins. As the car edged backward, a stray shot crashed into the horn and caused it to blare loudly. The other officers, thinking the horn was a signal of the Barrows' surrender, held their fire.[8]

Clyde used the delay to move behind the steering wheel; he ordered W. D. to stand on the running board with a Browning machine gun. Since Buck and Blanche had not left their room, he jumped out and ran around the car to the left cabin side door. He met Blanche coming out supporting a semiconscious Buck, whose blood was streaming from two wounds in his head. Before Clyde could help, the weight of Buck became too great and she collapsed in a flood of tears and wailed, "We can't go on. He's dying."

Ignoring her, Clyde picked up Buck and loaded him into the car. Blanche got in beside Buck and held him in her arms. Clyde dashed back around the car to the driver's seat, started the motor, and yelled for the others to hang on tightly. Pressing the accelerator all the way to the floorboard, he released the clutch pedal; the car volleyed out of the garage, taking the lawmen assembled around the armored car unprepared. The outlaws' car spun around with W. D. bombarding the officers with his Browning from the right running board. The lawmen held their ground and fired at the car as it flashed past them.

Bullets crashed through the careening car's windows, and shattered glass shards struck Blanche in the eyes. Blood gushed down her face as she screamed, "Oh, my God. They've blinded me."

Clyde dodged the patrol cars parked around the cabin, sped out of the court grounds onto the highway and raced toward Platt City at seventy miles per hour while the authorities ran to telephones and called ahead to set up a roadblock. Clyde found a deserted country lane; he turned off his lights and drove along the road until he found an open field. Spreading newspapers and using a flashlight, he helped Buck and Bonnie to lie down and tried to treat Buck's wounds. W. D. brought the physician's bag. Clyde searched through it for medication, found a bottle of hydrogen peroxide, and poured the solution into Buck's open head wounds. When Buck screamed out in agony, Clyde loaded the group back into the car and sped away. The other gang members were in painful but less serious condition. Blanche was experiencing a great amount of pain from slivers of glass in her eyes. (Despite surgeons' best efforts during four operations while she was in Missouri State Prison, she ultimately lost sight in her right eye.) W. D. was slightly wounded; Bonnie's leg was in great pain, but there was no relief for it. Clyde felt it was too dangerous to stop long enough to change her dressings.[9]

Back at the shooting site, lawmen carried their wounded to hospitals. Deputy George Highfill received medical help for his wounded knees at St. Joseph's Hospital in Kansas City, Missouri. Sheriff Coffey, who had a neck wound, and his son, Clarence, who had come to the fire fight as a spectator and received a severe arm wound, were treated at Bethany Hospital in the same city.[10]

Meanwhile, Clyde continued to race through the night without stopping for sleep or food. By morning, he had covered a great distance. His fatigue was exacerbated by the dreadful conditions inside the car. Buck was feverish and delirious, Blanche alternately cried about her eyes and about Buck, and Bonnie moaned with her untreated burns. Finally Clyde halted for a brief period beside a stream near Mount Ayr, Missouri. He changed Bonnie's dressings, washed out Blanche's eyes with fresh water, and bathed Buck's forehead with a cold compress. Starting to move again, he had no real destination. Blanche begged, "Clyde please stop at a hospital or at least at a doctor's office."

"No," he said. "We ain't stopping. Shut up about it." When Buck became rational, at infrequent intervals, he agreed with Clyde. They desperately searched for a hiding place to rest and get food and water. Hundreds of miles from Texas and family, Clyde viewed everyone they met as a potential enemy and possible executioner. By early evening of the second day following the Platt City gun battle, Clyde found a wooded spot between Dexter and Redfield, Iowa, called Dexfield Park. The area, about twenty-five miles west of Des Moines, ironically was located in Dallas County. The site encompassed approximately twenty acres and was exactly what Clyde needed. Thick woods and heavy underbrush furnished cover, and a branch of the Middle Raccoon River running through the park supplied fresh water for the gang while they recovered.[11]

Clyde drove into a small clearing, got out, and walked around. The battered members of his little band continued to moan in the car while he checked for other people. Returning to the car, Clyde called on W. D. to help him make beds for Bonnie and Buck out of old clothing and newspapers. They carried Buck to the improvised bunk while Blanche walked alongside holding her husband's hand. Bonnie was taken from the car and placed near Buck so Blanche could care for both. Clyde told them that he and W. D. were going into the nearest town to get food and to steal another car. They drove into Perry, a large town about eighteen miles northwest of the hideout. Clyde bought food, alcohol, medicine, stole a car belonging to Edward Stoner, and arrived back at the hiding place on Sunday morning. Loading Bonnie into Stoner's sedan, Clyde drove through the park and looked over the terrain for possible escape routes. A large paper bag of used bandages from both Bonnie's and Buck's wounds lay on the seat. At a secluded spot, Clyde stopped the car, placed the bag on the ground, and set fire to it. He watched the bag burn for a time, then climbed back into the sedan and drove away.[12]

A few hours later a local farmer, Homer Penn, happened onto the partially burned dressings. Recalling a radio news broadcast from Des Moines about wounded Texas outlaws who were suspected of being in the Dexfield area, Penn called Sheriff C. A. Knee in Adel, the county seat. The sheriff called in Special Deputy John Love of the Vigilantes of Dallas County and they began to plan a trap for the Texans. They immediately sent two deputies to Dexfield Park to watch the area around the original campsite. The officers quickly scouted the park and located the two cars and the wounded bandits. One officer kept watch while the other hurried to a nearby telephone to advise Sheriff Knee.[13]

Just before nightfall on Monday, 23 July 1933, Clyde gathered all the weapons, carefully cleaned them, and loaded all of them into the cars. He checked on Bonnie to make sure she was resting comfortably, then walked to his brother who lay on the makeshift bed. Clyde looked at Buck for several minutes. In the fading light, he saw that Buck's skin tone was gray and leathery, and he knew his brother was near death. Seated beside Buck, Blanche looked up at Clyde with her one good eye. He gave her a weak smile and hurried over to the cars to help W. D. check on the condition of the motors. Clyde had promised his mother several times that should he or Buck become mortally wounded, they would be brought home to die. Accordingly, he planned to lead the gang back to Dallas at sunrise.[14]

While Clyde made preparations to move, Officers Knee and Love were working furiously to gather every available man. The evolving force included members of the Des Moines Police Department and the Iowa State Board of Investigation. After reviewing the gun battle that had occurred in Platt City, Knee contacted an aide of Governor Clyde P. Herring about calling out a unit of the Iowa National Guard. As Clyde and W. D. worked on the cars, the lawmen began taking up positions around the campsite. Shortly after midnight on 24 July, the two outlaws finished tuning up the cars and lay down for a brief sleep. The officers, the Guardsmen, and about one hundred local farmers armed with squirrel rifles also settled down for the night. Sheriff Knee held a conference with leaders of the various groups and decided to place about forty men around the park and the remainder on the several roads leading out of the area. The trap was set to spring at daylight when the posse would move on Knee's signal.[15]

The bandits awoke just before dawn. Blanche checked on Buck who, obviously in pain, still slept fitfully. W. D. started a small fire and roasted a few weiners. All eyes of the posse members were on Sheriff Knee, who gave the signal to move into position.[16]

Bonnie noticed the posse first and yelled, "Clyde, it's the law."

Clyde leaped for the car where the weapons were stored. He threw a Browning automatic rifle to W. D. and grabbed another for himself. Both men opened fire and scattered the posse members by spraying the surrounding woods. Unable to walk by herself since the accident at Wellington, Bonnie now ran to the car and jumped into the backseat. Blanche helped Buck to his feet and supported him as they painfully struggled to get across the few lethal yards to the auto. Bonnie held onto the strap inside the car and reached out to assist Buck. Clyde and W. D. continued to fire at the posse members while running toward the cars and climbing inside. Starting the car, Clyde quickly drove a few yards before a sharp-shooting vigilante smashed his left arm with a shotgun blast. Clyde lost control of the steering wheel and ran into a large tree stump. Jumping out of the stranded auto, Clyde and W. D. first tried to free the bumper. When Clyde realized the car would not budge, he ordered everybody into the Stoner car.[17]

With Bonnie and Blanche helping, Buck staggered toward the other car as Clyde and W. D. fired bursts from the Brownings to provide cover. Seeing the three wounded moving shakily toward the other auto, the posse concentrated their fire power against them. Several pieces of buckshot struck Bonnie, but she was unaware of the wounds until she noticed her dress covered with blood. Buck was twice knocked off his feet when struck by bullets. Both times a cursing Bonnie and a hysterically sobbing Blanche helped him.

As W. D. stepped from behind the impaled car, a bullet hit him in the chest, and several shotgun pellets struck him in the face. He recoiled and noticed that blood gushed from his head wounds. When Clyde and W. D. saw Buck, Bonnie, and Blanche had reached the new auto, they also ran to get in. The posse, relieved of the two machine guns' frightening fire, moved closer and concentrated their salvos on the Stoner car. Bullets from all sides shattered the windows, flattened the tires, and punctured the gas tank in several places.[18]

Clyde yelled for the gang to jump out and hide in the surrounding thickets. Buck was assisted out of the right rear door by Blanche, but several more bullets slammed into his chest and back and he collapsed a few yards from the car. Blanche screamed frantically, "Clyde, come help us," as she lay down beside Buck and tried to shield his body.

Clyde leaped from the car and ran to where Buck and Blanche

lay; he was thrown around as another bullet caught him in the leg. Gripping his wounded leg with the good arm, Clyde ordered the couple to sit tight; he promised to get another car and return. Buck tried to focus his eyes on Clyde, "Take Blanche with you. Don't leave her here."

Blanche screamed loudly, "No, Daddy. I'm not leaving you."

Clyde yelled to W. D., "Take care of Bonnie. I'll be back with another car," and hobbled toward the river. A bullet, its momentum nearly spent, ricocheted off a nearby tree, and hit him in the head; it failed to break the skin but momentarily dazed Clyde and he staggered about for a few seconds before continuing toward the river. Reaching the edge of the water, Clyde discovered that he carried a pistol containing only empty shells. Meanwhile, Blanche tried to hide herself and Buck behind a log; she pulled his bloody form, severely shattered by several bullets in the body, closer to her for protection. When the rain of bullets slacked, Blanche screamed, "Hold your fire. He's dying. You don't have to shoot anymore."[19]

W. D., blinded by blood from his head wound, continued to help Bonnie toward the river. They stopped briefly and heard the posse's guns firing rapidly. Bonnie, suspecting that Clyde had been killed, sobbed loudly and collapsed to the ground. W. D. lay down beside her and began to cry. After several minutes, they heard a noise in the shrubs and then a hiss. Bonnie raised up and saw Clyde crawling toward them. Helping Bonnie and W. D. to their feet, Clyde led them to the water. About halfway across the stream, the lawmen sighted them and opened fire. Bullets sang over their heads and splayed into the water nearby. When Bonnie passed out, Clyde carried her the remainder of the way. Leaving Bonnie and W. D. in a cornfield, Clyde ran toward a nearby house where three men—Valley Fellers; his son, Marvin; and Walter Spillars—stood on the front porch watching the gun battle.[20]

Clyde waved his empty pistol at the men and said, "I'm in a hurry. Give me your keys or I'll kill you." When Fellers quickly pulled a chain of keys from his pocket, Clyde whistled to Bonnie and W. D., who shakily emerged from the cornfield. Clyde placed Bonnie in the backseat, waved W. D. into the passenger seat, and rapidly drove away.[21]

Back at the battle zone, the posse cautiously approached Blanche and Buck. Blanche looked at the possemen with blood-filled eyes:

"Please get him a doctor. He's dying." She sobbed and watched as a physician, a member of the posse, warily checked Buck's wounds. As officers pulled Blanche away from Buck, she fought to stay nearby. Local newsmen snapped photos of her, dressed in the tan riding breeches, struggling to get free. The officers hurriedly drove Buck and Blanche to the King's Daughters Hospital in Perry, Iowa. The news of the wounding and capture of Buck and Blanche shattered their families. Emma Parker, her daughter Billie, Mrs. Barrow, and her son L. C. quickly prepared to drive to Perry.[22]

In the escaping stolen car, Bonnie felt her consciousness slipping away again and awoke after dark. Clyde, having washed W. D.'s eyes so that he could drive, also collapsed. Just after daybreak W. D. stopped at Polk City, Iowa, to steal a better car, and they continued to drive west toward Denver. The next day the gangsters neared Colorado City and stole a newspaper from a mailbox. An article said Bonnie was hidden in a Denver hospital with severe wounds.

Clyde shook his head. "So much for Denver. Turn south. Everybody will be looking for us in Denver." They found a wooded area off a rural lane and hid out for several days. With the passage of time, the wounds began to heal. When Clyde recovered enough to drive, W. D. ran away.[23]

Arriving in Perry, the relatives found the hospital like an armed camp. The hospital doors were barred, Buck's room was locked, and only hospital personnel were allowed inside. Several lawmen guarded the front and back doors and walked the halls. Mrs. Parker thought the officers attributed some supernatural powers to Bonnie and Clyde. The lawmen appeared to fear that Bonnie and Clyde would dash into town, snatch Buck from his death bed, and escape in a cloud of smoke. When she ridiculed the gaggle of lawmen, one officer said, "Mrs. Parker, we don't consider your children as supernatural; we see them as Texas rattlesnakes that slither into a striking position and leave death in their wake." Inside the hospital, Buck emerged from a coma at one point and answered officers' questions.[24]

A. M. Saylers, who had witnessed the slaying of Marshal Humphery, arrived from Alma, Arkansas; he sat beside the bed and asked, "Buck, do you recognize me?"

Buck struggled to focus his eyes. "Yeah, I know you. Me and W. D. shot at you over in Arkansas when you scooted for that barn."

The reserve officer stood up and walked into the hall where Sheriff Knee stood talking to member of the Iowa National Guard. "I'm satisfied he was the one that shot Marshal Humphery in the gunfight. In my opinion, Clyde wasn't in on the killing."[25]

The lawmen and reporters, mindful that Buck's life was slipping away, remained close to the hospital. When Buck died on 29 July, relatives made arrangements for the body to be moved to Dallas. Lawmen and newspapermen prepared for the funeral. [26]

The Sparkman-Holtz-Brand Funeral Home conducted the services for approximately fifty persons. Officers and the public watched the crowd of mourners carefully because of a rumored appearance by Bonnie and Clyde. Later, people who were present at the graveside swore that they recognized Clyde dressed in a long cotton dress and bonnet. The Reverend Frank P. Dailey of the Cedar Valley Baptist Church offered prayers to the gathered mourners, which included Buck's ex-wife, Elizabeth Quick, and her son, Marvin Ivan Barrow, Jr. When the funeral directors closed the casket for the final time, Quick fainted and was caught by Buck's brother L. C. [27]

Frequently Bonnie and Clyde were credited with committing crimes when they were in another part of the state. One such offense occurred in the oil fields of east Texas. On the morning of Wednesday, 8 November 1933, F. E. Jarrett and Rufus Brene, truck drivers from Palestine, were working on the loading rack of the McMurray Refinery near Arp, Texas. The men failed to notice an approaching dark 1933 Ford sedan, which held a man and woman in the front and another man in the back. The two men got out of the car and walked to the loading dock; they pulled guns from their pockets and said, "This is a stick-up, boys. Get into the office."[28]

Two other workers, J. N. Maynor and Hebert Owens, were in the office working on company records when the intruders marched Jarrett and Brene inside. Studying the gangsters carefully, Maynor noticed that they were between the ages of twenty and twenty-five, tall, and very well-dressed.

The robbers said, "This is a hold-up. Where's the money?"

Maynor indicated a twelve-inch well casing embedded in the concrete floor that served as a safe. "All the money is in there, and nobody but Mr. McMurray has the key."

One of the outlaws waved his gun at the employees. "Well, you better find a crow bar damn quick and pry that thing up." When the safe broke free from the floor, he nodded to the truckers. "That's better. Now take it out to our car." The other outlaw kept his pistol trained on the two office workers.

While loading the safe into the robbers' car, one of the dock workers noticed the Oklahoma license plate and that the number was either A95-475 or A96-475. When the safe was loaded, the outlaw leader pointed the gun at the office. "Now you boys go back in the shack until we're completely gone. That way nobody will get hurt." The thieves quickly drove away.

After waiting until the robbers were out of sight, the two dock workers ran to their own car and hurried to Tyler, the county seat of Smith County, where they reported the robbery.[29]

Sheriff Earl Price immediately called his deputies together and ordered them to various sections of the county to establish roadblocks and halt all dark, four-door 1933 Ford sedans; he passed on the suspected license number and ordered the men to be on the lookout for the safe inside the car. None of the roadblocks proved successful and Price expanded the alert to authorities as far away as Dallas.[30]

When officers in Sheriff Schmid's office learned of the Arp robbery, they immediately suspected Bonnie and Clyde. Since authorities were unaware of W. D. leaving the gang, they presumed he was the second man. Smith County officers identified the robbers as Mr. and Mrs. W. J. "Whitey" Walker and Irwin "Blackie" Thompson. Nevertheless, Dallas officers continued to blame Bonnie and Clyde. Deputy Ted Hinton accused Bonnie and Clyde of the crime despite subsequent identification of other crime victims by Walker and Thompson in east Texas. The Walkers and Thompson robbed the Robinson State Bank in Palestine, Texas, of $4,300 on 26 October and were identified by the bank staff. After the Arp robbery, Palestine authorities sent the photographs on to Smith County Sheriff Price, who showed them to the refinery workers. The four McMurray employees identified the suspects as the robbers. Hinton later claimed to have visited refinery owner, James McMurray, who identified pictures of the robbers but refused to file charges when Hinton told him they were Bonnie and Clyde. Hinton ignores the fact that McMurray was not present.[31]

9

The Road Gets Dimmer and Dimmer

When Bonnie and Clyde arrived in the Dallas area in late November 1933 to visit their families, local officers had another opportunity to catch or kill them in an ambush. Clyde wanted to visit his mother on her birthday, 21 November. The Barrow and Parker families carried food and a cake to a rural location in west Dallas County. The family groups seldom met in the same location for two days in a row, but for the sake of convenience they agreed to meet at the same place again the next night.

A farmer who lived in the area became suspicious and notified authorities; he pointed out the meeting site to officers and swore he had been close enough to recognize Bonnie and Clyde. Hoping the gangsters would change their pattern and meet there again, the lawmen set up an ambush.[1]

Arriving at the meeting place just before nightfall, the relatives could see a great distance but could not detect lawmen nestled in ditches; they parked about twenty-five yards from Highway 15 on the right shoulder of the lane facing away from the main highway. There was still enough light available that Mrs. Parker recognized the fugitives as they drove slowly along Highway 15. Clyde appeared reluctant to go down the unpaved lane and drove a short distance down the main road. When the families did not follow him, Clyde turned around, returned to the lane entrance, hesitated, drove down the dirt road, and passed the parked cars. Thinking Clyde wanted them to follow along, the relatives started their cars and turned on their headlights. The light beams made Clyde's car a clear target for the hidden officers, and they opened fire. Mrs. Parker saw Clyde speed up and Bonnie break out the rear window with her pistol. The authorities' opening volley had blown out the left front tire, wounded both Bonnie and Clyde in the knees, and flattened the spare tire. The bandits' car bumped down the dirt road, with both Bonnie and Clyde firing as they could.[2]

The damaged car continued south and soon turned onto the Fort Worth Pike, or West Jefferson Avenue, near the present entrance to Hensley Air Force Base. Clyde used their car to block the path of a Model B Ford sedan occupied by Thomas R. James and Paul Reich from Fort Worth. The men were enroute home from a Scottish Rite function in Dallas. When they objected to giving up their car, Clyde fired a shotgun blast into the driver's window, which showered both men with flying shards of shattered glass. Bonnie and Clyde quickly transferred their spare weapons into the James auto and abandoned their own bullet-pocked Ford. As they drove away into the night, another Scottish Rite member, Wade Collier, passed and rushed the two victims to a doctor's office in Grand Prairie. When officers towed the outlaws' car into the pound, they found splashes of blood on the front seat and floor, quilts, medicine, cosmetics, shaving equipment, flatware, canned food, a sack of pennies, eleven different license plates of various states, and the latest detective magazines containing stories about the two fugitives. Dallas deputies found shell casings from two different .45 caliber pistols. A closer examination the next morning indicated that the steel body of the Ford had turned several of the officers' bullets away. It was clear that only a high- powered weapon like the Browning automatic rifle would penetrate the tough shell of the auto.[3] This was one reason Clyde preferred Ford automobiles. He always stole Fords, especially the new styles with the eight cylinder engines in a *V*. Six weeks before his death, he wrote Henry Ford a letter praising the V-8 for its speed and low maintenance needs.[4] Sheriff Schmid and Deputy Ed Caster studied the riddled Ford for some time and arranged to borrow the required weapons from the Texas National Guard.[5]

Bonnie and Clyde now began to plan a prison break. Lee Simmons, director of Texas prisons, later investigated the breakout and told newsmen that just after the first of the year, Bonnie and Clyde received a message that their former gang member, Raymond Hamilton, who was serving a sentence of two hundred and sixty-three years for the murder and armed robbery of John Bucher, wanted their help to escape from the Texas prison farm at Eastham. Simmons found that several other Texas criminals were already involved in the scheme. Fred Yost, a farm trusty, agreed to serve as the contact inside the prison. A tall, thin man with a receding chin and calm demeanor, Yost grew up in west Dallas near Clyde's home. Another involved inmate, James Mullin, also known as Jimmie Lamont, who was a small sharp-faced man with nervous gestures; like the Barrows and Hamiltons, his family had migrated to Dallas in the mid-1920s. He was scheduled for a parole from the Eastham prison farm shortly before the end of 1933.

A few weeks before Mullin's release, Hamilton sat down beside him in the mess hall. "I want to make you a deal, Mullin. I'll pay you a thousand if you'll set up a meeting with Bonnie and Clyde and help them break me out of here."

Mullin nervously looked at Hamilton. "Whadda I have to do?"

"First, get in touch with my brother Floyd. Tell him you want to meet with Clyde. When you do, tell Clyde you're to help him spring me. He'll take care of the rest."[6]

Mullin agreed to do it for $1,000. When released, he hurried to Dallas to contact Clyde through Floyd Hamilton. On Sunday, 14 January 1934, Floyd Hamilton arrived at the prison farm to see his brother and complete the final details. Around 2:00 A.M. the following morning, James Mullin and Floyd Hamilton hid two automatic pistols near a woodcutting area. Later that day, Yost, using his cover as trusty, retrieved the weapons and smuggled them into the barracks; he passed the guns to Raymond and Joe Palmer, another friend of Raymond who was serving a twenty-five year sentence for kidnapping a child. Palmer was a tall, slim, cold-blooded criminal with thinning blond hair and a prominent Adam's apple. Both Raymond and Palmer felt confident the weapons hidden in their clothing would not be discovered the next morning, since guards seldom searched prisoners as they left the sleeping areas.[7]

The day of the prison break dawned cold and foggy. Inside the corrugated metal barracks, guards blew whistles and ordered the inmates out of their cots. Both Palmer and Hamilton looked about the huge room. The other prisoners were preparing for a work day. Satisfied no one was looking in their direction, the two inmates pulled pistols from under their mattresses and hid them under their heavy prison jackets. The two men followed the others out of the building and lined up together. After breakfast Raymond reported to Palmer's woodcutting work squad instead of his own and marched away with the group into the dense woods.[8]

Meanwhile, Bonnie and Clyde arrived in the area and picked up Mullin, who directed them into the same woods. As Clyde drove the coupe in a grove of trees, the thinning fog parted briefly then closed again. Clyde and Mullin got out and looked around the area. Mullin closed the right door quietly and waited anxiously beside the car. Clyde calmly pulled a Browning automatic rifle and a .45 caliber automatic pistol from behind the seat; he pitched the hand gun to Mullin and looked into the car.

"Keep the doors locked, Sugar. There's no telling who's in these woods on a day like this."

Bonnie leaned across the seat and pulled the door closed; she lowered the window. "Don't worry about me, Silly. I'll be fine. You be careful."

Clyde looked around again. "When you hear the caps popping, start honking the horn for Raymond to run toward. Don't stop 'til you see us coming."

Bonnie nodded and raised the window. From the seat, she took a Big Chief notebook and started composing a poem. The fog began to clear as the two men walked through the trees. They reached a shrub-covered area twenty yards from the clearing. Mullin looked at Clyde and said quietly, "This's where the detail has been cutting."

Clyde nodded and squatted behind a large bush with the machine gun cradled in his arms. "Just keep your mouth shut and don't shoot until I start."[9]

Palmer and Hamilton walked side by side in the ranks. As they approached the cutting site, Palmer leaned toward Hamilton and whispered, "Now listen, they may spot you when Dog Sergeant Bozeman assigns the work details. If they do, just follow my lead. Henry Methvin's gonna take all the guards' guns when we get the drop on them. What we got to worry about now is the mounted guard with that Winchester. They pick them guys for their marksmanship. We can handle Bozeman and the other walking guards. But them riders are different. You never know where they are." Hamilton nodded.[10]

Joseph Crowson, a veteran prison system guard, always rode his horse with the butt of his .30-.30 Winchester rifle sitting on his right leg; his finger rested lightly in the trigger. That morning, he watched the various squads move from the barracks complex through the dissolving fog toward their assigned work areas.

Alan Bozeman ordered the prisoners to halt when they reached the clearing. He had served as a guard at Eastham for several years. A kindly man who treated the inmates humanely, Bozeman allowed none of his prisoners to shirk their duties or slip off to easier jobs. As Dog Sergeant, he assigned several men to get axes and begin cutting wood; he told others to clear away undergrowth. Bozeman looked carefully at each man's face as they passed by another guard to receive their tools. When he noticed Raymond, the guard stopped.

"What are you doing in this section, Hamilton?"

Raymond looked blank. "Why, Sergeant, this is where I'm supposed to be ain't it?"

Bozeman looked disgustedly at the prisoner. "You know damn well it ain't." He looked about and signaled to Crowson, who sat on his horse about seventy yards away. Crowson galloped to the group and reined in a few yards from the cluster of inmates. Bozeman and the other guards walked toward the horseman. The horse guardsmen were selected for their courage and marksmanship; their purpose was to ride the perimeters of the work areas, particularly when the squads were in dense woods.

In his book, *Assignment: Huntsville,* Lee Simmons outlined the primary task of the mounted force. It was to remain apart from the prisoner groups and be prepared to shoot any inmate who tried to escape. The mounted riflemen also served a psychological factor. The convicts were intimidated because they never knew precisely where the riders were located. The squad guard and the rider both violated the prison directors' expressed orders when the horseman rode over to the woodcutting area.

Crowson frowned. "What do you want? You know Simmons said we're not to come too near a work detail."

"Yeah, but a man jumped his squad and came out with us."

"Alright," said Crowson, "I'll run him back to the barracks. Who is he?"

"Raymond Hamilton," said Bozeman.

Crowson called out, "Hamilton, you know better than this. Come out here and get in front of the horse. You're going to run all the way back to the barracks."[11]

Clyde raised up from behind the shrubs. "Get ready, Mullin," he said. "Here's where the boys will make their play."[12]

Both Hamilton and Palmer walked toward the guards; as they drew near, they jerked out their automatic pistols. Hamilton pointed his weapon at the walking guards; Palmer aimed his at Crowson. In a steady voice, Palmer said, "Okay, boys, don't move and there won't be any shooting." He signaled Henry Methvin to move in.

Crowson whirled in the saddle to fire at Palmer, but his horse reared in fright and knocked his Winchester from his hands. The scene exploded in a mass of confusion. Palmer opened fire at Crowson, Raymond fired at the other guards, and Clyde fired his Browning automatic rifle over the heads of the entire group, terrifying both prisoners and guards alike. One bullet struck Crowson in the abdomen and another in the head. Bozeman swung his shotgun around and fired twice; his shots missed the gunmen. Both Palmer and Raymond now turned on the Dog Sergeant. One bullet hit the guard in the hip and knocked him off his feet.[13]

Clyde yelled, "Fire cover over their heads," and both gangsters fired their weapons above the group in the clearing. With Clyde's bullets barking over everyone's heads, two work groups, including their guards, fled from the area.

Back in the car, Bonnie heard the shots echoing through the woods. Within seconds she recognized the clatter of Clyde's automatic rifle. Slipping behind the wheel, she mashed the horn button. The blaring sound echoed loudly through the trees and floated over the landscape.[14]

Palmer waved his pistol toward the blare of the automobile horn. "Head for that noise," he said and began running. Raymond and Methvin followed quickly. W. H. Bybee, who was serving a life sentence, and J. B. French, who had been sentenced for twelve years, ran after the three escaping men.[15]

One officer, C. W. Bullard, pointed his shotgun at the prisoners in his area, ordered them to lie down, and vowed to shoot the first one who raised his head. Facing another Long Arm guard who galloped toward him, Bullard yelled, "Ride to the office quick and tell Captain Monzingo that we've got guards shot and prisoners escaping." The rider raced off toward the prison office.[16]

Clyde and Mullin hurried back to the car and arrived just ahead of the five prisoners. Mullin shook visibly and screamed, "Nobody but Raymond and Palmer are going."

Clyde whirled on the man and shouted, "Shut your damn mouth, Mullin. This is my car and I'm handling this. He pointed to the trunk. "Four of you can ride back there. I guess four of us can make it up here." He raised the trunk lid, waved Palmer, Methvin, French, and Bybee into the space, and lowered the door until it rested on the lock. Mullin moved into the right seat beside Bonnie; Clyde drove; Raymond sat on Mullin's lap.[17]

The farm manager B. B. Monzingo and his assistant, Tom Small, stood in the prison office discussing the proposed planting schedule. Hearing the noise of a racing horse's hooves outside, they stopped talking. Within seconds, the Long Arm Guard burst through the door and cried, "It's a break, Mr. Monzingo. Some guards are shot in the woodlot, and a bunch of prisoners got loose."

Monzingo waved Small toward the door. "See to that," he said, and picked up the telephone. "I'll call an ambulance from Crockette and let Huntsville know about the breakout." Small ran out to his pickup and raced toward the woodlot.

Director Lee Simmons sat at his desk in the headquarters building of the Texas prison system in Huntsville. When the telephone bell rang, he picked up the receiver.

"Mr. Simmons, this is Monzingo at Eastham. We've had some trouble. Some of my guards have been wounded, but I don't know how bad yet. An ambulance is on the way. Some prisoners may have gotten loose."

Simmons leaned forward in his chair. "Transfer those wounded officers to the main hospital here as soon as they can be moved. I'll alert the doctors to be ready to receive them." When Monzingo hung up, Simmons dialed his secretary: "Call the Highway Department in Austin; request them to send out an all-points bulletin on outlaws involved in a jail break at Eastham. Ask them to also relay the information to the radio and newspapers. Then tell Warden Waid I'm coming by to pick him up to go with me to Eastham."[18]

When Small arrived at the shooting site, he found Bullard guarding the remaining prisoners and trying to aid Bozeman and Crowson. The inmates that had run into the woods began returning. Small looked around. "Where are the other guards, Bullard?"

"I don't know, Mr. Small. They took off when the shooting started." Small jumped on Crowson's horse and searched the nearby woods; he flushed a few prisoners from their hiding places and found three guards standing together in a patch of trees about one-quarter mile from the woodlot.[19]

The outlaws sped northwest over back roads toward Dallas. After several miles Clyde stopped the car, opened the trunk lid and pointed to Bybee and French. "Boys, we're going to have to cut you loose. If we split up there's less chance of getting caught." Clyde watched Bybee and French climb out of the trunk and stand on the side of the dirt road; he pulled a pistol from his pocket and handed it over to French. "This is the best we can do for you."

French took the gun and pocketed it. Bybee grinned: "That's alright, Clyde. I get you. It's the panhandle for me. Everybody watch yourselves."

Clyde nodded, jumped back into the car, and drove away. In the rearview mirror he saw French and Bybee stick out their thumbs at an approaching car.[20]

Back at the prison, several guards loaded Crowson and Bozeman into the back of Small's pickup truck. Small called one of the Long Arm men over. "If I go too fast, it'll do more harm than good. You hustle up to the dispensary and tell them we're coming. Ask Captain Monzingo to send the ambulance there." The rider pulled his hat tighter on his head and raced off.

Simmons and Waid arrived at the Eastham Farm and watched the two guards being transferred from the pickup bed to the ambulance. After interviewing Bullard and some of the prisoners, the officials estimated the number of inmates at five and soon identified them. Warden Waid said, "You can bet that the operator of the machine gun was Clyde Barrow, especially since Hamilton bragged that Barrow would break him out."

Simmons nodded. "And Barrow is known to favor the Browning." Convinced that Monzingo and Small had taken steps to prevent further problems, Simmons and Waid returned to Huntsville.[21]

Meanwhile, Bybee stole a car and drove to the Texas panhandle; later he was captured when a female hitchhiker recognized his description and notified authorities. J. B. French broke into a cabin and was captured by its owner, Gabe Wright; he was returned to Huntsville the next day.[22]

By 9:00 A.M., the gangsters, using back roads, neared Hillsboro. "Look for a station with nobody around," said Clyde. "The tank's about dry." They continued on for a short distance and spotted a

Sinclair station. As the car pulled into the driveway, an attendant came out to greet them. Clyde leaned his head out the window and said, "Fill it up."

The man nodded and began filling the tank. He looked at the passengers. "I'll get your windshield in a minute."

Clyde got out of the car and reached for his wallet. "That's okay. It don't need cleaning."

The attendant continued to pump gasoline. "Man alive. Did you hear about the prison break down near Crockette? Somebody broke Raymond Hamilton out. They think it was Bonnie and Clyde. About twenty other convicts got loose, too. They say people were dropping like flies. That's all you can hear on the radio. The cops must have every road between here and Dallas blocked."

Clyde took the money from his wallet. "Yeah," he said. "We heard all about it."

"Don't you think it was Bonnie and Clyde that done it?"

Clyde thrust the money at the man. "Look here, I don't give a damn about all that. Are you going to take this money or not?" As he drove out of the station, Hamilton asked, "Why didn't you just draw down on him and not pay for the gas?"

Clyde snorted. "Cause every law in this part of Texas would be here within an hour." After continuing north for several minutes, Clyde pulled over to the side of the road. "Now that I think about it, that big mouth may be right. Every law in the state is trying to get between here and Dallas. Let's go to Houston." He turned the car around and headed south.[23]

Simmons and Waid waited outside the operating room where surgeons worked to remove the bullets from Crowson and Bozeman. Waid sat staring at the swinging doors, but Simmons paced.

"I'll tell you one thing, Waid, we're going to get the ones responsible for this. We can't have our guards shot down like dogs. When a prisoner kills one of our officers, the juries just add another life sentence. Well, it's not going to work like that this time." Forty-five minutes later, Simmons was still pacing when Dr. William Veazey, chief prison physician, came out of surgery. Simmons hurried up to him. "How are my men doing, Doctor?"

Veazey removed his surgical cap and ran his hand through his hair. "Bozeman will be all right. No problems there. But Crowson is different. We've done everything we can. But despite all our best efforts, I only give him a slight chance for recovery."

"When can I see him?" asked Simmons.

The physician looked at his watch. "He'll be under the influence of the ether for some time. I seriously doubt if he will know you before this evening. Perhaps after 6:00 or 7:00." When Simmons turned to leave, Veazy called out, "That is, if he wakes up at all. His situation is critical at best."

Simmons returned at 7:00 and talked briefly with Bozeman and Crowson. Later that night he was unable to sleep. Staring at the ceiling, he mulled over a plan to get the people responsible for the prison break. The next morning, officers returned J. B. French to Eastham, and Simmons went to interview him. "Who was involved, French?" they questioned.

The manacled prisoner sullenly answered. "I don't know anything. I just took off after Hamilton and Palmer lit out. I was in the trunk of the car with Palmer and Bybee and Methvin the whole time."

Waid said, "Don't lie to me. Who gave you the gun the officers found on you?"

"Okay. Clyde gave it to me when they put me out. I didn't know anybody else. I'll tell you one thing, though. You ain't ever going to get Clyde Barrow alive."[24]

Forty-eight hours later, the fugitives returned from Houston. Since Raymond had promised Mullin $1,000 Clyde planned to rob a bank in Lancaster, Texas, a small town just south of Dallas near the Ellis County line. Three days after the bust-out, Bonnie, Clyde, Mullin, Raymond, Joe Palmer, and Henry Methvin drove to a rendezvous with Floyd Hamilton and L. C. Barrow; they met northwest of Fort Worth near the small town of Rhome. Raymond, Palmer, and Methvin still wore their prison clothing and desperately needed to change. Clyde gave Mullin money to buy clothing for the convicts and sent him back to Dallas with Floyd Hamilton and L. C. Barrow. The entire group planned to meet again at Vernon, Texas, within a few days.[25]

Crowson died two days after the prison break. Simmons stood beside his grave and swore he would not rest until the killers were caught and punished. His first step was to learn as much as possible about everyone connected with the break. Checking prison records,

Simmons and Waid discovered that James Mullin was a close friend of Raymond Hamilton; they immediately suspected that he was involved in the breakout and ordered him arrested. The director slammed Mullin's file down on his desk. "I'm convinced that Mullin is our man, especially since he was released just before the break."

Waid nodded. "Sure. He would know where Hamilton was working and what to bring along."

Simmons narrowed his eyes. "You know he would. Besides that, Hamilton bragged at his trial that Bonnie and Clyde would bust him loose. I'd wager my teeth they're the ones in the woods with the horn and machine gun." Simmons's continuing research revealed that Mullin had an extensive criminal record and had served sentences in eight different penitentiaries. Within weeks, when the Dallas Police Department caught Mullin, Simmons hurried north to interview him. Confronting the man in an interrogation room, Simmons outlined Mullin's options. "Jimmy, you know the U.S. Government wants you for stealing weapons from a National Guard armory. Now, if you come clean with us about the break I might make you a deal."

Mullin nervously looked at Simmons. "What kind of deal?"

"The State of Texas will surrender you to the United States Justice Department. If you're convicted, it will mean a term in a nice, clean, safe, federal Pen."

Mullin looked perplexed. What sort of deal is that?"

Simmons raised his eyebrows. "Well, the alternative is that you go back to Eastham where you can serve out your time under Bozeman and the other guards who were close friends of Crowson. In fact, I can guarantee that you will be assigned to them."

Mullins paled. "Mr. Simmons, I can't go back there. They'll kill me for sure."

Simmons bristled. "Are you accusing my guards of being killers?"

Mullin shivered. "What do you want to know?"

"I want the names of everybody involved in the breakout. And I mean everybody. If you hold out on me, the deal is off."

"I'll tell you everything I know," said Mullin.

Simmons slept little until he put his plan into operation. First, he requested and received from the Prison Control Board and the Comptroller of Public Accounts permission to create an entirely new position, special investigator for the Texas prison system. Two lawmen were finalists in Simmons's selection process; both were former Texas Ranger captains and were chosen because of their fearlessness. He needed the approval of Governor Miriam Ferguson, but hesitated because he knew one of his choices, Frank Hamer, was her unrelenting political enemy. After interviewing various witnesses, Simmons knew that Clyde had sworn he would never be taken prisoner and that Bonnie had vowed that she would go down with him. So the new investigator would place his life on the line when he confronted the outlaws.

After considering all factors, Simmons chose Frank Hamer. He had been an acquaintance of Hamer for more than thirty years, but he knew the former Ranger openly disagreed and disapproved of the governor. Simmons decided on Hamer on 1 February 1934 and drove up to the executive mansion in Austin to talk with the governor. When he was shown into Governor Ferguson's office, Simmons opened quickly with, "Ma'am, I want to take Bonnie and Clyde off the road."

"Mr. Simmons, as you may know, we've assigned Texas Rangers to pursue Bonnie and Clyde as well as offering a $1,000 reward for them, dead or alive."

"Yes, Ma'am, I know. But I want to assign a special agent or two to chase them until they run them to ground."

"Who do you have in mind?"

"I was thinking about Captain Frank Hamer. As you know, he used to be in the Texas Rangers. I realize you and Mr. Ferguson have had differences with Captain Hamer in the past, but I believe he is the only man for the job. I think he can put Bonnie and Clyde out of business."

Governor Ferguson smiled. "We don't hold a grudge against Frank Hamer and we'll approve him."

"Well, I've got another request, Governor. I may need you to offer amnesty or a pardon in exchange for help in trapping Bonnie and Clyde."

Governor Ferguson nodded slowly. "Whatever it takes to get these killers off the streets."

Simmons drove from the governor's mansion near the capitol to Hamer's home in another part of Austin. Hamer greeted him at the door. After they were seated, Simmons came right to the point. "I want you to come back to work for the state of Texas as a special agent for the prison system. Your main job will be to get Bonnie and Clyde."

Hamer looked thoughtful. "Lee, I work for an oil company as a security consultant. They pay me $500 a month."

"I can't match that. I can only offer one hundred and eighty. But I know money doesn't mean a damn to you. What matters to you is law and order."

Hamer smiled. "I'll own up to that. But what about the Fergusons? They never will approve of me."

Simmons grunted. "They already have." He leaned forward in his chair. "I promise you that you will be completely in charge and backed to the limit."

Hamer exhaled a puff of smoke. "How long do you think this job could take?"

Simmons hesitated; he knew that other agencies, such as the Dallas Sheriff's Department, had pursued the outlaws for over two years without success, but he had confidence in Hamer's ability to track and corner bandits. "It might take six months or even longer, but regardless of how long it takes, you will be supported. These people have a hell of a record. They'd as soon drill you as to look at you. I think the thing for you to do is just put them on the spot, know you are right, and then shoot everybody in sight."

Hamer sat staring into space for several seconds while continuing to puff on his Bull Durham cigarette. Looking back at Simmons, he said, "Okay, Lee. I'll take the job."

Simmons kept the assignment secret; he knew Bonnie and Clyde closely monitored radio news broadcasts and might flee the state if they knew an experienced tracker was on their trail. When Hamer and Simmons communicated, they conferred in a hotel room in Austin or Dallas. They never met in Huntsville.[26]

Meanwhile, the gangsters who were hiding just south of Wichita Falls, Texas, had other concerns. Raymond contacted Mary O'Dare, wife of Gene O'Dare, who had been arrested with him in Michigan in December 1932. Mrs. O'Dare was living with a man named Pitts while her husband served his prison term. However, when Raymond knocked on her door and invited her to join him as his mistress, she agreed.

Around 19 February 1934 the Barrow and Parker families traveled from Dallas to Greenville to meet the gangsters. When the reunion broke up, the relatives came back home, and the crooks drove to Ranger, Texas, to burglarize a National Guard armory for new weapons. Late the following day, Floyd Hamilton met the fugitives at a prearranged spot between Dallas and Lancaster; he took the weapons to hide until the next planned bank robbery and agreed to meet the gangsters again one week later near Cedar Hill and pull a daring bank robbery at Lancaster, Texas.[27]

10

Sometimes You Can Hardly See

The Lancaster bank robbery encompassed two phases. The first maneuver included stealing fresh automobiles. The group drove from Dallas to Wichita Falls on Sunday, 25 February 1934. That evening as they drove along the city's streets, Clyde selected a car belonging to C. J. Waggoner; it was parked in front of his home at 1600 Buchanan. Raymond jumped out, cross-wired the car, and drove it away. Outside of town, the gang divided into two parties with three to four members in each car. During the night they traveled south to Temple, Texas, arriving early Monday morning, 26 February. They abandoned their original car, gathered in the Waggoner car, and drove through Temple seeking another fresh vehicle. They took the second escape auto from the front of Earl Johnson Motor Company in downtown Temple. Raymond, the expert automobile thief, again stole the car and the gang once more divided while enroute to Dallas. The six outlaws met the Barrow and Parker families during the evening of 26 February, then spent the night at the familiar abandoned farmhouse near Grand Prairie. Clyde and Raymond had used this hideout just after the Neuhoff robbery in August 1932.[1]

The following morning, Tuesday, 27 February, the gangsters began the second phase of their crime; they drove both cars to Wilmer Road near the small community of Kleberg. Clyde, Raymond, and Henry Methvin loaded their weapons into the Waggoner car and continued southwest to Lancaster. Clyde parked the car beside the R. P. Henry and Sons Bank. Leaving Methvin as lookout, Clyde and Raymond walked along the side of the bank to the main entrance while carrying their weapons under heavy top coats. They entered the front door, threw back their coats, and whipped their guns into view.

L. L. Henry, one of the bank's owners, stood behind a teller's window serving a customer, Olin Worley. Clyde pointed his sawed-off shotgun at Henry and said, "You, open the safe. Don't try any fast stuff, and you'll live through this." Raymond shoved his pistol against Worley's back and ordered, "Mister, you need to sit down right here on the floor." As Worley slid to the floor, Hamilton noticed that he had three one-dollar bills in his hand and snatched them away.

When Henry opened the safe and stepped back, Clyde pointed the barrel of his shotgun toward where Worley sat and told Henry to sit down. Keeping Henry and Worley covered with the shotgun, Clyde watched the front as Raymond ran behind the counter and hurriedly began gathering up all the money in view. From his seated position, Henry watched Clyde's eyes and marveled at his extremely calm manner. He was intrigued by the steady, unwavering barrel of the shotgun. When Raymond finished removing all of the money from the safe and tellers' drawers, he came back around the counter and headed for the rear of the bank. Clyde pointed his weapon toward the back and ordered the seated men to open the side exit near the rear of the building. Both Clyde and Raymond kept Henry and Worley in view as long as possible to prevent them from raising an alarm.

Waiting at the door for Clyde, Raymond reached into a bag, pulled out three one-dollar bills and threw them to Worley. Clyde looked at the two men for a long moment with an icy expression that startled Henry; he then calmly followed Raymond through the door. Hearing the car doors slam and the motor roar as the car raced away, Henry ran to the telephone and called the sheriff's office. Within minutes, Deputy Sheriff John Ciesa arrived and asked the banker to disturb nothing in the safe so as to preserve evidence, but if possible, to determine the loss. When Henry and Worley described the bandits, Ciesa told them the robbers were probably Clyde Barrow and Raymond Hamilton. Reporters arrived shortly and asked Henry to describe Clyde's actions. He thought for a moment and said, "You could tell by looking at him that he would shoot in an instant if he thought it necessary." Ciesa interviewed a witness who had passed the bank while the robbers were inside and learned that nothing appeared suspicious except the car parked beside the building with the motor running and a tall, dark-haired man seated behind the wheel. When Henry totaled the loss, it amounted to $4,138.50.[2]

A farmer near Kleberg spotted Bonnie, Mary O'Dare, and Joe

Palmer waiting in a car for over an hour near his property. After he saw Clyde, Raymond, and Henry Methvin drive up, park in front of the first car, and the two women and a man jump into the second car, he called the sheriff's office. Deputy Brian Peck raced to the scene and talked with the witness. Searching the abandoned auto, Peck soon decided it was the one stolen the previous week.[3]

As the gang drove north toward Oklahoma with Clyde, Bonnie, and Henry Methvin in the front and the others in the back, a problem developed. In the rearview mirror Clyde saw Raymond stealing some of the undivided money. As officers threw up roadblocks throughout north Texas, Clyde drove the group out of the state and headed for Indiana.

Joe Palmer, now regarding Raymond with tremendous contempt, called him a blabbermouth and a punk. Later, near Joplin, Missouri, while Palmer slept in the floorboard, Raymond pulled a gun and tried to shoot him. Clyde reached into the backseat, slapped and disarmed Raymond, lost control of the car, and went into a ditch. Since the left wheel was broken, Clyde had to steal another car. Additionally, conflict between the two women led to a severe split in the gang. Bonnie, Clyde, and Henry Methvin came back to Texas. Within a few days, a Dallas newspaper reported that police received a tip that Bonnie and Clyde would be spending the night in an abandoned farmhouse near Grapevine. The officers searched several deserted houses without locating the bandits.[4]

Raymond Hamilton and Mary O'Dare soon returned to Texas and competed with Bonnie and Clyde for authorities' attention. After robbing a Grand Prairie bank of more than $1,500, Hamilton wrote a disjointed letter to Assistant District Attorney Winter King in Dallas disavowing any connection with Clyde Barrow; his warm gratitude to Bonnie and Clyde for freeing him from prison had turned frosty because of the exchange between Bonnie and Mary O'Dare.[5] Authorities were naturally skeptical about the alleged split and treated it as a nonevent. On Saturday, 31 March 1934, the day before Easter, Raymond drove up to a bank in the small town of West, a Czechoslovakian American community in central Texas. Leaving Mary O'Dare in the car, he dashed inside and took more than $1,200. Just south of town Raymond lost control of the car on rain-soaked country roads and slid into a ditch. He jumped out, stopped a passing car that contained Mrs. Cameron Gunter and her small son, and forced her to drive him and Mary to Houston where he freed them.[6]

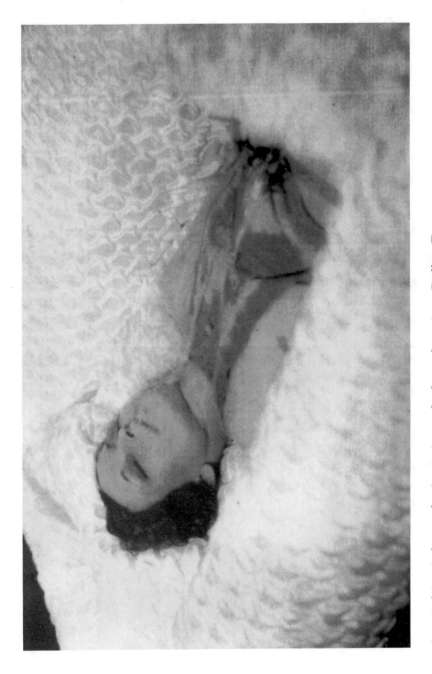

Bonnie lying in her casket just prior to the funeral services, Dallas, Texas. Courtesy of Dr. Allen B. Campbell, Jr.

Pallbearers removing Bonnie's remains from the McKamy-Campbell Funeral Home, Dallas, Texas. Courtesy of Dr. Allen B. Campbell, Jr.

(Top) *Bonnie's headstone, Dallas, Texas. Photograph by E. R. Milner.*

(Bottom) *Dual headstone of Clyde and his brother Buck, Dallas, Texas. Photograph by E. R. Milner.*

*The Dallas Theater promotes a newsreel on Bonnie and Clyde, aided
by the McKamy-Campbell hearse and its driver, Johnny Bullock.
Courtesy of Dr. Allen B. Campbell, Jr.*

"Some day they'll go down together." Marker at the ambush site. Photograph by E. R. Milner.

11

They Wouldn't Give Up 'Til They Died

Bonnie and Clyde continued their practice of always trying to get home on holidays. Since officers frequently watched their parents' homes, the gangsters devised methods to arrange meetings. Occasionally, they drove by one of the relatives' homes and threw out a soft drink bottle with a message inside that specified the location where they would be that night; other times, they sent one of the lesser recognizable gang members to the relatives' homes with the plan.

With the approach of Easter, Bonnie bought a white rabbit for the holiday and planned to give it to her mother. On Easter Sunday, 1 April 1934, Joe Palmer hitchhiked into Dallas to deliver the rendezvous information; he found nobody at either of the relatives' homes. Around midmorning the black, 1934 Ford V-8 sedan carrying Bonnie, Clyde, and Henry Methvin moved east on Texas Highway 114 and turned north on Dove Lane, a dirt trail that crossed the main road about six miles west of the little town of Grapevine. William Schieffer, local farmer, was sitting under a tree on his property across the highway and watched the cars pass; he saw the black car park and two men, one larger than the other, get out and walk around. Within a short time the two men returned to the car. It was not uncommon during the Great Depression for travelers to park on side roads for a nap, so Schieffer suspected nothing sinister about the car. Actually, both Bonnie and Clyde were weary and napped while Methvin kept a lookout.[1]

Dallas Morning News reporters later learned from the Texas

Highway Patrol that the north Texas headquarters had assigned three motorcycle officers to cruise that stretch of Highway 114 to watch for speeders. Officers E. B. Wheeler, H. D. Murphy, and Polk Ivy had monitored the traffic since before noon and had noticed the black sedan parked on the side road. The three officers stopped on another side lane, checked the oil in their cycles, and fired a few practice pistol shots at a nearby deserted hill. Officer Ivy finished first and returned to the highway to patrol.

Around 2:30 P.M. Mr. and Mrs. Fred Gizzal left their Dallas home for a Sunday drive on Highway 114 toward Rhome, a small community in Wise County. As they drove along the highway, Officers Wheeler and Murphy pulled onto the road about one hundred yards in front of them. The Gizzals saw the two officers look at the black sedan as they neared Dove Lane and signal one another to check on the parked car.[2]

From inside the car Bonnie heard the cycles and looked out the back window. Seeing the officers pull into the lane, dismount, and put their cycles on stands, she woke Clyde by whispering, "It's the law." Clyde jumped up quickly and saw that the patrolmen expected no danger. They leisurely approached the car without drawing their weapons. Methvin, who had been sitting inside the car, looked at Clyde for guidance. Clyde nodded to Methvin and said, "Let's take them." Henry had been with Bonnie and Clyde only a short time and was not familiar with their practice of kidnapping officers and releasing them later to embarrass them. As an escaped convict, possibly drunk, and certainly quite scared, he understood Clyde to mean open fire and he did.[3]

Hearing shots echoing from the area near the black car as they passed, the Gizzals saw Wheeler, struck by several bullets, fall to the ground. He died almost instantly. Murphy, walking behind Wheeler, stopped and reached into his pocket for shells for his shortened shotgun. He had told Ivy earlier that he was concerned about an accidental discharge of the weapon and carried it unloaded. As Murphy grabbed for the shells, Methvin ran around the car, shot the officer, and jumped into the sedan. Clyde gunned the motor and wheeled onto the highway.

Meanwhile, west of Dove Lane, Officer Ivy turned around and rode back to find his friends; he met Gizzal who frantically signaled him to pull over. Gizzal, shocked by the shootings, gasped, "Go back to the last dirt road. Somebody just shot two of your officers." Ivy looked in both directions. "Find the nearest phone," he said. "Call the police and an ambulance. Tell them to come to Highway 114 and Dove Lane just west of Grapevine."

The Foust Funeral Home in Grapevine dispatched Corbin Crews to the crime scene. Crews found Wheeler already dead and Murphy barely alive; he rushed Murphy to the office of Dr. J. A. Ellison in Grapevine, but the man was dead on arrival.[4]

Like Simmons, Captain L. G. Phares, chief of the Texas Highway Patrol, was a traditional law enforcement officer who held the Old Testament philosophy of an eye for an eye. The day after the slayings, Phares issued bulletin number 259, which described the suspects' automobile and offered a reward of $1,000; he was determined to avenge the deaths of his two patrolmen. Bonnie and Clyde did not yet know it, but they had, with the prison break and the slaying of the highway patrolmen, aroused the two lawmen in Texas that had both the determination and the resources to track them to the end. The foxes were now pursued by snarling, blood-thirsty hounds who would never tire, never quit, and never rest until the chase ended in death. No longer were Bonnie and Clyde confronting woefully incompetent small-town sheriffs and "Keystone Kop" deputies; they now were pursued by hard-eyed, Old West-type professionals.

Having heard some Austin gossip that Frank Hamer had been hired as Simmons's investigator, Phares telephoned Mrs. Hamer and insisted that she ask her husband to contact him as soon as possible. When Hamer called, Phares pressured him, "Frank, you've got to let me assign one of my men to join you. Those bastards killed two of my young officers in cold blood."

Hamer tried to stall. "Chief, I really prefer to work alone. Besides, I don't have the final say. Lee Simmons created this job. You'll have to check with him."

Phares refused to be dissuaded. "If you see Lee before I do, tell him the Highway Department will work with you boys any way you like. But I've got to have a patrolman in on the kill."

In a subsequent meeting between Hamer and Simmons, they considered Phares's offer. Simmons posed the question, "How do you feel about working with somebody?"

Hamer shook his head. "I would just as soon not. But I guess it depends on who Phares assigns. Some of his boys are ex-Rangers. I know most of them."

Simmons nodded. "I'll pass that along to Phares. If it's alright with you, we may try to work something out."[5]

When the Highway Patrol suggested Manny Gault, Hamer readily agreed, and the patrolman joined in the pursuit. Gault, like Hamer, was a former Texas Ranger. A quiet man with pleasant features and an easy smile, Gault dressed plainly in a single-breasted gray suit and a beige farmer's hat. He looked more like an insurance salesman or a grocer than a fearless peace officer. He had served in the same Texas Ranger company as Hamer and on several occasions proved to be extremely cool under fire. The two officers soon stopped at a roadside cafe for lunch, and Hamer shared with Gault the traveling pattern of Bonnie and Clyde that he had observed. "I compare these outlaws to wild horses that move around on an open range. They always go in the same circle. I've traced their route from Dallas northeast through Oklahoma and Kansas to Joplin, Missouri, south to the northeastern part of Louisiana, and back to Dallas." Hamer had readily discovered the travel pattern of Bonnie and Clyde. The Dallas lawmen who had pursued the outlaws for two years had never discerned the system.

Gault nodded. "And what we have to do is break the circle."

Hamer blew out a puff of smoke. "That's the way I see it."[6]

Simmons recognized that while Hamer and Gault needed no help in tracking and capturing criminals, they weren't familiar enough with Bonnie and Clyde to instantaneously identify the outlaws; he contacted Dallas authorities and requested help. Judge Roland G. Williams of the Criminal District Court Number Two ordered Sheriff Schmid to assign two deputies to advise and assist the state lawmen. Deputy Bob Alcorn, who knew Bonnie and Clyde on sight as well as their personal habits, and Deputy Ted Hinton, who was friendly with the Barrow family, were selected.[7] Alcorn was a tall, thin man with a lantern jaw and dark eyes set in a hardwood face that was partially obscured by a tan Stetson pulled low over his eyes; he appeared immutably grim. Hinton was a large-boned man and a flamboyant dresser; he favored light suits and a dark hat worn at a rakish angle with the left side of the brim turned down. Alcorn and Hinton, having pursued Bonnie and Clyde unsucessfully for almost two years, were very weary. On 3 April 1934 the four officers joined forces, with Alcorn and Hinton in one car and Hamer and Gault in another.

During one of their conferences, Simmons and Hamer discussed the possibility of involving a gang member in a betrayal plot.

Simmons reminded Hamer, "I've got the governor's permission to grant clemency or a pardon to anybody that helps us."

Hamer rolled a cigarette and struck a match. "Henry Methvin's people live in northwestern Louisiana. That's on the outlaws' circle. Let me speak quietly with the lawmen in the area. I'll let you know how I come out." Within a few days Hamer contacted Henderson Jordan, sheriff of Bienville parish, where the Methvins lived. Jordan knew the elder Methvin well and arranged a session between Hamer and Methvin.[8]

A late winter sun warmed the two men as they sat on a park bench on the lawn of the Arcadia, Louisiana, courthouse. Hamer rolled a cigarette and lit it. Methvin placed a dip of snuff into his mouth from a small canister.

Hamer looked across the lawn. "Bonnie and Clyde are going to get your boy killed. You know that as well as I do. What will it take to get you to set them up?"

Methvin spit onto the grass. "I don't want my boy to go back to no Texas prison. That's all I ask."

Hamer nodded. "Alright, I can get that fixed. What I need from you is word where they will be at a certain time. It'll have to be away from innocent bystanders. We'll take it from there."

"You'll be careful not to hurt my boy?"

Hamer blew out a puff of smoke. "I can't make any guarantees, Methvin. But I'll promise you we will do the best we can."

Hamer forwarded the demand via Simmons to Governor Ferguson. She wrote a letter of intent stating that "under certain conditions involving . . . assistance to the law" Henry Methvin would receive a full pardon from the State of Texas." Neither Simmons nor Governor Ferguson knew that Henry was the killer of both of the Texas highway patrolmen on Easter Sunday near Grapevine.[9]

The four tracking companions, using Hamer's theory of a continuous and clockwise circular route, drove north on Highway 77 from Dallas through Sherman toward the Red River and eastern Oklahoma. As the officers halted occasionally for gasoline, service station operators passed on information about the bandits that they had heard on the radio. The officers speculated that the outlaws' ultimate destination was Methvin's home in northeastern Louisiana.

Wednesday, 4 April 1934, dawned bright, clear, and mild in southern Oklahoma. Following a cold winter and rainy spring, the people of the area crowded into Durant, the major town of the area. Cars lined the streets and dozens of people shopped and visited. Early in the afternoon the two unmarked police cars arrived in town; the deputies' car in front was followed by the state policemen. Through the jammed traffic Bob Alcorn saw a car coming down the street going in the opposite direction. "Here they come," he said. They then pulled off the road, and when Hamer and Gault stopped alongside, they told them of the sighting. Both cars rapidly turned about and began the chase, but the car had disappeared.[10]

After spending the night off the main road, Bonnie, Clyde, and Henry reached Texarkana, Texas, about noon. Shortly after 1:00 P.M., Bonnie told Clyde she was hungry. He stopped near a drugstore and waited in the car with Henry as she went inside to eat. Bonnie had eaten half her sandwich, when Clyde became agitated.

"Go in there and signal her to move it."

Methvin walked inside, looked at her, and came back to the car. Bonnie quickly got in the car, and they drove away. Several hours later, they stopped at a lunch counter about five miles north of Texarkana. Finishing their meal, they crossed the Index tollbridge over the Red River and headed for Ottawa County in the northeast corner of Oklahoma where they had hidden out in the past.[11]

The following day, Thursday, 5 April 1934, witnesses spotted the fugitives in Commerce, Oklahoma, when they drove through town just after daylight, and again about 9:00 A.M. as they parked near the First State Bank of Commerce. Just before noon other citizens saw the outlaws drive west out of Commerce toward Miami in an area known as the Lost Trail Mine. Rain had fallen intermittently for several days, and most county roads were quagmires. A short distance out of Commerce, Clyde got stuck in a mudbank. He and Methvin jumped out and waved their guns at a passing motorist, but the man managed to pass the bandits before they could fire their weapons. Reaching the county seat at Miami, the driver reported the gunmen to Chief of Police Percy Boyd and Constable Cal Campbell. When the officers arrived at the site, Clyde and Henry had freed the car. Seeing the lawmen approach, Clyde jammed the car into reverse and backed up rapidly. When the car spun in the mud and slid into the ditch, Boyd and Campbell got out and walked toward the car. Campbell, in the lead, saw the men brandishing guns; he yelled to Boyd, "Look out, Percy." The constable pulled out his pistol. Clyde and Henry opened their car doors; Clyde fired twice with his shotgun and grabbed his automatic rifle. Campbell fired three shots while Boyd shot his pistol four times. One of Boyd's shots narrowly missed Clyde, and he heard the air loudly snap as the bullet passed near his head; two of the officer's bullets crashed through the gangsters' windshield.

Clyde and Henry continued to fire as they moved closer. Their bullets knocked both lawmen to the ground. Boyd knew he had been struck in the head but couldn't determine how badly he was wounded. He heard Campbell groaning and then grow quiet. The two outlaws stopped to talk for a moment; Henry cautiously came closer while Clyde ran to a nearby farmhouse.

Charles Dobson, local trucker who hauled freight over much of eastern Oklahoma, was driving between Miami and Commerce about that time. Hearing gunfire ahead, he sped to the shooting site. Pulling up near Campbell's body, Dobson saw Clyde hurry back onto the roadway and point a machine gun at him. As he held the gun on Dobson, Clyde called out to Henry to hook the truck chain onto their car and pull it out of the ditch. When another motorist, Jack Boydston, drove alongside, Clyde pointed the Browning at him and yelled, "Get out and help free that stuck car." Boydston quickly looked around the area and later was able to tell investigators every detail. For example, he noticed that the main gunman was barefooted and had a big toe missing from his right foot. He also saw Bonnie sitting in the front seat of the stuck car, calmly smoking a cigarette. Hurriedly, he scanned and memorized the criminals' license plate number, Oklahoma 231-047. When the car was freed from the mud, Clyde led Boyd around to the right side of the car. "Okay, Lawman, get inside." Dobson noticed blood flowing down the left side of the officer's head and onto his chest.

Clyde jumped behind the steering wheel, rolled down the window, and signaled to Dobson and Boydston to come over. When they cautiously approached, Clyde coldly said, "Tell the officers if they lay off following us, we won't kill the cop. If they follow us and cause us any trouble, we'll kill him." He gazed at the two men for several seconds, rolled up the window, and sped away toward the west across the Neosho River Bridge.[12]

Inside the car Bonnie and Henry began bandaging Boyd's head wound. Dobson and Boydston hurried to Miami to report the shooting-kidnapping to Sheriff Dee Watters. When the witnesses told Watters that the first man and the woman were both in their twenties, slightly built, and that the second man had a severe skin problem, the sheriff said, "Boys, you just met Bonnie and Clyde." When Watters telephoned law enforcement agencies in the area requesting help, fifteen officers raced toward Miami. The sheriff drove to the shooting scene to search for evidence and studied the area where Campbell's body lay.[13]

Meanwhile in Miami, County Attorney Perry Porter interviewed Jack Boydston about the shootings. Porter disagreed with Sheriff Watters as to the identity of the suspects; he pointed out that Jim Clark and Wilbur Underhill, major Midwest criminals who had recently escaped from the Kansas State Penitentiary, fit Boydston's description of the bandit leader, and he ordered the information broadcast on the radio. Within a short time, however, the Department of Justice office in Dallas, Texas, telephoned to tell him that the killer was probably Clyde Barrow.[14]

During all of this, the outlaws continued their getaway. Three miles from the death scene, near Timber Hill Farm, they met two farmers, A. N. and John Butterfield, whose small truck was stuck in the mud, blocking the road. Clyde and Henry jumped from the car and yelled, "We've just killed two men, and we're in a hurry. The law is after us." Then they helped the brothers move their truck out of the road, returned to their own car, and sped away toward Chetopa.[15]

Watters arrived back in Miami with Campbell's body, which was taken to the Mitchelson Undertaking Company. Within minutes the officers summoned from the surrounding area began arriving. Piling into squad cars, the group raced to pick up the trail. Presently, they met the Butterfields and learned that the fugitives were still driving west. The lawmen were concerned that the farmers had seen nothing of Boyd, and many speculated that Clyde had killed him and dumped the body.[16]

In Dallas, Lee Simmons was in the office of veteran detective Will Fritz to discuss ways of catching Bonnie and Clyde. An officer ran into the office and breathlessly said, "Turn on the radio, quick. Oklahoma officers are working a dragnet for Bonnie and Clyde."[17]

Clyde continued driving westward toward Highway 73. Just east of Chetopa, they met Blaine Boone, a U.S. Postman, on a muddy side road and nearly forced him into the ditch. Boyd, who was unaware of

Clyde's practice of doubling back, keeping to side roads, and occasionally parking, was puzzled and felt the driver had become confused.[18]

Miami authorities enlisted a local pilot, Andy Walker, to join the search. He took off from the Miami Municipal Airport about 11:15 A.M. and flew over all the roads leading to Chetopa looking for the dark blue Ford sedan. Clyde soon spotted the plane circling nearby and hid the car under a small grove of trees; he got out and walked around. Boyd was struck by the coolness and unruffled manner of the killers.[19]

Boone soon met members of the posse; he flagged down the officers and advised them that Clyde was heading directly for Highway 73, which ran between Chetopa and Welch. But Clyde had already doubled back; slipping along back roads, he continued to evade the search parties. Southwest of Chetopa Clyde passed another mailman, Jim Allen. Within minutes members of the posse waved the letter carrier over and learned that the bandits were still in the Chetopa area. The officers found a letter torn into small pieces near a schoolhouse. The handwriting appeared to have been written by a woman. Searching through the scraps, lawmen found bits of phrases such as, "He's not guilty" and "police officers."[20]

Inside the getaway car, Boyd tried to become friendly with the outlaws. Intrigued with Clyde's coolness and calm outlook during the escape, Boyd also felt disgust with the arrogance of the man, and in his mind he applied a contemporary phrase: "He acted like he owned the earth." Despite these feelings, he continued the conversation with the bandits. After several minutes of small talk, Clyde told Boyd he was sorry Campbell had been shot, but he had to do it to survive. At first Boyd accepted Clyde's apparent remorse; later he was shocked at the gangsters' joking about shooting Campbell.

Boyd assumed that the killers had ample money; he had $25 in his wallet, but the crooks never searched him. Since Boyd's shirt had become stained with blood, Clyde gave him a new one as well as a necktie. After several hours of conversation, Boyd asked about the two highway patrolmen killed on Easter Sunday.

"Percy, we didn't have a damn thing to do with that," said Clyde. "All we know about those two was what we read in the newspapers."

Boyd looked at Bonnie. "Do you have a message for the world?"

Bonnie snorted. "You're damn right. Tell the papers that I don't smoke cigars. The Joplin reporters spread this lie after that gun battle in Joplin. We had to leave a bunch of snapshots and one of 'em was a joke picture of me. I just took the cigar from Clyde and put it in my mouth for the picture."

Occasionally, Boyd glimpsed the roadside despite the muddy windows and recognized the area as being south and west of Chetopa. Shortly, Clyde turned the car northwest. When arriving in Bartlett, Kansas, he stopped at a service station for gasoline before turning toward Fort Scott.[21]

When Sheriff Watters and members of the posse arrived in Bartlett and canvased the various businesses, the service station attendant remembered the dark Ford sedan but recalled no wounded man in the car. Watters, now deeply concerned about Boyd's safety, relayed the information to County Attorney Porter before pressing on with the chase.

As afternoon passed into early evening, peace officers were on the move throughout the region. Dozens of lawmen, confident that Clyde and his gang would return to Ottowa County to hide out, guarded nearby highways and bridges. The Kansas Highway Patrol joined sheriffs, deputies, and city policemen from Kansas, Missouri, Arkansas, and Oklahoma in the search. Frightened citizens sent officers on several erroneous leads. A man called the Missouri Highway Patrol to report having seen Bonnie and Clyde in Minden. Lawmen from Kansas City, Jefferson City, and Springfield converged on Minden in radio-equipped patrol cars. The sighting proved to be false. In Dallas local authorities checked out misleading reports. A man stated that while passing through the Oakland Cemetery about 5:30 P.M., he had been stopped by Clyde, Raymond Hamilton, and two women. Two other citizens reported seeing the Barrow gang between Oak Cliff, a section of south Dallas, and Lancaster. Checking out these sightings, deputies found all to be erroneous.[22]

The federal government soon became involved. From his office in Washington, D.C., Attorney General Homer Cummings instructed the Investigation Division of the Department of Justice to advise all field officers in the affected states to cooperate with local authorities and offer every assistance in capturing Bonnie and Clyde.[23]

Late Friday evening the gang arrived in Fort Scott. After driving around town for nearly an hour, Clyde stopped near a drug store while Henry ran inside to buy a newspaper. For the first time, they learned that Constable Campbell had died of his wounds. While Bonnie read the article aloud, Clyde drove up and down Main Street and once passed the police station. Later he parked near a grocery store while Henry went inside to buy food, then drove out of Fort Scott on Highway 69 and parked while the group ate.[24]

As the evening passed, reporters pressed Sheriff Watters about Boyd's chances. The lawman said, "They'll probably hold him for protection as long as they can and then kill him." Once again, however, as they had with lawmen throughout the South and Midwest, Bonnie and Clyde released their captive unharmed. Shortly before midnight on Friday, 6 April 1934, Clyde stopped the blue sedan about nine miles south of Fort Scott and turned to look at Boyd in the backseat. "You can get out here, Chief. I don't care what you tell the other laws as long as it is the absolute truth."

Boyd nodded, got out of the car, watched the taillights disappear into the night, and began trudging back into town. When he reached the police station, authorities placed a telephone call for him to his wife and children. While waiting for the Miami police car to come for him, Boyd told officers and local reporters of his experiences. When he arrived back in Miami, he briefed county and Department of Justice officials on his impressions of Bonnie and Clyde. After a visit to the Miami hospital for treatment of his head wound, he arrived home about 7:00 A.M. Less than twenty-four hours had passed since he and Campbell had answered the alarm raised by a fearful motorist on the Commerce Road.[25]

Bonnie, Clyde, and Henry slept in their car on a side road near Fort Scott and the next morning drove south to Stillwater, Oklahoma. They stopped at a cafe but ran to their car and sped away when a uniformed officer appeared. They raced south from Stillwater and turned west at an area known as Nine Mile Corner. Pursuing lawmen stopped to question a stalled motorist. He reported seeing a sedan containing two men, a woman, and a bulldog pass him traveling very fast and disappear into the woods. Officers lost the trail but began concentrating their search along the Red River next to Texas and the Cookson Hills of eastern Oklahoma, an area the gang had used as a hideout in the past.[26]

Texas Highway Patrol Chief Phares speculated to reporters that the killers would return to Texas because they were so familiar with the roads, and he vowed, "We'll be watching for them when they come."[27]

In New Orleans, Raymond Hamilton and Mary O'Dare read the accounts of the Miami shootings in the Saturday morning newspapers. Raymond considered surrendering, since he was suspected of being the second man. Mary O'Dare persuaded him to wait. Her advice proved correct.[28]

After sleeping a few hours, Percy Boyd again talked with agents from the Department of Justice and looked at several police photographs. He could not identify Raymond Hamilton as the second man in the blue sedan but did recognize Henry Methvin.[29]

On Saturday afternoon Raymond mailed a letter to his Dallas attorney disclaiming any connection with crimes in which persons had been killed, and he attached his thumbprint for identification. The lawyer made the letter public when he received it on Monday.[30]

12

Death Came Out to Meet Them

As the spring progressed, the pursuit of Bonnie and Clyde reached a new intensity. The slaying of Major Crowson during the Eastham Prison breakout had aroused Lee Simmons and led to the placing of Frank Hamer on their trail; the killing of the two Texas Highway Patrol officers had severely angered Highway Patrol Chief Phares; the death of Constable Campbell and shooting of Chief Boyd stirred the emotions of people in Kansas, Oklahoma, and Arkansas.

Bonnie and Clyde's continued freedom increased the possibility for them killing more citizens and law officers. This knowledge rested heavily on public officials. At this point the deaths caused by the outlaws numbered twelve in slightly over twenty-four months, an average of one slaying for each two-month period the killers remained free. Even more chilling to officials was the thought that the number could have been nearly twice as high if Bonnie and Clyde had been the wanton killers some pictured them to be. The evidence clearly indicates that they never killed for the sake of killing. Every slaying had been in the heat of battle or on a one-to-one confrontation. On six different occasions, they kidnapped private citizens and officers rather than murdering them: beginning with gasoline station operators in east Texas; continuing with Deputy Sheriff Joe Johns near Carlsbad, New Mexico; next the capture of Motorcycle Officer Thomas Persell in Springfield, Missouri; then the brief kidnapping of H. D. Darby and Sophie Stone in Ruston, Louisiana; next Town Marshal Tom Hardy and Sheriff George Corry near Wellington, Texas; and finally, the capture and subsequent release of Police Chief Percy Boyd outside Miami, Oklahoma.

While Hamer and his small automobile posse drew closer to their prey, other ordinary citizens in all parts of the American South and Midwest were drawn into the gruesome pageant that was playing itself out. One example was Jesse and Ruth Warren of Topeka, Kansas. They had recently bought a new Ford V-8, four-door sedan. Its finish, called Desert Sand by the Ford Motor Company, glistened in the spring sunshine. The Warrens had carefully chosen the automobile. The extra equipment inside included deluxe seat covers and an Arvin hot water car heater. Outside options were bumper guards, a steel cover for the spare tire, and a chrome greyhound in the jumping position atop the radiator cap. The car had been produced at the River Rouge plant in February and was a popular style. Despite the severe economic depression, Ford dealers had already sold nearly one million cars just like the one purchased by the Warrens.[1]

Ruth Warren had driven her automobile slowly, according to Ford Company instructions, for more than 1,000 miles. Toward the end of April, the car was considered "broken-in," and Ruth planned to see just how fast the tan auto would run on the last weekend of April. Sunday, 29 April 1934, dawned bright and clear in Topeka. The day was pleasantly mild, and Ruth drove her car for a short speed run and planned a faster drive in the afternoon. When she arrived back home a short time later, she pulled into the driveway and left the keys in the switch.

Neighbors along Ruth's street noticed a young couple driving through the area in a Plymouth coupe. The man and woman had circled the block several times as if looking for an address. Late that afternoon the couple returned to the Warrens' street once more with the man standing on the right running board. As the coupe slowed near the Warren driveway, the man stepped down; he quickly ran to the tan Ford sedan, jumped inside, and drove away. Witnesses immediately alerted Ruth, who notified authorities.

Topeka police told reporters that they suspected the thieves were Bonnie and Clyde, who were known to favor Ford cars. Clyde had even written a letter to Henry Ford praising his steel-bodied V-8 automobiles, stating that he always stole a Ford when he could get one. The little cars used less gasoline and could travel great distances at very fast speeds without requiring maintenance. Most appealing of all to Clyde was that with one million copies on American roads, he could change license plates and appear to be another law-abiding citizen.[2] The next day Bonnie and Clyde picked up Henry Methvin and

Joe Palmer and robbed a Kansas bank of $2,800; they divided the money. Four days later Joe Palmer decided to leave the gang temporarily. His stomach pained him constantly, and he needed a rest. Concerned about his friends, Palmer warned Bonnie and Clyde about going back to Louisiana. Bonnie and Clyde told Palmer not to worry and promised to link up with him again when he had recovered; they worked their way south toward Dallas, arriving there on Sunday, 6 May. Clyde drove by the Barrow gasoline station and threw out a bottle with instructions that they could meet after dark on a special rural road just east of the Dallas city limits.[3]

The relatives passed the word by telephone and later met with Bonnie, Clyde, and Henry Methvin. While Clyde talked with his mother and sister Nell, Bonnie spoke with her mother and shared some pictures of Clyde and her. Obviously preoccupied, she fell silent for a long time then spoke very seriously and softly with her mother and made two macabre requests.

"When they kill us, don't let them take me to an undertaking parlor, will you? Bring me home."

Her mother cried out in anguish. "Don't Bonnie. For God's sake."

Bonnie calmed her mother with soothing words, then continued, "Now Mama, don't get upset. Why shouldn't we talk it over? It's coming. You know it. I know it. . . . Bring me home when I die. It's been so long since I was home. I want to lie in the front room with you and Billie and Buster setting beside me. A long cool, peaceful night together before I leave you. That will be nice and restful. Another thing, Mama, when they kill us, don't ever say anything ugly about Clyde. Please promise me that too."

After Mrs. Parker promised, Bonnie gave her mother a poem she had just completed, "The Story of Bonnie and Clyde."

> You've read the story of Jesse James
> Of how he lived and died
> If you're still in need of something to read
> Here's the story of Bonnie and Clyde.
>
> Now Bonnie and Clyde are the Barrow Gang,
> I'm sure you all have read

how they rob and steal and those who squeal
are usually found dying or dead.

There's lots of untruths to these write-ups
They're not so ruthless as that
Their nature is raw, they hate all law
Stool pigeons, spotters, and rats.

They call them cold-blooded killers
They say they are heartless and mean
But I say this with pride, I once knew Clyde
When he was honest and upright and clean.

But the laws fooled around and taking him down
and locking him up in a cell
'Til he said to me, "I'll never be free,
So I'll meet a few of them in hell."

The road was so dimly lighted
There were no highway signs to guide
But they made up their minds if all roads were blind
They wouldn't give up 'til they died.

The road gets dimmer and dimmer
Sometimes you can hardly see
But it's fight man to man, and do all you can
For they know they can never be free.

From heartbreak some people have suffered
From weariness some people have died
But all in all, our troubles are small
'Til we get like Bonnie and Clyde.

If a policeman is killed in Dallas
And they have no clue or guide
If they can't find a fiend, just wipe the slate clean
And hang it on Bonnie and Clyde.

There's two crimes committed in America
Not accredited to the Barrow Mob

They had no hand in the kidnap demand
Nor the Kansas City Depot job.

A newsboy once said to his buddy
"I wish old Clyde would get jumped
In these hard times we's get a few dimes
If five or six cops would get bumped."

The police haven't got the report yet
But Clyde called me up today
He said, "Don't start any fights, we aren't
working nights, we're joining the NRA."

From Irving to West Dallas viaduct
Is known as the Great Divide
Where the women are kin, and men are men
And they won't stool on Bonnie and Clyde.

If they try to act like citizens
And rent a nice little flat
About the third night they're invited to fight
By a sub-gun's rat-tat-tat.

They don't think they're tough or desperate
They know the law always wins
They've been shot at before, but they do not ignore
That death is the wages of sin.

Some day they'll go down together
And they'll bury them side by side
To few it'll be grief, to the law a relief
But it's death for Bonnie and Clyde.

Clyde called out to her, "Honey, we need to get going." Bonnie
kissed her sister, Billie, gave her mother one last hug and ran to the
tan Ford to join Clyde. She crawled into the front seat beside him,
rolled down the window and leaned out as the car pulled away. Waving wildly, she called out, "We'll be back in two weeks. I promise."
But their families never saw them alive again.[4]

The unfolding drama moved to Louisiana as more and more officers joined in the search, but only Hamer had developed the correct theory of actually tracing them. The other lawmen served as unsuspecting native-type beaters in a depression-devastated, rural jungle. Over the next two weeks, the people of northern Louisiana saw more of the outlaws in the tan car with ever-changing license plates. When in the area, the couple often stopped at the Sailes Crossroads convenience store for soft drinks and snack food. The red-haired woman usually came in to make the purchases while the man remained in the car looking up and down the road. Since the woman always paid with change, the shopkeeper was almost certain that he recognized the couple. One day when the tiny woman paid him with a fifty-cent piece, he kept it for himself, certain that Bonnie and Clyde had paid him. Unquestionably, the money was stolen, but to him it was special and he carried it for the rest of his life. Twenty years later the coin was still in his pocket when he was buried.

One person in northern Louisiana who knew the Barrow gang and where they were staying was Ivan Methvin, Henry's father. Neighbors didn't know too much about the Methvins except that Ivan was a drunkard who drove a logging truck that was on the verge of collapse and that his son was in prison in Texas.

There were several old deserted houses in the area that had been abandoned for one reason or another. Otis Cole's family owned such a house. A primitive dwelling, it had unpainted raw wood siding, a tin roof, and only four rooms, two on each side with an open passage through the center. Cole's father, mother, and two sisters had died of tuberculosis while living in the house. Furniture still remained in the house, but none of the family had been there for four years. Neighbors notified Cole that someone was living there and suggested an investigation. Cole and his wife drove out from Gibsland, walked through the woods to the house, and found Ivan Methvin sitting on the front porch, obviously drunk. Cole left when Methvin asked him where he could get more whiskey. Walking away, the Coles noticed that someone was moving around inside. Later Cole concluded that the mysterious squatters were Bonnie and Clyde.[5]

On Saturday night, 19 May 1934, the two sedans carrying the Texas lawmen pulled into parking places at the Inn Hotel in Shreveport, Louisiana. The officers liked the hotel because they could park their cars beneath the hotel and walk up one flight of stairs to their assigned rooms. They left most of their firearms lying under blankets on the backseats of their locked cars. The automatic rifles and ammunition, however, remained in the automobile trunks. Between them the four officers had the firepower of an infantry squad.[6]

Just a few blocks away, Clyde parked his tan Ford sedan in front of the Majestic Cafe. As was the custom, Bonnie sat beside him, with Henry in the backseat. After discussing what each wanted to eat, Methvin got out and entered the cafe; he sat down at the counter, ordered several sandwiches and soft drinks, and asked that they be prepared to carry out. Outside Bonnie and Clyde carefully monitored the traffic on the street.

Within a short time, a police car, apparently on routine patrol, drove along the street. Clyde jerked his car into gear and hurriedly slipped his car away from the curb and sped down the street. The patroling policemen, who had not noticed the tan sedan until it raced away, began pursuit. In a very short time, however, the policemen gave up the chase and the tan Ford disappeared into the night.

Inside the cafe Henry heard the squeal of the tires and noticed Clyde driving away very fast; leaving before the sandwich order was ready, he calmly and quietly slipped out of the restaurant and blended into the busy Saturday pedestrian traffic on the sidewalk. For the last several days, his father had tried, very cautiously, to separate Henry from Bonnie and Clyde. Now they had left him. Clyde had told Henry that if they were separated, a rendezvous point would be a deserted spot on the Sailes highway south of Arcadia. Henry walked to the edge of Shreveport and began hitchhiking east toward Ruston. Arriving home, Henry told his father where and how he planned to rendezvous with Bonnie and Clyde. Ivan Methvin hurried from the house and drove to advise Sheriff Jordan.[7]

After a good night's sleep, the first time in a bed in several days, the four Texas lawmen ate breakfast in the hotel diner. Following the meal, they lounged, played poker, and after days of living in their police cars, wrote letters to their wives and families. Late that evening the officers telephoned Chief of Police Tom Bryan to advise him that they were in town and to inform him of their purpose. Bryan invited the Texans to come to his office for additional information; he described the odd behavior of the Majestic Cafe customers the previous evening and outlined how he personally had gone to the cafe to interview the waitress that had served the mysterious customer. The woman had told Bryan that she had never seen the man before but would know him next time because of his severe skin problem. The following morning, 21 May 1934, Bryan and the Texas officers went to the Majestic Cafe for breakfast. The police chief waved the manager over to the table. "These gentlemen are Texas peace officers. We need to talk to the waitress that was on duty Saturday night."

"Sorry, Chief. She's not scheduled to come on duty until much later today."

"Please telephone her home and tell her we desperately need to talk with her. Believe me, it's very important." The manager hurried to the telephone; he returned shortly and said, "Okay. She'll be here in a few minutes."

When the lady arrived, Hamer handed her a group of photographs. "Do you recognize anyone that could be the man who walked out on the sandwich order Saturday night?"

Scanning the pictures, the waitress immediately selected one; after looking at it carefully, she handed the picture of Henry Methvin back to Hamer. "That's the guy. I'd know him anywhere because of the strange eyes and blotched skin."

Hamer sat in the cafe stirring his coffee; he was certain this was the opportunity he had been waiting for. Now was the time to contact his Judas and prepare the ambush. After several minutes of silence, he turned to the others. "We will go to Arcadia. Henry has had time to get home by now. I expect Henry's Daddy has talked to Sheriff Jordan." He stepped to the telephone and dialed Jordan's number. Returning to the table, he nodded. "Old Man Methvin has already seen the sheriff. A meeting has been set."

The officers hurried to the motel; they loaded their luggage into the cars and quickly drove toward Arcadia. After talking with Sheriff Jordan the next day, 22 May, Hamer stopped at a public telephone about 8:00 P.M. and telephoned Huntsville, Texas. When Simmons answered the call, Hamer simply said, "The old hen is about ready to hatch. I think the chickens will come off tomorrow." Simmons answered okay and hung up.[8]

In Bienville Parish, Sheriff Henderson Jordan sighed; he had a round face with deep-sun grin lines and eyes virtually covered by the brim of his fawn-colored Stetson western hat. His heavy beard gave the appearance of a devious person, but Jordan was an outgoing man with a friendly air that characterized southern politicians. He now called his main deputy, Prentis Oakley. "Pick up your rifle and come down to the office." Oakley was a thin, wiry, reserved man with a receding chin and narrow, gaunt face; he resembled a rural school teacher more than an ambush squad member. Only his eyes, narrow icy-hard slits, indicated boldness and determination. Shortly after Jordan hung up the phone, the Texas officers arrived, and Hamer stepped into the sheriff's office.

"Is it all set up?" he asked.

Jordan nodded. "The old man is cooperating fully. He will do what we talked about."

The six lawmen quietly drove out of Arcadia and hurried to the ambush site; under Hamer's direction, they took up their positions. The night passed slowly and the officers' muscles felt stiff and sore as the sun finally rose. Just after dawn on 23 May, Ivan Methvin arrived in his logging truck and pulled off the road near where the officers waited; he jacked up the truck's front end and removed the right front wheel. Hurrying to the rear of the truck, he dragged out a spare tire and dropped it to the ground. Looking both ways to ensure that no one saw him, Methvin ran to the shrubbery on the east side of the road and hid with the posse.[9]

Around the same time William Lyon picked up a load of pulp wood logs and started north on the Sailes road toward the mill. His truck strained up the small hills and coasted down the inclines. Reaching another rise, Lyon saw a tan Ford sedan approaching in the distance from the north.[10]

As the officer responsible for identifying Bonnie and Clyde, Bob Alcorn also had seen the Ford; he knew that this car matched the description of the auto that Clyde had stolen in Topeka and had driven in Shreveport. Watching the car draw near at high speed, Alcorn's expectations grew; few people drove like Clyde. When the car came closer, Alcorn recognized Bonnie and Clyde and turned to Hamer. "It's them," he said.[11]

The motor roared as the Ford reached the crest of the hill but slowed as it neared the truck parked off the road. Lyon slowed his logging truck to allow the tan sedan to have sufficient room while passing the parked truck with the wheel removed. Clyde slowed to a crawl and looked at Methvin's truck. Behind the bushes Hamer raised his rifle to a firing position. Following his lead the other officers raised theirs as well. Inside the car Clyde looked away from the truck toward the east and saw the officers with pointed rifles. He grabbed for his gun and the authorities opened fire. Dozens of bullets rained into the tan Ford.

Lyon stopped his truck and fell into his seat as the bullets continued to tear into the sedan. With dozens of rounds striking their bodies, Clyde's head flew back and Bonnie toppled forward. Clyde's foot slipped off the brake pedal and the car lurched forward, careened to the left, and ran into a sand bank. The posse continued to fire into the car as the motor idled.[12]

Finally, Hamer lowered his rifle and signaled the others to stop firing. The lawmen stood looking at the bullet-riddled car for several seconds. When no return fire came from the car, the officers approached the auto carefully with their guns poised. Looking inside, they relaxed their weapons. Bonnie and Clyde sat in grotesque positions of death. They would never kill again.

Ivan Methvin came running from behind the sand mound. "They hadn't met up with my son, had they?"

Hamer shook his head. "He wasn't in the car."

Methvin hurried to his truck and mounted the wheel; he looked at the tan Ford for several seconds and drove away. Deputy Hinton returned to his hidden car and picked up a 16-mm movie camera; he walked to the death car and began filming the holes in the automobile and the bodies inside.

Hamer turned to Gault. "How about driving to Gibsland to arrange for a tow truck?" Looking at Alcorn, Hamer said, "Why don't you and Deputy Oakley go to Arcadia to find the Parish coroner?"

Having heard the massive gunfire, nearby farmers began arriving to investigate and soon milled about the death scene in rapt fascination. Hamer and Jordan ordered the farmers to stand back and began an inventory of the contents of the tan Ford. They noted that the car displayed Arkansas license plates and found fifteen more sets of spare plates in the backseat from Texas, Arkansas, and Louisiana. Near the plates Hamer discovered a traveling bag containing clothing. Under a blanket on the floor, he found fifty clips of ammunition for the automatic rifles. Additional weapons in the backseat included various pistols and rifles. Hamer checked the trunk and found camping equipment, more clothing, and weapons.[13]

Meanwhile, Gault arrived at Gibsland; he had trouble locating a tow truck and waited to escort it to the death scene. Alcorn and

Oakley reached Arcadia and located Dr. Wade, the parish coroner. "Doc, we're part of a posse that just killed Bonnie and Clyde. We need you to come to the site and make a ruling on the cause of death."

Wade picked up his black leather physician's bag. "Just a minute," he said, "this will probably take some time. Wait 'til I call my wife and tell her I'll be late for lunch."

Alcorn nodded. "That's fine. I need to find a public phone and call my sheriff in Dallas." Wade sat at his rolltop desk and asked the operator to ring his home. The operator dialed the number, covered the mouthpiece with her hand, and listened along with Dr. Wade to the rings at the other end of the line. When his wife answered, Wade said, "I'm going to be late because I have to go down between Mount Lebanon and Sailes. A posse has just killed Bonnie and Clyde there."

The operator's eyes opened wide, and she pulled the plug of her headset; she ran out the door of her office and began screaming the news to everyone within earshot. People jumped into their cars and hurried out the Gibsland Road. Running back inside, the operator called the *Bienville Democrat*. The paper put the story on the telegraph to the rest of the nation.[14]

At approximately 10:00 A.M., the wire service message about the successful ambush reached the officers of the *Dallas Morning News*. Managing Editor John E. King called his state editor, Thomas J. Simmons, to his office and signaled the picture editor to send in a photographer. While the reporter stood by, the editor turned to his assistant. "Contact Long and Harmon Air Charter Service at Love Field. Tell them we want to charter an airplane to northeast Louisiana." As his assistant went out, Carl Moore, the photographer, came into the editor's office.

Leaning back in his chair, King smiled at Simmons and Moore. "I'm sending you two on the story of the decade. Lawmen have just killed Bonnie and Clyde in Louisiana. Take that airplane and get as close as you can. Then rent a car or taxi and get to a town named Arcadia as quickly as possible. This is the location of the funeral home that will receive the bodies."

The assistant stepped back into the office. "A plane will be warmed up and ready to go at 11:00 o'clock."

Dallas County Sheriff Smoot Schmid was sitting at his desk talking with a reporter when Alcorn's call came in. Schmid hung up the telephone and stared into space. His team had pursued the outlaws for so long it seemed strange the chase was over.

The newsman broke the silence. "Sheriff, you know who will be as thrilled about the ambush as anyone else? W. D. Jones and Raymond Hamilton. How about permission to talk with W. D.?"

Schmid turned to a deputy. "Take the reporters in to see W. D. I'm going to Arcadia, Louisiana."

One journalist looked through the bars at Jones, who was lying on his cot. "Say, Jones, a group of officers have just put your buddies, Bonnie and Clyde, on the spot."

Jones, who had been dozing, raised up and looked sleepily at the reporter. Grasping the significance of the message, he came to the cell door and gripped the bars with his hands. He shook his head. "I admit that I am relieved."

As the deputy and reporter walked back toward the main office, the lawmen said, "He's been a willing prisoner since he got here. He hasn't even inquired about bail."

The reporter stepped through the barred door the guard held open, then looked back as the gate closed with a bang. "Wouldn't you be scared after spilling the beans about all of Clyde's hideouts that maybe led to the ambush?"

The officer laughed and nodded.[15]

Across town Emma Parker was making a dress on her sewing machine when a newspaper reporter called.

The reporter asked hesitantly, "Are you alone, Mrs. Parker?"

"No," she said and waited for him to continue. Newsmen called almost daily to get statements or stories about the desperadoes. The families of Bonnie and Clyde always cooperated with them because they usually made the sheriff's office look incompetent. But this time the reporter asked to speak to another family member.

"I don't have time to call somebody else to the phone. Ask me."

"Okay. Have you heard yet that cops killed Bonnie and Clyde in Louisiana?"

Mrs. Parker dropped the phone and fainted. Buster rushed over to her and helped her to the couch. When she regained consciousness, Mrs. Parker burst into tears and looked up at Buster. "The law caught the kids. Somewhere in Louisiana."

Buster swore. "Don't believe that reporter, Mama. We've heard the same thing a hundred times, and it's never true."

Mrs. Parker shook her head. "No. Something tells me that this time it's different."[16]

When a reporter told Clyde's parents the news, Mrs. Barrow screamed and sobbed, "Oh my Lord. Only last night, I prayed to God that I might see him alive just one more time." When asked about his plans, Mr. Barrow turned away and mumbled, "I guess my wife will be going to Louisiana."[17]

At the Retriever Prison Farm near Huntsville, Roy Thornton, who had been married to Bonnie since 1925, listened carefully as Captain Ike Kelly told him of his wife's death. Reporters, allowed to observe Thornton's briefing, asked, "Thornton, do you have anything to say to the newspapers?"

The convict slowly shook his head.

One journalist asked, "When did you last see Bonnie?"

Thornton looked thoughtful and answered, "About three years ago."

As the reporters turned to leave, he called out, "I'm glad Bonnie and Clyde went out like they did because it's better than getting caught."[18]

In the Denton County Jail, newsmen rushed to Raymond Hamilton's cell. "Ray, aren't you relieved at the news of the ambush?"

Hamilton sneered, "I ain't scared of anybody."

One newsman laughed and said, "Mary O'Dare told police that you began dodging Bonnie and Clyde since shortly after the Lancaster bank robbery."

Hamilton bristled, "That's a damn lie. Clyde was my good friend."[19]

In Oklahoma, reporters contacted Percy Boyd, wounded and kidnapped by Bonnie and Clyde just a few weeks before near Miami, Oklahoma. Advised of the death of his captors, Boyd remembered the image of his friend, Cal Campbell, lying dead on the muddy highway after being killed by Clyde; he quietly told reporters, "I think it's lucky that more officers were not killed."[20]

In Oklahoma City, Joe Palmer sat in the lobby of the Huckins Hotel listening to a news report on the radio. Since his face was not as well known as those of Bonnie and Clyde, Palmer moved about freely. He stayed on the main streets, talked openly with lawmen, and generally avoided acting suspiciously. When the announcer told of the ambush, Palmer recalled that Clyde had said that he knew the lawmen were closing in. Clyde had asked Bonnie to write a letter to Dallas authorities offering to surrender, but Bonnie refused and said they would die together.[21]

In Austin, Texas, reporters hurried to the headquarters section of the Texas Highway Patrol. L. G. Phares, director of the agency, had offered Mrs. E. B. Wheeler, widow of one of the two highway patrolmen killed near Grapevine on Easter Sunday, a position in the bureau's office. She had accepted and had begun work shortly after her husband's funeral. News reporters now crowded around her desk and asked for her reaction. She told the newsmen that she thanked God.[22]

Meanwhile, Deputies Alcorn and Oakley arrived back at the death scene with Dr. Wade at approximately 10:15 A.M. The coroner made a brief examination of the bodies of the two bandits; he looked around the site and made several notes. Scanning the area, Wade was amazed at the number of people present at the scene. Some of them had driven out from Arcadia and had arrived before the coroner and deputies. Nearly everyone had begun collecting souvenirs such as shell cases, slivers of glass from the shattered car windows, and bloody pieces of clothing from the garments of Bonnie and Clyde. One eager man had opened his pocket knife and was reaching into the car to cut off Clyde's left ear. The doctor noted that one of the lawmen continued to move about the site shooting film with a movie camera. Realizing that there was no hope of conducting an investigation in the circuslike atmosphere of the ambush site, Wade turned to Hamer for help. The lawman, who had been talking with some of the gathered citizens, agreed, and he instructed the deputies to keep spectators away from the car.

Within minutes Gault returned from Gibsland with the tow truck. Sheriff Jordan and Deputy Oakley jumped into their car and drove in the lead position of the procession. They were followed by Hamer, Gault, and Dr. Wade in the unmarked Texas police car. Next in line came the wrecker pulling the Desert Sand Ford with its dreadful cargo. The death car was followed by Dallas County Deputies Alcorn and Hinton. Last, some of the spectators climbed into their cars and fell into line behind the pitiful parade. By the time the caravan reached Gibsland, the moving gallery had grown to almost twenty cars. Around 10:40 A.M. the column briefly stopped near the Gibsland

High School. Hearing the news, all the students ran out of their class-rooms and gathered around the battered Ford sedan. One girl jumped upon the right side running board and gasped as she discovered she was staring into what was left of Bonnie's mutilated face. The features were almost unrecognizable because of the fifty-odd bullet holes that had bashed her body. One shot in particular had struck the left jaw, passed through the mouth, smashing the front teeth, and gone out through the lips. The sight of caked blood nauseated the schoolgirl. She tried to jump off the running board and away from the sight, but her classmates wanted a closer look and pushed her up against the car door. The girl fainted but could not fall because of the crush of the crowd.[23]

Other reporters arrived at the Barrow and Parker homes and begged relatives for information about the upcoming funerals. Newsmen were told that both services would be conducted by the Reverend Clifford Andrews, pastor of the Gospel Lighthouse Church. When pressed about the possibility of a double funeral, Mrs. Barrow categorically stated that her son would have a separate service. Simultaneously, Emma Parker refused to allow her daughter to be buried alongside Clyde; she told reporters that Clyde had her daughter in life but now Bonnie belonged to her.[24]

While other newsmen talked with the relatives, Simmons and Moore, of the *Dallas Morning News,* arrived at Love Field and raced to the Long and Harman Air Charter hanger. Pilot Merrill Brock sat in the cockpit watching the dashboard gauges as the motor idled. When the journalists climbed into the airplane, Brock signaled the control tower that he was ready to taxi. Receiving a sign of clearance, he took off and headed east. Simmons waited until the aircraft had settled on a steady course and asked, "Where are we going to land?"

The pilot said, simply, "Shreveport."[25]

Meanwhile, reporters in Dallas newsrooms speculated on the amount of reward monies that would be presented to the posse for killing Bonnie and Clyde. Checking with the Dallas Police Department, they discovered that the amount could reach as high as $3,000. However, some of the reward offers were based on the stipulation that Bonnie and Clyde were convicted or proven responsible for specific crimes. Officers explained that many of the offers were posted for capture, dead or alive, of Bonnie and Clyde. Several tenders made in Texas were for the killers of the highway patrolmen on 1 April. Though many lawmen felt Bonnie and Clyde were responsible for this double murder, Floyd Hamilton and Billie White, Bonnie's sister, were being held for the slayings. Veteran officers speculated that these particular rewards might be held up pending disposition of the case. When journalists asked officers to review the total proposed prizes offered for the two outlaws, policemen ticked off $1,000 reward offered by L. G. Phares of the Texas Highway Patrol; $500 offered by the state of Texas; $600 pledged by a group of citizens in Joplin, Missouri; $100 from the state highway employees of Lufkin, Texas; $100 by the Chamber of Commerce of Seguin, Texas; and $340 by the Dallas Police Department.

Phares previously had stated that nearly $4,000 had been subscribed in a special fund to help pay for bringing Bonnie and Clyde into custody and that all remaining monies left in the account would be given to the men responsible for their capture. Dallas policemen told the reporters that Phares recently had intimated that there was a considerable amount of money not yet spent.[26]

Back in Gibsland, Louisiana, students were cleared away and the caravan of officers' cars, the wrecker pulling the death car, and the morbidly curious began to move again. Arriving in Arcadia, the motorcade moved along the main street and stopped at the entrance to Conger's Furniture Store and Funeral Parlor. The news had spread throughout the region, and the regular population had more than doubled. As the gaping onlookers pressed closer in the noonday heat, Dr. Wade jumped out of Hamer's car and hurried into the furniture store. He returned shortly with his helper, C. F. "Boots" Bailey, and two stretchers. Forcing his way through the crowd, Wade created a small space so the remains could be taken from the tan car. As Clyde was moved from his position behind the wheel, his partially shattered sunglasses fell into the street. Several people in the horde dived to grab them. When Wade and Bailey placed Clyde's body on the stretcher, several coins slipped from the pocket and rolled onto the street. People shoved one another for the precious souvenirs. When the men removed Bonnie's body, the crowd gasped as the amount of damage to the girl became evident. The murmur of the mob evaporated as the two bodies were carried into the store. Speaking for the gathering, one man uttered disillusionment that Clyde was so physically small in size. A writer concluded that the group felt foolish and frustrated because such a small outlaw had terrified them for so long.[27]

Around 11:20 A.M. Hamer slipped through the crowd to a public telephone and talked with Lee Simmons at the main office of the Texas Prison System in Huntsville. After hearing a complete description of the ambush, Simmons hung up and called for his driver to take him to Arcadia. Hamer next called Chief Phares of the Texas Highway Patrol. Learning of the two gangsters' deaths, Phares congratulated Hamer and then chartered a plane.[28]

When Hamer returned to the dusty main street, he found the officers straining to hold back the crush of people. As the bodies disappeared into the furniture store, a throng estimated by newsmen to be more than five hundred people jammed into the building. Wade and Bailey carried the stretchers through a door in a plywood wall into a huge mortuary room with large cadaver tables and embalming equipment.[29]

Deputy Sheriff Ted Hinton felt nauseated and began to shake. Looking around he saw that his friend Bob Alcorn was visibly trembling as well. The lawman shoved spectators aside and began making his way out of the store. The more Hinton saw of the crowds, the more he became convinced that the entire group had gone insane. In his book, *Ambush,* Hinton says that as he stepped from the front door of the furniture store, a woman grabbed him and kissed him. Astonished, the deputy looked closely at the woman. "Do I know you, Ma'am?"

"No, sir," said the woman.

"Then why did you kiss me?"

The woman beamed. "Deputy, I am Sophia Stone, a home demonstration agent from Ruston. Bonnie and Clyde kidnapped me last year. I am grateful to you for catching them."[30] Sophia Stone Cook remembers no such meeting.[31]

Inside the funeral parlor, Sheriff Jordan became concerned about his image with the parish voters, whom he would soon face again for reelection. As a good politician, he was eager to give the people an opportunity to view the bodies. Walking to the embalming table, he spoke softly to Dr. Wade. "How much longer will you need?"

Wade, who was thoroughly disgusted with the lack of control, snapped, "I'll work 'til I'm finished. Now leave me alone and let me do my job."

Jordan entered the furniture section of the store and announced repeatedly, "Folks, very soon the bodies will be placed on display." Despite Jordan's assurances, many of the more aggressive throng members climbed upon an arrangement of caskets placed against the plywood wall. Apparently, they expected to be able to see through the lattice work above the plywood wall. When the climbers found the wall was too high for them to see, they furiously jumped down on new furniture displays. Other spectators, unaware that the first climbers could not see, clambered upon the stacked coffins. S. A. Conger, the furniture store and funeral parlor director, soon realized that the climbers were damaging his new caskets and furniture and pleaded with the crowd to stay back from the wall. When the mob ignored him, Conger begged the lawmen to keep the mass of people off his equipment. The milling, overheated crowd refused to obey the orders of the authorities. Conger gave up trying to keep the group off his equipment and concentrated on holding the shoving throng out of the mortuary by stationing two employees to guard the door.

Bailey, a mortician with Conger's firm, helped Dr. Wade in the autopsy and arranged the evidence for the coroner's jury; he stopped for a moment to telephone his assistant, King Murphy, who was also an amateur photographer. Bailey suggested he bring his camera if he wanted to make some extraordinary photographs.[32]

Meanwhile, the clock struck 12:00 noon at the Parker home in Dallas. Within a few minutes, a hearse from the McKamy-Campbell Funeral Home arrived to pick up a member of the family to accompany the driver to Arcadia. Bonnie's mother wanted to go but her son, Buster, refused and insisted that he accompany the vehicle. Almost at the same time, Clyde's father and brother Jack left in another car. An ambulance followed them within a short time to pick up their relative's body.[33]

Back in Arcadia, Dr. Wade completed a brief cleaning of the remains and convened a coroner's jury consisting of M. W. Barker; G. C. Taylor; F. W. Pentecost, Jr.; B. G. Theus; and J. R. Goff. With Conger and Bailey assisting in the movement of the bodies and with the five jurors reluctantly looking on, Wade picked up a pad of notebook paper and pulled a stub of a pencil from his pocket. He looked once more at the shoving, milling crowd pressing against the plywood wall and began the grisly task by writing *Clyde Barrow* at the top of the page. Wade studied the body for several seconds to locate the distinguishing marks and tattoos. He first noted a description of the design on the outer right arm, a drawing of a girl with the name Grace printed underneath. On the inner right arm, Wade described the design of an anchor and a shield with the letters U. S. N. On the left arm, the coroner found a drawing of a dagger through a heart and the three letters E. B. W.; it had been there since he had dated the young lady in Dallas when he was sixteen. Turning to specific bullet wounds, Wade found that one missile had entered in front of the left ear, passed through the brain, and exited approximately two inches above the right ear. Another penetrated the forehead at the hairline just above the left eye. Wade discovered several wounds in and near the left shoulder joint and at least seven bullet holes in the inner part of the right knee. Another bullet had struck the fleshy section of the left thigh.

Two jurors became nauseated from the ghastly sights, the increasing sounds of the pressing crowd, and the oppressive odors of the funeral parlor; they ran out the back to an alley for a breath of fresh air. After patiently waiting for their return, the doctor turned Clyde's body over and described eight various gunshots in the right side of the back from the base of the neck downward. Approximately midway of the trunk, one of the eight bullets had destroyed the backbone. Wade jotted down several lacerations from the shattered window glass, surveyed the body one more time, and signed the report.[34]

About the time Wade was finishing Clyde's autopsy, Moore and Simmons, the two *Dallas Morning News* reporters finally arrived in Arcadia. After their chartered airplane landed in Shreveport about 1:00 P.M., they rented a car at the airfield and drove east on Highway 80. Arriving in Arcadia, they flashed their press passes and forced their way through the furniture store. They told the city marshal, who stood guarding the door in the plywood wall, that they were friends of Sheriff Schmid, and he admitted them to the examination area. Moore wanted to take pictures, but Dr. Wade insisted he wait until the examinations were complete. After watching Wade, Conger, and Bailey working in the close quarters, listening to the rising demands of the surly crowd, and suffering in the oppressive heat, the newsmen shoved their way outside. Jotting a few notes in his reporter's pad, Simmons looked at Moore, "Those people were shot to pieces."[35]

Back inside, Wade now turned to the table containing Bonnie's body; he decided to first list her personal belongings because several of Clyde's possessions, including a diamond stick pin, were missing from the box where Bailey had placed them. Wade recorded two diamond rings, a gold wedding ring on the third finger of her left hand, a lady's watch on her left wrist, a three-acorn broach pinned to the front of her dress, and a Roman Catholic crucifix on a chain around her neck. The coroner jotted down that her body was dressed in red shoes and a red dress; he removed the garments and underclothing and turned the body on its back. Wade found only one tattoo, located six inches above her right knee, with twin hearts and an arrow through them. On the right side of the hearts was the word *Roy* and on the left side, *Bonnie*.

Wade grimly began locating the numerous gunshots; he found one in the edge of the girl's hair approximately one and one-half inches above the left eye. Another had passed through the mouth on the left side. A third had entered the left side of the head and exited through the top of the skull. Wade continued his terrible work of finding bullet holes, jotting down the locations with the stubby pencil, and looking for more wounds. After several minutes he completed the ghastly physical survey and hurriedly signed the bottom of the page.

Wiping the perspiration from his brow, Wade glanced at the plywood wall. On the other side of the barricade, the sullen mutterings of the crowd rose and fell. Wade disgustedly shook his head and turned to the next job of outlining the statements indicating that Bonnie and Clyde had died from gunshot wounds inflicted by law enforcement authorities. He handed the pages to M. W. Barker, who quickly signed them and passed the documents on to the others. One by one the members of the coroner's jury attested to the causes of the deaths. While the two sheets passed about the room, Wade wrote out his final note of a statement of identification based on information furnished by Deputy Bob Alcorn. Wade finished writing the final note and handed it to the officer. As Alcorn signed the statement, Wade turned to the two morticians. "I'm through. As soon as the embalming is complete, you can let the vultures in, I suppose." After washing his hands, Wade followed Alcorn out of the funeral parlor. The jurors blankly looked at one another and followed.

Conger and Bailey hurriedly worked to complete the task of embalming the two bodies. Murphy grabbed his camera and snapped several flash pictures before the remains of the two outlaws were covered partially with sheets. Finally, the morticians wheeled the remains out to be viewed by the crowd. As the line quickly formed and began filing past the two bodies, the morticians checked their watches and saw that they indicated 2:15 P.M. Bonnie and Clyde had been dead about seven hours.[36]

On the main street outside Conger's store, local citizens told newsman Tom Simmons that Sheriff Jordan had been in charge of the ambush. The reporter tried to arrange an interview, but Jordan insisted that he was too busy. When the six posse members gathered for photographs, Simmons soon realized that Frank Hamer was the officer in charge. All the other authorities, especially Jordan, deferred to the former Ranger. After the photo session, Simmons identified himself, asked Hamer for a few minutes, and the two men strolled away from the crowd toward the courthouse. As they slowly walked across the courthouse lawn, Hamer described the ambush in detail. Simmons felt he saw the old lawman's eyes glisten with the excitement of the hunt as he outlined the massive firepower of the six posse members against the outlaws' car. The two men stood directly in front of the courthouse.

Hamer pointed to a bench on the side and said, "A few weeks ago, I sat on that seat and mapped out the plan that was carried out this morning." The old Ranger looked back at the Conger Furniture Store where the crowd continued to push and shove one another; he shook his head and rolled another cigarette. Simmons, knowing the officer would talk more when he was ready, remained silent.

Finally, Hamer continued, "The posse has been a great distance in the last two months. We've traveled through half a dozen states, but I always thought we would trap them around Arcadia."

To Simmons that statement verified what he had heard from several citizens in the Arcadia streets: that Ivan Methvin was the man who set up Bonnie and Clyde. He looked at Hamer. "Several people said Henry Methvin's father helped you. Anything to it?"

Hamer blew out a puff of smoke. "The idea's ridiculous."

Simmons looked away and smiled. He knew that Hamer's reputation for protecting his informants was the reason he continued to claim Methvin was not involved. Snitches trusted him and knew their confidence would never be betrayed.

As Hamer and Simmons sauntered back toward the milling crowd, a car carrying Clyde's father and brother arrived and pulled up to the Conger Furniture Store. When the old man identified himself and asked to see his son's body, the crowd melted back amid waves of whispers, "Clyde's daddy is coming in." Simmons checked his watch and saw that it was just after 3:00 P.M.[37]

After viewing his son's remains, the white-haired old man came back to the front of the store. An employee offered him a rocking chair, and the man sat down. The afternoon sun blazed in through the store windows as the grief-stricken man sat rocking. He alternated fanning and wiping his face with a large, white handkerchief. At times emotion overcame the old man and he wept into the cloth.[38]

Tom Simmons went back outside the store just as Lee Simmons, the Texas prison system director, arrived. Hamer joined him, and the two talked quietly. Tom Simmons edged closer and heard the Ranger say, "Well, they died with their guns in their hands." Rolling another cigarette, he said, "I've always had a fear of shooting women and children, though I've been a peace officer for a long time." Hamer took another puff of his cigarette. In the windless overheated afternoon, the smoke drifted straight up, and Hamer watched it rise. He shook his head, looked at Lee Simmons and said, "As guilty as I knew Bonnie to be and as well as I knew that she would get me if I didn't get her, I still had a funny feeling in my stomach when I saw her with her head slumped between her knees and the body riddled with bullets." Seeing reporters from the various newspapers approaching, Hamer, who earlier had refused to make a general statement to the press, now pointed to Lee Simmons and called out, "Okay, boys, here is the boss. I've been acting on his instructions, and any general statement will come from him."

As Tom Simmons continued to walk about the crowd, he saw Sheriff Smoot Schmid and Deputy Bill Decker arrive. Feeling that these lawmen could contribute nothing to the story, he pulled his photographer Moore into their cab and rode out to the ambush site; they arrived about 5:00 P.M. Souvenir hunters were frantically chopping down trees in the immediate area to dig out stray bullets. Others scanned the ground to find empty shell casings. A few people scrounged the area east of the road where the posse had waited. When an onlooker learned that the men were reporters from the *Dallas Morning News,* he proudly showed them bullets he had stolen from ammunition bags in the death car; the man acted as if the metal items had some intrinsic magical power. Totally disgusted, Simmons ordered the taxi to return them to Shreveport, and they flew back to Dallas.[39]

By evening the long lines of curious lookers had at last gotten their fill of gore; the milling crowd had finally tired of the excitement and drifted away. The ambulance that was to carry Clyde's body back to Dallas arrived, and the attendants made the arrangements for the removal of the body. The hearse hired to pick up Bonnie's body did not arrive until much later. Buster Parker and the driver, Johnny Bullock, had mistaken Acadia for Arcadia. But by midnight both bodies were enroute to Dallas.[40]

Epilogue

Clyde's remains were carried to the Sparkman-Holtz-Brand Funeral Home. During all of Thursday night and much of Friday, more than 30,000 eager citizens paraded past the casket. The Reverend Clifford Andrews of the Gospel Lighthouse Church conducted the services Friday in the funeral home chapel. Deputy Sheriff Ted Hinton who, like Deputy Bob Alcorn, knew the Barrow family well, attended the funeral. After the graveside ceremony, an airplane swooped down to drop a large spray of flowers on the grave. Clyde is buried on the left side of his brother Buck in a cemetery that sits on a small hill overlooking one of his favorite escape routes, U. S. Highway 80 in west Dallas. Souvenir hunters chipped away the first two headstones that the family placed at the grave site. Today their resting place is indicated by a marker that is encased in concrete.

Bonnie's body was not taken home as she had wished. Crowds blocked the street to her mother's home. Buster, Bonnie's brother, and Johnny Bullock, the hearse driver, decided to detour to the McKamy-Campbell Funeral Home. The following day, Friday, 25 May 1934, thousands lined Forest Avenue around the funeral home to view the tiny, shattered body. Emma Parker had maintained a life insurance policy on Bonnie all during the time she and Clyde were on the run. The proceeds of this policy paid for a magnificent funeral conducted by the Reverend Andrews in the funeral home chapel. Originally, Bonnie was buried in the old Fish Trap Cemetery. Later, the family moved her remains to a bright, open burial ground in north Dallas near Love Field. Hinton, who also attended Bonnie's funeral, estimated that about 150 family and friends sat inside the small sanctuary while hundreds waited outside. Dallas newspaper statistics indicated that between Wednesday, when Bonnie and Clyde were killed, and Saturday, when Bonnie was buried, readers eagerly purchased almost one-half million newspapers, which described the various events that occurred, beginning with the time the peace officers set up their ambush early Wednesday morning.

Frank Hamer, the leader of the posse that slew Bonnie and Clyde, remained in law enforcement and security work. He and a former police chief of Houston formed a security company that guarded various businesses in the area around Houston for more than a decade. Hamer sold his interest in the firm in 1949 and retired to his home in Austin. After suffering a heat stroke in 1953, Hamer never recovered his health; he died at age seventy-one on Sunday, 10 July 1955.

Ted Hinton remained a deputy for some time before going into the motel business. For many years Hinton's Motor Lodge was located on U.S. Highway 80, a short distance from the burial plots of Clyde and Buck Barrow. Hinton completed his manuscript for the book, *Ambush,* shortly before he died on 27 October 1977.

Henderson Jordan, who had been sheriff of Bienville Parish for eight years, was elected for another four-year term shortly after the ambush. Jordan attempted to keep the 1934 Ford sedan Bonnie and Clyde had stolen from Ruth Warren in Topeka, Kansas, in April 1934, but Mrs. Warren filed suit in U.S. District Court and forced him to give up possession. Jordan's chief deputy and fellow posse member, Prentiss Oakley, succeeded him. Both men passed away in the 1960s.

Raymond Hamilton was returned to the main Texas prison at Huntsville; his co-conspirator, Joe Palmer, who had been captured a short time afterward, joined him. Whitey Walker and Blackie Thompson, the two men who had actually robbed the McMurray Refinery on 8 November 1933, helped Hamilton and Palmer escape again on 22 July. In late March 1935, Hamilton and Ralph Fults reunited. Fults had been with Bonnie, Clyde, and Raymond when they burgled the hardware store in Kemp, Texas, back in 1932; he had taken the blame for the crime so Bonnie could go free. Fults and Hamilton robbed a bank in Mississippi in the spring of 1935. Several farmers joined the lawmen to pursue the two robbers. Stopping their getaway car near a dozen of these armed citizens, Fults and Hamilton asked the farmers, "What are you doing out here on the highway armed to the teeth?"

The leader replied, "We're looking for the bank robbers."

The outlaws leveled machine guns at the farmers and replied, "Well, you've found 'em." The outlaws kept the posse captive for several hours before releasing them unharmed. Both Ralph Fults and Raymond Hamilton were later captured and returned to Huntsville. Fults finished his sentence, became a celebrated anticrime speaker in the Dallas-Fort Worth area, and passed away in March 1993. Ironically, his last employment before retirement was as a security guard.

Joe Palmer, who was unknown by Dallas authorities, attended graveside services for Clyde; this hardened criminal and murderer was sickened by the disrespect of spectators who ripped souvenir flowers from Clyde's grave. After the funeral Palmer boarded a train for St. Louis and Chicago. Within a few days, he returned and was captured; he and Hamilton were defendants on trial for the death of Joseph Crowson, the Texas prison guard slain during their escape from the Eastham prison farm in January 1934. Lee Simmons helped the prosecution to ensure both men received the death penalty. In court Palmer attempted to shield Hamilton by saying that he himself had done all the shooting. Simmons, however, produced depositions from witnesses to the crime and demanded that Hamilton also pay with his life. He was successful: both Raymond Hamilton and Joe Palmer were sentenced to be electrocuted on the evening of 10 May 1935. Because Hamilton was terrified, Palmer agreed to go into the execution chamber first. Raymond Hamilton regained his composure and calmly followed his friend within five minutes.

Henry Methvin, whose father had assisted the officers in the ambush, was given a pardon by the state of Texas; he was not so fortunate in dealing with the state of Oklahoma. For the murder of Oklahoma Constable Calvin Campbell, Methvin was sentenced to death; he appealed the conviction on the grounds that Clyde had actually fired the fatal shots. Oklahoma later considered his cooperation with Louisiana and Texas authorities to be justification for clemency and reduced his sentence to life imprisonment. Paroled after ten years, Methvin returned home to Louisiana, where he operated a restaurant near a Minden, Louisiana, defense plant until the end of World War II. He was later struck and killed by a freight train; his father died in a massive car crash.

W. D. Jones, who told officers that he had been held prisoner by Bonnie and Clyde, was sentenced to fifteen years in prison for his involvement in the slaying of Malcolm Davis, the Tarrant County deputy sheriff. In 1968 when the movie *Bonnie and Clyde* was playing to packed theaters all over the world, Jones wrote an article for *Playboy* magazine about his adventures while riding with Bonnie and Clyde. He was later slain in Houston, Texas, by an unknown assailant wielding a shotgun.

Blanche Barrow was wanted on several charges: flight to avoid prosecution; harboring a fugitive; as an accomplice in the theft of Darby's automobile; and the kidnapping of Darby and Stone in Ruston, Louisiana, in 1933. The state of Missouri tried her as an accessory in the slaying of Constable Wes Harriman, and Joplin, Missouri, policeman Harry McGinnis in the gun battle in Joplin in April 1933. She received fifteen years. While she was confined in Missouri State Prison, doctors performed four surgeries on her right eye, which had been filled with automobile window glass during the fire fight at the Red Crown Tavern on 19 July 1933. Her current whereabouts and condition are unknown.

The mothers of the two outlaws, Cumie Barrow and Emma Parker, were tried for harboring fugitives. They were convicted but Federal Judge William Atwell allowed the women to sentence themselves. They chose a sentence of thirty days each. The two mothers tried repeatedly to gain possession of their infamous children's shotguns, rifles, and pistols. The ambush team kept them and later donated the entire arsenal to the Texas Rangers Museum, Fort Fisher, in Waco, Texas. Bonnie's mother lived until 1946. Clyde's mother was slightly wounded by a shotgun blast by an unknown attacker in 1938; she died of natural causes on 14 August 1942. Clyde's father survived his infamous sons and his wife until 19 June 1957. Despite all his grief and misery, Henry Barrow lived until age eighty-four. The Parker home was demolished to make way for a Sears office building. The Barrow home/service station is now a tortilla factory.

Bonnie's sister, Billie, had harbored neither Bonnie nor Clyde. Though cleared of the charge of the Texas Highway Patrolmen slayings on Easter Sunday in 1934, near Grapevine, the court found that she had aided the outlaws while caring for Bonnie when she was burned in the Wellington, Texas, car crash. She drew a sentence of one year and one day.

Mary O'Dare, the mistress of Raymond Hamilton, who some

considered responsible for the split between Bonnie and Clyde and Raymond Hamilton, also received a sentence of a year and a day.

Sheriff Holt Coffey, who was shot while trying to arrest Bonnie and Clyde at the Red Crown Courts in Platte City, Missouri, on 19 July 1933, recovered and served for many years as sheriff. Clarence Coffey, his son, who was wounded several times when he ran to help his father, survived and became a physician.

Officer Jimmy Persell, who was kidnapped by Bonnie and Clyde in Springfield, Missouri, on 31 January 1933, completed his career with the Springfield Police Department and retired.

Of all the people involved in the slaying of Bonnie and Clyde, Ruth Warren, owner of the auto that the couple had stolen in Topeka, Kansas, in April 1934, gained most from their ambush. Dr. Carroll Rich, retired University of North Texas professor, grew up in Arcadia, Louisiana, and thoroughly researched the history of Bonnie and Clyde's last days as well as the pilgrimage of the car. He found the purchase price of her 1934 Ford sedan was $835. After Clyde had added 2,500 miles to the odometer and the posse had riddled the desert tan body with more than 150 bullets, collectors' offers ranged from $3,000 to $25,000 for the death car. When Ruth Warren arrived in Bienville Parish to claim her car, Sheriff Henderson Jordan, one of the ambush team, refused to turn it over. Jordan told Mrs. Warren the release of the auto would cost her $15,000 and directed her to his attorneys. Mrs. Warren hired an Arcadia attorney, W. D. Goff, to represent her. Goff soon realized that Jordan had allowed avarice to overwhelm his better judgment. Goff pointed out that by setting the value of the death car at a price exceeding $3,000, Jordan had ensured the case would be heard in federal court. Sheriff Jordan initially refused to surrender the car to U.S. marshals sent by the court to Arcadia to retrieve it. Federal Judge Benjamin Dawkins threatened Jordan with jail if the car was not produced. Mrs. Warren got her car and drove it to Shreveport, Louisiana, where it was put on a truck and moved back to Topeka, Kansas. For several days the tan Ford sat in the Warren driveway, complete with 160 bullet holes and an interior that reeked with dried blood. Mrs. Warren leased the death car to John Castle of United Shows. When he broke the contract, she repossessed the car and rented it to a carnival operator named Charles Stanley.

When the Warrens later divorced, Ruth kept the title to the car. Stanley later bought the car from Mrs. Warren for $3,500 and exhibited it at an amusement park in Cincinnati, Ohio, from 1940 to 1952. Ted Toddy bought the car from Stanley in 1952 for $14,500. After sitting in a warehouse for years, the car became famous again with the Warren Beatty-Arthur Penn movie, and a new generation of car fans emerged. Toddy told Rich, "I've seen people kneel before it or do the sign of the cross. Women have walked away weeping." Rich estimates the auto has earned over one million dollars.

Bonnie and Clyde still fascinate Americans though nearly sixty years have passed since they died in the ambush. Perhaps the main reason is their romantic involvement. Few writers agree on the exact circumstances of their criminal acts; most agree that they were in love. W. D. Jones said, "Clyde trusted one person: Bonnie."

Next, the couple's exploits received a great deal of publicity from the contemporary media. The outlaw couple were good copy and helped sell newspapers during the most dreadful part of the worst economic depression in the history of the United States. Editors and publishers not only gave extensive coverage to every incident involving Bonnie and Clyde but enlarged the news story whenever possible. Moreover, the bandits themselves covertly but happily contributed both snapshot pictures and primitive poetry to nourish the legends that rapidly grew up around them.

Third, Bonnie and Clyde's apparent ability to escape various police traps by dashing through huge ranks of officers contributed to their charisma and captivation. Barrow's driving skills, usually at seventy miles per hour, certainly aided the many escapes, but careful examination of available evidence indicates that the bandits were not so much infallible as the pursuing lawmen were disorganized, intimidated by news reports, and incompetent.

Fourth, though Clyde was a criminal, he never murdered in cold blood; he killed swiftly when angered, as with Howard Hall in Sherman, Texas, or to escape as in the deadly Joplin, Missouri, shootout. Compared, however, with a contemporary such as Mad-Dog Coll or a 1990s style drive-by shooter, he was relatively moderate.

Finally, the events surrounding the deaths of Bonnie and Clyde enhanced the public's perception of their charm. Reports stated that they died simultaneously and virtually in one another's arms. Many citizens viewed the gruesome climax as a modern Shakespearian tragedy played out on a dusty lane in rural Louisiana.

Today that road is covered with asphalt. Also paved is a roadside area that indicates the spot where the lives of Bonnie and Clyde ended in a barrage of machine guns, rifles, and shotguns so long ago. A simple white granite rectangle sits on a stone slab at the side of the Sailes Road, and chiseled into the face is:

At this site May 23, 1934
Clyde Barrow
and
Bonnie Parker
were killed by
law enforcement officials
Erected by
Bienville Parish Police Jury

From the site, the road stretches out north and south through lovely, quiet woodlands with no houses visible. The area is peaceful and extremely quiet. The people that live near the road are hard-working, friendly, and not given to fabricating stories. But some of them claim that occasionally, on moonless spring nights when the weather is very humid, you can hear a Ford V-8 automobile traveling along the deserted road at high speed—perhaps as fast as seventy miles per hour.

Notes
Index

Notes

1. Bonnie and Clyde

1. Jan Fortune, *Fugitives: The Story of Clyde Barrow and Bonnie Parker* (Dallas, np., 1934), p. 31.
2. Carroll Y. Rich, "The Day They Shot Bonnie and Clyde," *Hunters and Healers* 9, no. 2 (1976): 35.
3. *Denton (Texas) Record Chronicle*, 24 May 1934; *Fugitives*, pp. 27–32.
4. *Fugitives*, pp. 25–27.
5. *Dallas Morning News*, 24 May 1934.

2. A Legacy of Violence

1. *Fugitives*, p. 28.
2. *Ellis County, Texas, Vital Statistics*, volume 1909.
3. Ted Hinton, *Ambush* (Austin: Shoal Creek Publishers, 1979), p. 173.
4. Personal interview, Mrs. Charles Kilgo, Dallas, Texas, 29 October 1975.
5. *Fugitives*, p. 29.
6. Ibid.
7. Ibid.
8. *Denton (Texas) Record Chronicle*, 30 November 1929.
9. Ibid.
10. Ibid.
11. Ibid.
12. Ibid.
13. Newspaper interviews with Denton Police Officers Clint Starr and T. E. Jones in *Denton (Texas) Record Chronicle*, 30 November 1929.
14. *Fugitives*, p. 30.
15. Newspaper interview with County Attorney Earl Street in *Denton (Texas) Record Chronicle*, 14 January 1930.
16. *Fugitives*, p. 31.
17. *Denton (Texas) Record Chronicle*, 14 January 1930.
18. *Fugitives*, p. 31.

3. Bonnie and Clyde Are the Barrow Gang

1. *Fugitives*, p. 32.
2. Ibid.
3. *Ambush*, p. 8.
4. *Fugitives*, p. 33.
5. Ibid.
6. Ibid.
7. Ibid.
8. *Waco (Texas) News-Tribune*, 10 and 12 March 1930.
9. Ibid.; *Fugitives*, p. 33.
10. Newspaper interviews with the jailer I. P. Stanford and Mrs. J. M. Byrd in *Waco (Texas) News-Tribune*, 23 March 1930; *Fugitives*, p. 33.
11. *Fugitives*, p. 33.
12. Newspaper interview with Clyde Barrow in *Waco (Texas) News-Tribune*, 23 March 1930.
13. Newspaper interviews with Sheriff Leslie Stegall and Assistant District Attorney Jimmy Stanford in *Waco (Texas) News-Tribune*, 23 March 1938.
14. Newspaper interview with Assistant District Attorney Frank Williford in *Waco (Texas) News-Tribune*, 23 March 1930.
15. Ibid.; *Fugitives*, p. 34.
16. *Ambush*, p. 11.
17. *Fugitives*, p. 35.
18. Ibid.
19. Ibid.
20. Ibid.
21. Ibid.; *Dallas Morning News*, 10 June 1984.
22. *Dallas Morning News*, 10 June 1984; personal interview with Ralph Fults, Dallas, Texas, 21 October 1981.

23. *Fugitives*, p. 36.
24. *Dallas Morning News*, 10 June 1984.

4. They Call Them Cold-Blooded Killers

1. Newspaper interviews with Bedell Jordan and Marvin Kitchen in *Hillsboro (Texas) Evening-Mirror*, 14 March 1933.
2. Newspaper interview with Martha Bucher in *Hillsboro (Texas) Evening-Mirror*, 14 March 1933.
3. *Fugitives*, p. 102.
4. *Hillsboro (Texas) Evening-Mirror*, 14 March 1933; *Fugitives*, p. 107.
5. *Dallas Morning News*, 7 May 1932.
6. *Fugitives*, p. 111.
7. Newspaper interviews with Elsie Wullschleger, Joe Neuhoff, Henry Neuhoff, Dallas Police Captain A. F. Deere, and Dallas Police Sergeant Roy Richburg in *Dallas Morning News*, 2 August 1932.
8. Ibid.; *Fugitives*, p. 39; *Dallas Morning News*, 7 August 1932.
9. *Atoka (Oklahoma) Indian Citizen-Democrat*, 11 August 1932.
10. *Fugitives*, p. 114.
11. Newspaper interviews with Special Officer L. C. Harris, County Attorney J. B. Maxey, Cleve Brady, John Redden, Lonnie Redden, and Everett Milligan in *Atoka (Oklahoma)*

Indian Citizen-Democrat, 11 August 1932.

12. *Fort Worth Star-Telegram*, 8 August 1932.

13. *Fugitives*, p. 116.

14. Newspaper interview with Constable H. A. Hunt in *Fort Worth Star-Telegram*, 9 August 1932.

15. Newspaper interview with Everett Milligan in *Atoka (Oklahoma) Indian Citizen-Democrat,* 11 August 1932.

16. Personal memoir of kidnapping of Joe Johns. "Kidnapped by Bandits," *Carlsbad (New Mexico) Current-Argus*, 19 August 1932.

5. Hang It on Bonnie and Clyde

1. *Ambush*, p. 28; *Fugitives*, p. 126; Lee Simmons, *Assignment: Huntsville* (Austin: University of Texas Press, 1939), p. 121.

2. *Sherman (Texas) Democrat*, 12 October 1932.

3. Newspaper interviews with Homer Glaze, Mrs. L. C. Butler, Sherman Police Chief Gradie Thompson, Officer B. V. Atnip, and Deputy Sheriff O. J. Nearberry in *Sherman (Texas) Democrat*, 12 October 1932; *Fugitives*, p. 96.

4. Ibid.

5. Newspaper interviews with Sheriff Frank Reese, District Attorney Joe P. Cox, and A. B. Little in *Sherman (Texas) Democrat*, 13 October 1932.

6. *Fugitives*, p. 168.

7. *Dallas Morning News*, 15 December 1932.

8. Newspaper interviews with Dallas County Deputy Sheriffs Denver Seale and Ed Caster, Hill County Deputy Sheriffs P. F. Wilkerson and Kelly Rush in *Dallas Morning News*, 15 December 1932.

9. W. D. Jones, "Riding with Bonnie and Clyde," *Playboy* 15 (1968): 151.

10. Newspaper interviews with Tillie Johnson, Henry Krauser, and Clarence Krauser in *Temple (Texas) Daily-Telegram*, 26 December 1932.

11. *Fugitives*, p. 133.

12. *Temple (Texas) Daily-Telegram*, 26 December 1932.

13. *Fugitives*, p. 133.

6. They Say They Are Heartless and Mean

1. Newspaper interviews with W. A. Schumaker and Jesse Trigg in *Dallas Morning News*, 7 January 1933.

2. Ibid.; *Fugitives*, pp. 137–39.

3. *Fugitives*, pp. 140–41.

4. Newspaper interviews with Texas Ranger J. A. Van Noy, Tarrant County Deputy Sheriffs Dusty Rhodes and Walter Evans, and Dallas Deputy Sheriff Fred T. Bradberry in *Dallas Morning News*, 7 and 8 January 1933.

5. *Fugitives*, 137–40.

6. *Dallas Morning News*, 8 January 1933.

7. *Fugitives*, pp. 140–41.

8. Newspaper interview with John Persell in "Kidnapped by Bonnie and Clyde," *Kansas City Times*, 13 September 1972.
9. *Fugitives*, p. 145; "Riding with Bonnie and Clyde," p. 163.
10. *Fugitives*, p. 145–46;"Kidnapped by Bonnie and Clyde," *Kansas City Times*, 13 September 1972.
11. *Fugitives*, p. 145.
12. Newspaper interviews with Missouri Patrolmen George B. Kahler and W. E. Grammer, and Joplin Police Officer Tom De Graff in *St. Louis Post-Dispatch*, 14 April 1933.
13. *Fugitives*, p. 145.
14. Ibid.
15. Ibid.
16. Ibid.; *St. Louis Post-Dispatch*, 14 April 1933.
17. Newspaper interview with Dallas County Sheriff Smoot Schmid, *Dallas Morning News*, 15 April 1933.
18. *Ambush*, p. 39.
19. Ibid.; *Fugitives*, p. 58.
20. *Fugitives*, p. 152.
21. *St. Louis Post-Dispatch*, 15 April 1933.

7. From Heartbreak Some People Have Suffered

1. *Fugitives*, p. 61.
2. Carolyn Carver, "A Day with Bonnie and Clyde," personal interview with Sophia (Stone) Cook *North Louisiana Historical Association* II, no. 2 (1971): 60; personal interview with Sophia (Stone) Cook, Ruston, Louisiana, 27 January 1982.
3. *Ruston (Louisiana) Daily-Leader*, 28 April 1933.
4. *Fugitives*, p. 162; personal interview with Sophia (Stone) Cook, Ruston, Louisiana, 27 January 1982.
5. Personal memoir of H. Dillard Darby of his kidnapping written for the *Ruston (Louisiana) Daily-Leader*, 29 April 1933.
6. *Fugitives*, p. 162.
7. Newspaper interview with Sheriff A. J. Thigpen in *Ruston (Louisiana) Daily-Leader*, 28 April 1933.
8. Ibid.; "A Day with Bonnie and Clyde"; *Ruston (Louisiana) Daily-Leader*, 29 April 1933.
9. Newspaper interview with Nick Mialos in *Ruston (Louisiana) Daily-Leader,* 29 April 1933.
10. *Ruston (Louisiana) Daily-Leader*, 29 April 1933.
11. *Fugitives*, p. 174; *Redfield (Iowa) Review*, 27 July 1933.
12. *Hillsboro (Texas) Evening-Mirror*, 19 May 1933.
13. Newspaper interview with Marvin Kitchen, Knox Smith, and R. Q. Dehart in *Hillsboro (Texas) Evening-Mirror*, 14 June 1933.
14. *Hillsboro (Texas) Evening-Mirror*, 7 June 1933.
15. Ibid., 9 June 1933.
16. *Fugitives,* p. 168; *Ambush*, p. 50.
17. *Ambush*, p. 51; "Riding with Bonnie and Clyde," p. 165.
18. Newspaper interview with Tom Pritchard, Mrs. Tom Pritchard,

and John Cartwright in *Amarillo (Texas) Daily News*, 12 June 1933.

19. Ibid.; *Fugitives*, pp. 174–75.

20. *Fugitives*, pp. 174–75.

21. *Fugitives*, p. 175–76; *Ambush*, pp. 55–56; personal memoir of kidnapping of Paul Hardy as written by Paul Hardy and Jimmie Gillentine, "I Was Taken for a Ride," *True Detective* 28, no. 1 (April 1937): 46–51.

22. *Alma (Arkansas) Southwestern American,* 23 June 1933.

23. Ibid.; *Fugitives*, p. 176.

24. *Alma (Arkansas) Southwestern American,* 23 June 1933.

25. *Fugitives*, p. 177.

26. Ibid., pp. 178–81; *Alma (Arkansas) Southwestern American,* 23 June 1933.

27. *Fugitives*, p. 177.

**8. From Weariness
Some People Have Died**

1. *Fugitives*, pp. 185–86.

2. Newspaper interviews with Delbert Crabtree, H. D. Hauser, William Baxter, Holt Coffey, Thomas Witherspoon, L. A. Ellis, George Borden, George Highfill, and Lincoln Baker in *St. Louis Post-Dispatch*, 20 July 1933; "Shootout with Bonnie and Clyde," *Kansas City Star*, 7 September 1978.

3. Ibid.; *Fugitives*, p. 178.

4. *St. Louis Post-Dispatch,* 20 July 1933; "Shootout with Bonnie and Clyde."

5. *Fugitives*, p. 190.

6. "Kidnapped by Bonnie and Clyde"; "Shootout with Bonnie and Clyde."

7. "Shootout with Bonnie and Clyde."

8. Ibid.

9. *Fugitives*, pp. 191–93.

10. "Shootout with Bonnie and Clyde."

11. *Fugitives*, pp. 191–93.

12. *Fugitives*, p. 190.

13. Newspaper interview with Sheriff C. A. Knee and John Love in *Redfield (Iowa) Review*, 27 July 1933.

14. *Fugitives*, p. 192.

15. Ibid.; *Redfield (Iowa) Review*, 27 July 1933.

16. *Fugitives*, p. 193.

17. Ibid.

18. Ibid.; *Redfield (Iowa) Review*, 27 July 1933.

19. Ibid.

20. Newspaper interviews with Valley Fellers, Marvin Fellers, and Walter Spillars in *Redfield (Iowa) Review*, 27 July 1933; *Fugitives*, p. 193.

21. *Fugitives*, p. 193.

22. *Fugitives*, pp. 193–94.

23. Ibid.

24. *Fugitives*, p. 196.

25. Ibid.

26. *Dallas Morning News*, 30 July 1933.

27. *Dallas Morning News*, 1 August 1933.

28. Newspaper interviews with F. E. Jarrett, Rufus Brene, J. N. Maynor, and Sheriff Earl Price in *Tyler (Texas) Daily-Courier*, 8 November 1933.

29. Ibid.

30. Ibid.; *Dallas Morning News*, 10 November 1933.
31. *Troup (Texas) Banner*, 23 November 1933; *Ambush*, p. 98.

9. The Road Gets Dimmer and Dimmer

1. *Ambush*, pp. 103–4.
2. Ibid.; *Fugitives*, pp. 211–14.
3. *Fugitives*, pp. 105–6; newspaper interviews with Dallas County Sheriff Smoot Schmid, Deputy Ed Caster, Deputy Bob Alcorn, Deputy Ted Hinton, Thomas R. James, Paul Reich, and Wade Collier in *Dallas Morning News*, 23 November 1933.
4. Letter in Ford Motor Company files, Clyde Barrow to Henry Ford, 13 April 1934.
5. *Ambush*, p. 107.
6. *Fugitives*, pp. 222–23; *Assignment: Huntsville*, pp. 124–25.
7. *Ambush*, p. 116.
8. *Assignment: Huntsville*, pp. 124–25.
9. *Assignment: Huntsville*, p. 125.
10. *Assignment: Huntsville,* p. 165.
11. *Assignment: Huntsville*, pp. 124–25.
12. Ibid.
13. Ibid.; *Dallas Morning News*, 17 January 1934.
14. *Fugitives*, p. 222.
15. *Assignment: Huntsville*, p. 145.
16. *Assignment: Huntsville*, p. 125.
17. Ibid.; *Fugitives*, pp. 223.
18. *Dallas Morning News*, 17 January 1934; *Assignment: Huntsville*, p. 145.
19. Ibid.
20. *Fugitives*, p. 223.
21. *Assignment: Huntsville*, pp. 166–67.
22. *Assignment: Huntsville,* p. 145; *Dallas Morning News*, 6 April 1934.
23. *Fugitives*, pp. 223–24.
24. *Assignment: Huntsville*, pp. 166–67.
25. *Fugitives*, pp. 223–24.
26. *Assignment: Huntsville*, pp. 126–28; Walter Prescott Webb, *The Texas Rangers* (Austin: University of Texas Press, 1937), p. 540.
27. *Fugitives*, p. 224; *Ambush*, pp. 122–23.

10. Sometimes You Can Hardly See

1. *Dallas Morning News*, 28 February 1934; *Ambush*, p. 123.
2. Newspaper interview with L. L. Henry, Lancaster, Texas, *Dallas Morning News*, 28 February 1934; newspaper interview with Olin Worley, Lancaster, Texas, *Dallas Morning News*, 28 February 1934.
3. Newspaper interviews with Deputy Sheriff John Ciesa and Deputy Sheriff Brian Peck in *Dallas Morning News*, 28 February 1934.
4. *Fugitives*, p. 225.
5. Ibid.; *Dallas Morning News*, 31 March 1934.
6. Newspaper interview with Mrs. Cameron Gunter in *Houston Post*, 2 April 1934.

11. They Wouldn't Give Up 'Til They Died

1. *Fugitives*, p. 231.
2. Newspaper interviews with Patrolman Polk Ivy, Mr. and Mrs. Fred Gizzal, Corbin Crews, and Dr. J. A. Ellison in *Dallas Morning News*, 2 April 1934.
3. *Fugitives*, pp. 231–32.
4. *Dallas Morning News*, 2 April 1934.
5. *Assignment: Huntsville*, p. 132.
6. Ibid.
7. Ibid.
8. *The Texas Rangers*, p. 540; *Assignment: Huntsville,* pp. 130–31.
9. Ibid.
10. *Dallas Morning News*, 24 May 1934; *Ambush*, pp. 138–39.
11. *Ambush*, pp. 138–39; *Fugitives*, p. 232.
12. Newspaper interviews with Police Chief Percy Boyd, Charles Dobson, and Jack Boydston in *Miami (Oklahoma) Daily News-Review*, 8 April 1934.
13. Ibid.
14. Newspaper interview with Sheriff Dee Watters in *Miami (Oklahoma) Daily News-Review*, 8 April 1934; newspaper interview with County Attorney Perry Porter in *Miami (Oklahoma) Daily News-Review* 8 April 1934; *Dallas Morning News*, 10 April 1934.
15. Newspaper interview with A. N. Butterfield and John Butterfield in *Miami (Oklahoma) Daily News-Review*, 8 April 1934.
16. Ibid.
17. *Assignment: Huntsville*, p. 132.
18. Newspaper interview with Police Chief Percy Boyd and Blaine Boone in *Miami (Oklahoma) Daily News-Review*, 8 April 1934.
19. Newspaper interview with Andy Walker in *Miami (Oklahoma) Daily News-Review*, 8 April 1934.
20. Newspaper interview with Blaine Boone in *Miami (Oklahoma) Daily News-Review*, 8 April 1934.
21. Ibid.; *Dallas Morning News*, 10 April 1934.
22. Ibid.
23. *Dallas Morning News*, 10 April 1934.
24. *Miami (Oklahoma) Daily News-Review*, 8 April 1934.
25. Ibid.
26. Ibid.
27. *Dallas Morning News*, 10 April 1934.
28. Ibid.
29. *Miami (Oklahoma) Daily News-Review*, 8 April 1934.
30. *Dallas Morning News*, 10 April 1934.

12. Death Came Out to Meet Them

1. Carroll Y. Rich, "Clyde Barrow's Last Car," *Journal of Popular Culture* 8, no. 3 (1977): pp. 631–32.
2. Ibid.

3. "Clyde Barrow's Last Car," p. 632; *Assignment: Huntsville*, pp. 165–66; *Fugitives*, pp. 239–41.
4. *Fugitives*, pp. 239–40.
5. Carroll Y. Rich, "The Day They Shot Bonnie and Clyde," *Hunters and Healers* 9, no. 2 (1977): 36.
6. Ibid.; *Assignment Huntsville,* pp. 166–67; *Ambush*, p. 157.
7. Ibid.
8. Ibid.
9. "The Day They Shot Bonnie and Clyde," p. 38.
10. Ibid.
11. *Dallas Morning News*, 24 May 1934.
12. "The Day They Shot Bonnie and Clyde," p. 38.
13. *Dallas Morning News*, 24 May 1934.
14. Ibid.; "The Day They Shot Bonnie and Clyde," p. 39; *Ambush*, pp. 168–71.
15. *Dallas Morning News*, 24 May 1934.
16. *(Dallas) Daily Times-Herald*, 24 May 1934.
17. *Fugitives*, p. 238.
18. *(Dallas) Daily Times-Herald*, 24 May 1934.
19. *Dallas Morning News*, 24 May 1934.
20. *Fort Worth Star-Telegram*, 23 May 1934.
21. *Assignment: Huntsville*, p. 133.
22. *Dallas Morning News*, 23 May 1934.
23. "The Day They Shot Bonnie and Clyde," p. 39.
24. "The Day They Shot Bonnie and Clyde," p. 40; *Fort Worth Star-Telegram*, 24 May 1934.
25. *Dallas Morning News*, 24 May 1934.
26. Ibid.; *Fort Worth Star-Telegram, 24 May 1934.*
27. "The Day They Shot Bonnie and Clyde," p. 39.
28. *Austin American-Statesman*, 24 May 1934.
29. *Dallas Morning News*, 24 May 1934.
30. *Ambush*, pp. 168–71.
31. Personal interview with Sophia (Stone) Cook, Arcadia, Louisiana, 27 January 1982.
32. Carroll Y. Rich, "The Autopsy of Bonnie and Clyde," *Western Folklore* 29, no. 1 (1974): p. 29.
33. *Shreveport Times*, 24 May 1934.
34. "The Autopsy of Bonnie and Clyde," pp. 29–30.
35. *Dallas Morning News*, 24 May 1934.
36. "The Autopsy of Bonnie and Clyde," pp. 30–31.
37. Newspaper interview with Frank Hamer in *Dallas Morning News,* 24 May 1934; "The Autopsy of Bonnie and Clyde," pp.31–32.
38. Ibid.; "The Autopsy of Bonnie and Clyde," pp. 31–32.
39. *Dallas Morning News*, 24 May 1934.
40. Ibid.; "The Day They Shot Bonnie and Clyde," p. 42; "The Autopsy of Bonnie and Clyde," pp. 32–33.

Index

Abernathy, Emery: participant, McClennan County, TX, jailbreak, 22–26

Alcorn, Bob: searched Joplin, MO, hideout, 65; physical description, 125; assigned to posse, 125; identifies Bonnie and Clyde at Durant, OK, 127; Shreveport, LA, escape of the Barrow gang, 140; firepower of the posse, 142; in position at the ambush site, 142; slaying of Bonnie and Clyde, 142–43; brought parish coroner from Arcadia, LA, 143–47; removal of Bonnie's and Clyde's bodies to Arcadia, LA, 147; experienced sickness at mortuary crowds, 150; signed Dr. Wades's statement of causes of deaths, 153

Allen, Jim: witness, Miami, OK, gun fight, 130

Andrews, Clifford: minister, funerals of Bonnie and Clyde, 148

Atnip, B. V.: investigator, Howard Hall murder, 50

Bailey, C. F. "Boots": assisted Dr. Wade in autoposies, 149, 151; helped embalm Bonnie's and Clyde's remains, 151; photographed remains of Bonnie and Clyde, 153

Baker, Lincoln: witness, Platt City, MO, gun fight, 90–92

Barker, M. W.: coroner's jury member, 151; signed Dr. Wade's coroner's report, 153

Barrow, Blanche (Caldwell): joined Barrow gang, 62–63; Joplin, MO, hideout, 63; witness, Joplin, MO, gun fight, 64–65; Dallas, TX, visit, 79; Commerce, TX, visit, 79; Platt City, MO, gun fight, 90–92; wounded in gun fight, 92; Dexfield, IA, gun fight, 95–96; Perry, IA, 97; life in prison, 160

Barrow, Clyde: no cold-blooded killer, 3; physical description, 5; Barrow family when Clyde was born, 9; birth recorded incorrectly, 9; love of guns and music, 9; obsession with guns, 9; disliked school, 9; employee of

Barrow, Clyde *(Continued)*
Proctor and Gamble, 9; considered proposing marriage to sister of co-worker, 10; arrested by police the first time, 10; in Wichita Falls, TX, Dallas, TX, with "Grace," 10; criminal career, 11; Henrietta, TX, burglary and car theft, 11–12; Denton, TX, burglary, 12–13; tried for car theft, 14; introduced to Bonnie, 15; arrested at Bonnie's home, 18; transferred from Denton, TX, to Waco, TX, 18; persuaded Bonnie to bring a gun to him in McClennan County Jail, 19–20; jail break, 23–24; captured at Middleton, OH, 26; accused of Howard Gouge murder, 27; transferred to Huntsvillle (TX) Prison, 28; encouraged Bonnie to stand by him, 28; depressed at death of yough prisoner, 29; fellow convict cuts off toes, 29; released from Texas prison, 29; appeared changed after prison, 29; visited Bonnie after prison release, 29; Wooster, MA, job 29–30; quits Wooster job, 30; criticized by sister Nell, 30; promised to avoid gangster friends, 31; robberies with Raymond Hamilton and Frank Clause, 32; Bucher gift shop and murder of John Bucher, 32-35; lied to his family regarding Bucher crimes, 36, 43; robberies with Frank Clause, 36–37; attitude after Atoka, OK, killing, 43; Howard Hall robbery and attacked by the posse, 143; description of death, 143; funeral, 157

Barrow, Cumie: physical description, 9; visited Clyde in McClennan County Jail, 27; Commerce, TX, visit, 79–80; Perry, IA, 97; Dallas, TX, reunion, 100–101; Dallas, TX, gun fight, 100–101; Lancaster, TX, bank robbery, 114–15; Greenville, TX, reunion, 112–13; Grand Prairie, TX, reunion, 114; last meeting with Clyde, 136–38; reaction to deaths of Bonnie and Clyde, 146; tried for harboring fugitives, 160; wounded by shotgun blast, 160; death, 160

Barrow, Henry: background, 8; reaction to deaths of Bonnie and Clyde, 146; drove to Arcadia, LA, to retrieve Clyde's body, 151; waiting to claim Clyde's body, 154–55; death, 160

Barrow, Jack: drove to Arcadia, LA, to retrieve Clyde's body, 151

Barrow, L. C.: accompanied Mrs. Barrow to Perry, IA, 97; at Buck Barrow's funeral, 98; Lancaster, TX, bank robbery, 114–15

Barrow, Marvin Ivan (Buck): physical description, 10; led Clyde into a criminal life, 10; convicted of theft over $50, 10; Henrietta, TX, burglary and car theft, 11–12; Denton, TX, burglary, 12–13; captured by Denton, TX, policeman, 14; tried for Denton, TX, burglary, 14–15; sentenced to Texas state prison system, 15; escaped prison farm, 29; married Blanche Caldwell, 29; surrendered to Texas prison authorities, 29; paroled from Texas prison, 61; plans to visit Clyde, 62; Joplin, MO, gun fight,

64–65; Darby-Stone kidnapping, 76–78; Commerce, TX, visit, 79–80; Alma, AR, bank robbery, 84; Fayetteville, AR, grocery robbery, 84–85; Alma, AR, slaying, 85; Washington County, OK, car theft, 86; Platt City, MO, gun fight, 90–92; wounded in gun fight, 91; Dexfield, IA, gun fight, 95–96; Perry, IA, 97; death of, 98; funeral, 98

Barrow, Marvin Ivan, Jr.: attends father's (Buck Barrow's) funeral, 98

Barrow gang: burst upon American scene, 1; films on, 2; the Great Depression and the gang, 3; smuggled weapons into Texas prison, 4; Kaufman, TX, burglary, 31; capture of Bonnie and Ralph Fults, 31–32; return to Dallas, 37; Prairie hideout, 39; trip to Oklahoma, 40; Atoka, OK shooting, 40–41; Clayton, OK, auto stolen, 41; Lonnie Redden kidnapped, 41; Grandview, TX, auto stolen, 42; Nettie Stamps' farm hideout, 43–44; Joe Johns kidnapped, 44–45; Victoria, TX, auto stolen, 46; Wharton, TX, shoot-out, 46–47; Grand murder, 47–49; Oronogo, MO, bank robbery, 51–52; Doyle Johnson murder, 54–56; Lillie McBride home, gun fight, 59–60; Persell kidnapping, 61–62; Joplin, MO, gun fight 64–65; Darby-Stone kidnapping, 76–78; Commerce, TX, visit, 79–80; Wellington, TX, accident, 81–82; nursed Bonnie, 83; Enid, OK, car theft, 87; Fort Dodge, KS, robberies, 89; Platt City, MO, gun fight, 90–92; Perry, IA, car theft, 93; Dexfield, IA, gun fight, 95–96; Dallas, TX, gun fight, 100–101; Dallas, TX, reunion, 100–101; Eastham prison farm break, 101, 106; Greenville, TX, reunion, 112–13; Grand Prairie, TX, reunion, 114; Lancaster, TX, bank robbery, 114–15; breakup of Barrow gang, 116; Easter slaying of Texas highway patrolmen, 123–24; Miami, OK, gun fight, 127–28; Topeka, KS, car theft, 135; last meeting with their families, 136–38; Shreveport, LA, escape, 140; deceived by Ivan Methvin at the ambush site, 142–43

Baxter, William; participant, Platt City, MO, gun fight, 80–90

Beatty, Carl: Clyde's alias, Joplin, MO, hideout, 65

Bissett, Lillian: witness, Howard Gouge murder, 27

Bonnie and Clyde: driving toward ambush, 5; physical descriptions, 5; clothing and sense of fashion, 5; accepted death as inevitable, 6; ambush site, 6; heritage and background, 8; poem: "The Story of Bonnie and Clyde," 136–38

Bonnie and Clyde (film), 2

Boone, Blaine: witness, Miami, OK, gun fight, 129

Borden, George: participant, Platt City, MO, gun fight, 90–92

Boyd, Ben: presided at Denton, TX, trial, 15

Boyd, Percy: victim, Miami, OK, gun fight 17–28; identified Henry Methvin, 133; reaction to deaths of Bonnie and Clyde, 146

Boyd, W. C.: presided at hearing about Denton, TX, burglary, 15

Boydston, Jack: witness, Miami, OK, gun fight, 128-29

Bozeman, Alan: victim, Eastham prison farm break, 103–5

Bradberry, Fred T.: participant, Dallas, TX, gun fight, 59–60

Brady, Cleve: kidnap victim, 41

Brene, Rufus: victim, McMurray Refinery robbery, 98

Brock, Merrill: piloted *Dallas Morning News* team to Shreveport, LA, 148

Bryan, Tom: investigator, Shreveport, LA, escape of the Barrow gang, 140–41

Bucher, John: gift shop owner, 33; murdered, 34–35

Bucher, Martha: witness, John Bucher murder, 34–35; reported murder, 35; identified Clyde and Raymond Hamilton, 35

Bullard, C. W.: prison guard, Eastham prison farm break, 105–6

Bullock, Johnny: ambulance chauffeur, transported Bonnie's remains, Arcadia, LA, to Dallas, TX, 156

Butler, Mrs. L. C.: witness, Howard Hall murder, 49

Butterfield, A. N.: witness, Miami, OK, gun fight, 129

Butterfield, John: witness, Miami, OK, gun fight, 129

Bybee, W. H.: participant, Eastham prison farm break, 105–7

Byrd, Mrs. J. M.: auto theft victim, McClennan County, TX, jail break, 24

Campbell, Calvin: victim, Miami, OK, gun fight, 127–28

Cartwright, John: witness, Wellington, TX, accident, 81–82

Caster, Ed: returned Raymond Hamilton from Michigan, 53; participant, Dallas, TX, gun fight, 101

Chambless, Odell: participant, Grapevine, TX, bank robbery, 57; kidnapped farmers, 57

Ciesa, John: investigator, Lancaster, TX, bank robbery, 115

Clark, Jim: suspect, Miami, OK, gunfight, 129

Clause, Frank: member of the Barrow gang, 10; physical description, 10–11; burglaries, 11; Bucher gift shop robbery and murder of John Bucher, 33–35

Coffey, Clarence: witness, Plattt City, MO, gun fight, 90–92; wounded in the gun fight, 91; later became a physician, 161

Coffey, Holt: participant, Platt City, MO, gun fight, 90; wounded in the gun fight, 91; retired as sheriff, 161

Cole, Otis: Bonnie and Clyde were squatters in his old family home, 139

Conger, S. A.: tried to keep crowds from damaging furniture, 151; embalmed Bonnie's and Clyde's remains, 153

Corry, George T.: called to Wellington, TX, accident, 82; Wellington, TX, kidnap victim, 83

Cowan, Nell (Barrow): speculated about brothers' lives of crime, 2; begged Clyde to return to parents' home, 10

Cox, Joe P.: posted a reward for Howard Hall's killer, 51

Crabtree, Delbert: motel clerk, Platt City, MO, 89–90

Crews, Corbin: picked up bodies after the Easter slaying of Texas highway patrolmen, 124

Crowson, Joseph: victim, Eastham prison farm break, 104–7; death, 109

Cummings, Homer: U.S. attorney general during the Miami, OK, gun fight, 131

Dailey, Frank P.: minister, Buck Barrow funeral, 98

Darby, H. Dillard: victim, Ruston, LA, auto theft, 75; kidnap victim, 77–78

Davis, Malcolm Lon: victim, Lillie McBride home gun fight, 59–60

Day, W. S.: participant, arrest of Raymond Hamilton, 53

Decker, Bill: deputy who drove from Dallas to Arcadia, LA, with Sheriff Schmid, 155

Deere, A. F.: pursuing officer, Neuhof Packing Co. robbery, 39

De Graff, Tom: participant, Joplin, MO, gun fight, 64–65

Dehart, R. Q.: witness, Marvin Kitchen kidnapping, 81

Dobson, Charles: witness, Miami, OK, gun fight, 128–29

Ellis, L. A.: participant, Platt City, MO, gun fight, 90

Ellison, J. A.: doctor, Easter slaying of Texas highway patrolmen, 124

Evans, Walter: participant, Lillie McBride home gun fight, 59–60

Farrie, Maggie: witness, Lillie McBride home gun fight, 59–60

Fellers, Marvin: victim, Dexfield, IA, gun fight, 96

Fellers, Valley: witness, Dexfield, IA, gun fight, 96

Ferguson, Mirian: governor of Texas, signed parole found after the Joplin, MO, gun fight, 65; agrees for Hamer to pursue Bonnie and Clyde, 111; agrees to grant amnesty to Henry Methvin as informant, 111

Fisher, Byron: participant, Platt City, MO, gun fight, 90

Ford, Henry: industrialist whose automobile was involved in the Dallas, TX, gun fight, 101

Fortune, Jan: ghost writer, *The Fugitives*, 2

Foust Funeral Home: received Texas highway patrolmen after the Easter slayings, 124

Freeland, John: sheriff, investigator, murder of John Bucher, 35; transported Raymond Hamilton, LaGrange, TX, trial, 80

French, J. B.: participant, Eastham prison farm break, 105–7

Fritz, Will: deputy who tracked the Miami, OK, gun fight, 127

Fugitives, The: (book by Jan Fortune and Barrow gang relatives), 2

Fults, Ralph: participant, Kaufman, TX, burglary, 31; captured, 31; claimed responsibility for burglary, 32; robbed Mississippi bank with Raymond Hamilton, 158–59; captured by authorities, 159; subsequent life, 159; death, 159

Gault, Manny: becomes Frank Hamer's partner, 125; physical description, 125; Frank Hamer's design for catching or killing Bonnie and Clyde, 125; Durant, OK, spotting of Bonnie and Clyde, 127; Shreveport, LA, escape of the Barrow gang, 140; posse firepower, 140; in position at the ambush site, 143; posse firing at Bonnie and Clyde, 143; got tow truck at Gibsland, LA, to remove "death car," 144, 147; removal of Bonnie's and Clyde's bodies to Arcadia, LA, 147

Gizzall, Mr. and Mrs. Fred: witnesses, Easter slaying of Texas highway patrolmen, 123–24

Glaze, Homer: witness, Howard Hall murder, 47–50; identified Clyde Barrow, 51

Goff, J. R.: coroner's jury member, 151

Gouge, Howard: muder victim, unrelated crime, 27

Goyne, Charles: investigator, Darby-Stone kidnapping, 77

Grammer, W. E.: participant, Joplin, MO, gun fight, 63

Gunter, Mrs. Cameron: kidnap victim, West, TX, bank robbery, 116

Hale, Hollis, accomplice, Howard Hall murder, 48–50; participant in the Oronogo, MO, bank robbery, 51–52; cheated Clyde, 52

Hall, Howard: murder victim, 48–49

Hamer, Frank: Texas Ranger captain hired to capture or kill Bonnie and Clyde, 4; ambush of Bonnie and Clyde, 4, 6; physical description, 6; accepts task of pursuing Bonnie and Clyde, 112; Easter slaying of Texas highway patrolmen, 124–25; agrees to have Manny Gault as partner, 125; design for capturing or killing Bonnie and Clyde, 125; Durant, OK, spotting of Bonnie and Clyde, 127; Shreveport, LA, escape of the Barrow gang, 140; posse firepower, 140; informed Lee Simmons about the impending ambush, 141; ambush, 142–43; inventoried contents of "death car," 143; removal of Bonnie's and Clyde's bodies to Arcadia, LA, 147–48; contacts Lee Simmons with ambush news, 149–50; interviewed by Tom Simmons about ambush, 158

Hamilton, Floyd: Dallas contact, 63; participant, Eastham prison farm break, 102; Lancaster, TX, bank robbery, 113

Hamilton, Raymond: in Denton County Jail, 7; physical description, 7; Bucher robbery and murder, 33–35; in Witchita Falls, TX, 37; stole car at Corsicana, TX, 39; Atoka, OK, shooting, 40–41; in Carlsbad, NM, 43–45; at Wharton, TX, shoot-out, 46–47; with father in Michigan, 47, 53; tried for bank robbery, 80; tried for murder, 81; Eastham prison farm break, 101–6; Temple,TX, car theft, 114; Lancaster, TX, bank robbery, 114–16; Grand Prairie, TX, family reunion, 116; breakup of Barrow gang, 116; Grand Prairie, TX, bank robbery, 116; West, TX, bank robbery, 116; reaction to deaths of Bonnie and Clyde, 146; escaped Texas prison, 158; robbed Mississippi bank, 158; captured by authorities, 159; tried for slaying of Joseph Crowson, 159; executed, 159

Hanna, Otto: jury foreman, LaGrange, TX, trial, 81

Hardy, Frank: accomplice, Howard Hall murder, 48–50; participant, Oronogo, MO, bank robbery, 51–52; cheated Clyde Barrow, 52

Hardy, Tom: victim, Wellington, TX, kidnapping, 83

Harriman, Wesley: victim, Joplin, MO, gun fight, 64–65

Harris, L. C.: investigator, Atoka, OK, gun fight, 42

Hauser, H. D.: participant, Platt City, MO, gun fight, 89–90

Henry, L. L.: victim, Lancaster, TX, bank robbery, 115

Henry, R. P. and Sons Bank: scene of the Lancaster, TX, bank robbery, 114

Herring, Clyde, P.: witness, Dexfield, IA, gun fight, 94

Highfill, George: participant, Platt City, MO, gun fight, 90–92; wounded in gun fight, 91

Hilburn, Lillian: witness, Lillie McBride home gun fight, 61

Hinton, Ted: met Bonnie Parker, 17; investigated the Joplin, MO, hideout, 66; pursued Clyde and Billie Parker, 84; McMurray Refinery robbery, 99; assigned to posse, 125; physical description, 125; Durant, OK, spotting of Bonnie and Clyde, 127; Shreveport, LA, escape of the Barrow gang, 140; posse firepower, 140; ambush of Bonnie and Clyde,

142–143; made movie of Bonnie and Clyde in "death car," 147; removal of Bonnie's and Clyde's bodies to Arcadia, LA, 147; experiences sickness at mortuary crowds, 150; attended Clyde's funeral, 157; burial site, 157; attended Bonnie's funeral, 158; life after the ambush, 158

Hullet, Thomas: participant, Platt City, MO, gun fight, 90–92

Humphery, Henry: victim, Alma, AR, bank robbery, 84; victim, Alma, AR, slaying, 85

Hunt, H. A.: investigator, Grandview, TX, car theft, 43

Ivy, Polk: investigator, Easter slaying of Texas highway patrolmen, 123–24

James, Thomas R.: witness, Dallas, TX, gun fight, 101

Jarrett, F. E.: witness, McMurray Refinery robbery, 98

Johns, Joe: kidnap victim, Carlsbad, NM, 43–45

Johnson, Doyle: murder victim, Temple, TX, 54–55

Johnson, Earl: victim, Temple, TX, car theft, 114

Johnson, Tillie: victim, Doyle Johnson murder, 54

Jones, T. E.: investigator, Denton, TX, burglary, 12–13; testified, Denton, TX, trial, 15

Jones, W. D.: wrote *Playboy* article, 2; described Clyde's violent temper, 2; Dallas County, TX, Jail, 7; physical description, 7; joined Barrow gang, 53; Doyle Johnson murder, 54–55: Lillie McBride home gun fight, 58–59;

Jones, W. D.*(Continued)*
Thomas Persell kidnapping, 61–62; Joplin MO, gun fight, 63–66; Wellington, TX, shooting, 81–83; Alma, AR, slaying, 84–85; Washington County, OK, 86; Platt City, MO, gun fight, 92; wounded in gun fight, 92; Perry, IA, car theft, 93; Dexfield, IA, gun fight, 95–96; reaction to deaths of Bonnie and Clyde, 145; article in *Playboy*, 160; killed by unknown person or persons, 160

Jordan, Bedell: testified about Bucher robbery and John Bucher murder, 33; testified about Marvin Kitchen kidnapping, 80–81

Jordan, Henderson: sheriff of Bienville Parish where the ambush was planned, 141–42; physical description, 141; ambush of Bonnie and Clyde, 142–43; inventoried contents of "death car," 143; confrontation with Dr. Wade, 150; assured Arcadia, LA, crowd that all would view bodies, 150–51; life after the ambush, 158; refused to deliver the Warren car to Ruth Warren, 161

Kahler, George: participant, Joplin, MO, gun fight, 63–65

Kimbrough, W. C.: physician who treated captured suspects in Denton, TX, burglary, 14

King, John E: assigned editor Thomas Simmons to cover ambush, 144

King, Winter: connected with the breakup of Barrow gang, 116

Kitchen, Marvin: testified about Bucher robbery and John Bucher murder, 33; kidnap victim, 80

Knee, C. A.: planned the Dexfield, IA, gun fight, 93–94

Little, A. B.: posted a reward for Howard Hall's murderer, 47, 51

Long, Fred: participant, LaGrange, TX, trial, 80

Love, John: helped plan the Dexfield, IA, gun fight, 94

Lyons, William: background, 7; ambush witness, 142–43; driving near the ambush site, 142; almost hit by posse firing at Bonnie and Clyde, 143

Maynor, J. N.: witness, McMurray Refinery robbery, 98

Maxey, J. B.: investigator, Aloka, OK, gun fight, 42

Maxwell, G. C.: victim and witness, Atoka, OK, gun fight, 40–41

McGinnis, Harry: participant, Joplin, MO, gun fight, 64–65

McMurray, James: owner, McMurray Refinery, 98–99

Methvin, Henry: participant, Eastham prison farm break, 105–8; participant, Lancaster, TX, bank robbery, 114, 116; Grand Prairie, TX, reunion, 114; Easter slaying of Texas highway patrolmen, 122–23; Miami, OK, gun fight, 127–28; identified by Percy Boyd, 133; Shreveport, LA, escape of the Barrow gang, 139–40; identified by Shreveport, LA, waitress, 141; pardoned by state of Texas, 159; sentenced to death in Oklahoma, 159; granted clemency by state of Oklahoma, 159; killed by freight train, 159

Methvin, Ivan: participant, ambush planning, 140; contacted Henderson Jordan to betray Bonnie and Clyde, 140; furnished hideout for Bonnie and Clyde, 142; at the ambush site, 142; death, 159

Milligan, Everett: member, Barrow gang, 39; Corsicana, TX, car theft, 39; Atoka, OK, gun fight, 40–43

Monzingo, B. B.: reports Eastham prison farm break, 106

Moore, Carl: photographer assigned to the ambush, 144; arrived in Arcadia, LA, from Dallas, 152

Moore, E. C.: participant, Atoka, OK, gun fight, 40

Moore, Sidney: burglar, 11; Henrietta, TX, burglary and car theft, 11–12; Denton, TX, burglary, 12–13; captured by Denton, TX, police, 13–14; tried for Denton, TX, burglary, 14–15; convicted of theft over $50, 15; sentenced to Texas state prison system, 15

Mullin, James (aka Jimmie Lamont): participant, Eastham prison farm break, 102–3, 105–6; Lancaster, TX, bank robbery, 109; revealed information about Eastham prison farm break, 110

Munroe, R. I.: judge, heard plea to reduce Clyde's sentence, 29

Murphy, H. D.: victim, Easter slaying of Texas highway patrolmen, 123–24

Murphy, King: assitant to Boots Bailey, 151; photographed bodies of Bonnie and Clyde, 153

Murray, William: governor, ordered investigation of Atoka, OK, gun fight, 41

Nearberry, O. J.: investigator, Howard Hall murder, 50

Neuhof, Henry: victim, Neuhof Packing Co. robbery, 38–39

Neuhof, Joe: victim, Neuhof Packing Co. robbery, 38–39

Oakley, Prentis: contacted by Henderson Jordan to prepare for the ambush, 142; physical description, 142; member of posse firing at Bonnie and Clyde, 142–43; brought parish coroner from Arcadia, 147

O'Dare, Gene: traveled to Michigan with Hamilton, 47, 53; arrested, 53; returned to Texas, 53

O'Dare, Mary: became Raymond Hamilton's mistress, 112; Grand Prairie, TX, family reunion, 114; Lancaster, TX, bank robbery, 114–15; breakup of the Barrow gang, 116; tried and sentenced for harboring fugitives, 160–61

Owens, Herbert: witness McMurray Refinery robbery, 98

Palmer, Joe: participant, Eastham prison farm break, 102–6: Grand Prairie, TX, reunion, 114; breakup of Barrow gang, 116; Lancaster, TX, bank robbery, 116; Easter slaying of Texas highway patrolmen, 122; left Barrow gang due to illness, 136; warned Bonnie and Clyde not to go to Louisiana, 136; reaction to the deaths of Bonnie and Clyde, 146-47; attended graveside services of Clyde, 159; tried for slaying of Joseph Crowson, 159; executed, 159

Parker, Billie: nursed Bonnie, 84, 87; accompanied her mother to Perry, IA, 97; last meeting with Bonnie, 136, 138; tried and sentenced for harboring fugitives, 160

Parker, Bonnie: pleaded to be brought home when slain, 6; composed poetry, 6; wrote poem entitled "It's Death for Bonnie and Clyde," 6; met Clyde for the first time, 15; background and family, 16; marriage to Roy Thornton, 16; begged Clyde to go straight, 18; saw Clyde in McClennan County Jail, 19; stole gun for Clyde, 20–22; personality change, 25; letters to Clyde in prison, 28; phony job in Houston, 31; captured, Kaufman, TX, 32; felt deserted, wrote "Suicide Sal," 32; no-billed at grand jury hearing, 37; vows never to see Clyde again, 37; Wichita Falls, TX, with Clyde and Hamilton, 37–38; at Emma Parker's before Neuhof robbery, 38; hid out after Neuhof job, 39; after Atoka, OK, killing, 42–43; family reunion, 53; Doyle Johnson murder, 54–55; McBride home gun fight, 58–60; Joplin, MO, gun fight, 64–65; Commerce, TX, visit, 79–80; Wellington, TX, accident, 81–82; Dexfield, IA, gun fight, 95–96; Dallas, TX, reunion, 100–101; Dallas, TX, gun fight, 100–101; Eastham prison farm break, 101, 106; Greenville, TX, reunion, 112–13; Lancaster, TX, bank robbery, 114–15; Grand Prairie, TX, reunion, 114; Easter slaying of Texas highway patrolmen,

123–24; Topeka, KS, car theft, 135; last meeting with her mother, 136–38; attacked by the posse, 142–43; description of death, 143; funeral, 157; burial, sites, 157

Parker, Buster: reaction to deaths of Bonnie and Clyde, 145; arrived in Arcadia, LA, to carry Bonnie's remains home, 156

Parker, Emma: moved to Dallas, 16; advised Bonnie to divorce Roy Thornton, 17; met Clyde, 17; change in Bonnie after McClennan County jail break, 25; Commerce, TX, visit, 79–80; arrived in Perry, IA, with Mrs. Barrow, 97; Dallas, TX, reunion, 100–101; Dallas, TX, gunfight, 100–101; Greenville, TX, reunion, 112–13; Grand Prairie, TX, reunion, 114; last meeting with Bonnie, 136–38; reaction to deaths of Bonnie and Clyde, 145; tried for harboring fugitives, 160; death, 160

Peck, Brian: investigator, Lancaster, TX, bank robbery, 116

Penn, Homer: participant, Dexfield, IA, gun fight, 93

Pentecost, F. W.: coroner's jury member, 151

Persell, Thomas: kidnap victim, 61–62; retired, 161

Phares, L. G.: enraged over Easter slaying of Texas highway patrolmen, 124–25; speculates where Bonnie and Clyde will be caught, 132–33; charters a plane to go to Arcadia, LA, for autopsies, 150

Porter, Perry: investigator, Miami, OK, gun fight, 129

Price, Earl: investigator, McMurray Refinery robbery, 99

Pritchard, Tom: witness, Wellington, TX, accident, 81–83

Pritchard, Mrs. Tom: witness, Wellington, TX, accident, 82; Wellington, TX, shooting, 83

Quick, Elizabeth: collapsed at the Buck Barrow funeral, 98

Redden, Joe: witness, Lonnie Redden kidnapping, 41

Redden, Lonnie: kidnap victim, 41

Reese, Frank: investigator, Howard Hall murder, 51; reward for Hall murderer, 51

Reich, Paul: victim, Dallas, TX, car theft, 101

Rhodes, Dusty: participant, Lillie McBride home gun fight, 59

Rich, Carroll, Dr.: research on Bonnie and Clyde, 1; research on the "death car," 161

Richburg, Roy: investigator, Neuhof Packing Co. robbery, 39

Risinger, W. D.: investigator, Darby-Stone kidnapping, 77, 79

Rogers, Mrs. Frank: victim, Washington County, OK, car theft, 86

Rush, Kelly: returned Raymond Hamilton from Michigan, 53

Saylars, A. M.: participant, Alma, AR, gun fight, 85–86; identified Buck Barrow at Perry, IA, 97

Schieffer, William: witness, Easter slaying of Texas highway patrolmen, 123

Schmid, Smoot: Dallas County, TX, assigned deputies to posse, 25; assigned deputies to search Joplin, MO, hideout, 65–66;

theory on McMurray Refinery robbery, 99; Dallas, TX, gun fight, 101; reaction to deaths of Bonnie and Clyde, 144–45; arrived in Arcadia, LA, 155

Schumaker, Les: kidnap victim, 57

Seale, Denver: returned Raymond Hamilton from Michigan, 53

Seals, Dennis: delivered police photos to Grayson County authorities, 51

Simmons, Lee: director of Texas prisons, 4; investigator, Eastham prison farm break, 101, 104, 106–7, 109–11; swears justice for Crowson's death, 109; interrogates James Mullin about Eastham prison farm break, 110; creates position of special investigator for Texas prison system, 110; selects Frank Hamer for new position, 111; gets permission of governor of Texas for Frank Hamer, 111; gets governor's promise for amnesty for Henry Methvin as informant, 111; persuades Fank Hamer to pursue Bonnie and Clyde, 112; Manny Gault assigned as Frank Hamer's partner, 125; drives to Arcadia, LA, for autopsies, 155

Simmons, Thomas J.: assigned to cover slaying of Bonnie and Clyde, 44; arrived in Arcadia, LA, from Dallas, TX, 152; determines that Frank Hamer was the leader of the posse, 154; interviewed Frank Hamer about slaying of Bonnie and Clyde, 154; became disgusted with souvenir hunters, 155

Small, Tom: witness, Eastham prison farm break, 106–7

Smith, Knox: witness, Kitchen kidnapping, 81

Spillars, Walter: witness, Dexfield, IA, gun fight, 96

Stamps, Nettie: witness, Joe Johns kidnapping, 43–45

Stanford, I. P.: jailer and victim, McClennan County, TX, jail break, 23–24

Stanford, Jimmy: assistant district attorney, McClennan County, TX, jail break, 26

Starr, Clint: investigator, Denton, TX, burglary, 12–13; testified at the Denton, TX, trial of Buck Barrow, 15

Stegall, Leslie: witness, McClennan County, TX, jail break, 26

Stewart, Les: participant, Grapevine, TX, bank robbery, 57; offered to help trap Bonnie and Clyde, 58

Stone, Sophia: witness, Ruston, LA, auto theft, 76; kidnap victim, 77–78

Stoner, Edward: victim, Perry, IA, auto theft, 93

Street, Earl: district attorney, Denton, TX, burglary, 14; prosecuted Ivan Barrow and Sidney Moore for Denton burglary, 15

Taylor, G. C.: coroner's jury member, 151

Theus, B. G.: coroner's jury member, 151

Thigpen, A. J.: investigator, Ruston, LA, auto theft, 76–78

Thompson, Gradie: investigator, Howard Hall murder, 50

Thompson, Irwin "Blackie":

participant, McMurray Refinery robbery, 99

Thornton, Roy: married Bonnie, 16; separated from Bonnie, 17; sentenced to reform school, 17; Red Oak, TX, robbery, 17; sentenced to Texas prison system, 17; reaction to deaths of Bonnie and Clyde, 146

Trigg, Jesse: kidnap victim, 57

Turner, William: physical description, 19; criminal background, 19; participant, McClennan County, TX, jail break, 19–24

Underhill, Wilbur: unjustly accused of participation in Miami, OK, gun fight, 129

Van Noy, J. A.: participant, Lillie McBride home gun fight, 59–60

Veazey, William: performed surgery on Alan Bozeman and Joseph Crowson after Eastham prison farm break, 108–9

Wade, J. L.: Bienville Parish, LA, coroner, 7; requested rule on cause of death of Bonnie and Clyde, 144; disgusted at spectacle at death scene, 147; removal of Bonnie and Clyde's bodies to Arcadia, LA, 147–49; conducted autopsies on Bonnie and Clyde, 151–53

Waggoner, C. J.: victim, Dallas, TX, car theft, 115

Waid, T. M.: prison warden during the Eastham prison farm break, 106–8; interviewed J. B. French, 109

Walker, Andrew: flew as spotter for Miami, OK, authorities, 130

Walker, W. J.: "Whitey": participant, McMurray Refinery
robbery, 99

Walker, Mrs. W. J.: accomplice,
McMurray Refinery robbery, 99

Walsh, Douglas: fingerprinted and
photographed Clyde, 14

Warren, Jess: victim, Topeka, KS,
car theft, 135

Warren, Ruth: victim, Topeka, KS,
car theft, 135; profited from the
"death car," 161–62

Watters, Dee: investigator, Miami,
OK, gun fight, 129

Wheeler, E. B.: victim of Easter
slaying of Texas highway
patrolmen, 123–24

Wheeler, Mrs. E. B.: reaction to
deaths of Bonnie and Clyde, 147

Wilkerson, Bob: returned Raymond
Hamilton from LaGrange, TX,
trial, 80

Wilkerson, P. F.: returned Raymond
Hamilton from Michigan, 53

Williams, Roland G.: Dallas
County, TX, judge who assigned
deputies to the posse, 125

Williford, Frank: assistant district
attorney, investigated the Howard
Gouge murder, 27

Wilson, Webber: witness, Alma,
AR, slaying, 85

Witherspoon, Thomas: participant,
Platt City, MO, gun fight, 90

Worley, Olin: victim, Lancaster, TX,
bank robbery, 115

Wright, Gabe: witness, Eastham
prison farm break, 107

Wright, Glenn: chief jailer,
McClennan County, TX, jail
break, 24

Wullschleger, Elsie: witness,
Neuhof Packing Co. robbery, 38

Yost, Fred: participant, Eastham
prison farm break, 102

E. R. Milner is a professor of history and government at Tarrant College, Forth Worth, Texas. He has published several articles on Texas history, served as editor of the *Tarrant Historical Review,* and participated in numerous oral history projects. He is the author and producer of two video documentaries, *History of Salisbury Cathedral* and *Making Movie Magic: The Filming of Casablanca*, and is currently working on the history of the Lost Battalion in the South Pacific in World War II.